I Am The Blues

The Willie Dixon Story

Willie Dixon with Don Snowden

DA CAPO PRESS

Library of Congress Cataloging in Publication Data

Dixon, Willie, 1915-
  I am the blues: the Willie Dixon story / Willie Dixon with Don
Snowden.
     p.   cm. — (A Da Capo paperback).
  "Supplemented with author emendations" — T.p. verso.
  Includes index.
  ISBN-10: 0-306-80415-8   ISBN-13: 978-0-306-80415-1
  1. Dixon, Willie, 1915–   . 2. Blues musicians — United States —
Biography. I. Snowden, Don. II. Title.
ML410.D68A3   1990   90-38862
[B]   CIP
                                       MN

This Da Capo Press edition of *I Am The Blues: The Willie Dixon Story*
is an unabridged republication of the edition published in London
in 1989, supplemented with author emendations. It is reprinted by
arrangement with Quartet Books.

Published by Da Capo Press, Inc.
A Member of the Perseus Books Group
www.dacapopress.com

Manufactured in the United States of America

CONTENTS

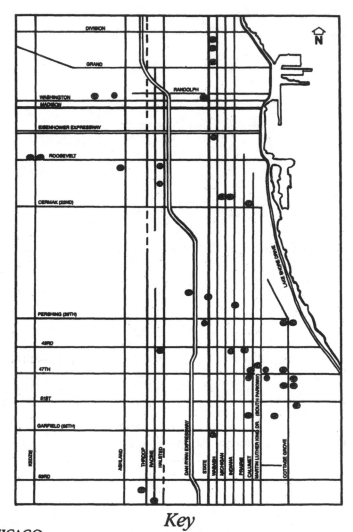

Key

CHICAGO

1 Willie's home on arrival in Chicago 1/4716 Forestville (1929)
2 Willie's place on arrival in Chicago 2/4837 Prarie (1936)
3 Eddie Nichols Gym South Park and 47/48th ('36–'38)
4 Jack L. Cooper's radio studio/43rd & Indiana ('37 or '38)
5 Bernardo Dennis' house/39th & Dearborn ('36–'38)
6 Club DeLisa/5515 Garfield (at State)
7 Martin's Corner/1900 W. Lake Street ('39–'40)
8 Pink Poodle/502 S. State St. ('40–'41)

NB: Madison Street is the dividing point between North and South in Chicago.

State Street marks the boundary between East and West in Chicago.

The area between 39th and 51st Streets and State and Cottage Grove has been enlarged in proportion to the rest of the illustration.

Locations 37 and 38 are actually further south than represented on the map.

To the world for all the unknown and unheard blues artists who never got a chance to make it, and to the memory of Little Brother Montgomery, Baby Doo Caston and Memphis Slim

—Willie Dixon—

ACKNOWLEDGEMENTS

Marie Dixon for patience and support in scheduling and putting up with the interviews.

Nancy Meyer and Scott A. Cameron of the Cameron Organization for co-ordinating and facilitating the project.

Cary Baker for his early involvement and encouragement.

Sandra Dijkstra for landing the deal, Chris Parker at Quartet for editing, and Yuval Taylor and Karen Brooks at Da Capo for handling revisions.

Barbara Meador at Bug Music and Barbara Cain at BMI in Los Angeles for enduring repeated questions about songwriting credits and cover versions.

Bob Koester of Delmark Records for supplying a historical overview of the pre-Chess Chicago recording scene.

Cash McCall, Dave Clark, Ray Funk and Dr. David Evans of Memphis State University for fleshing out the gospel context.

Horst Lippmann and Fritz Rau, Giorgio Gomelsky, Long John Baldry and Philippe Rault for the behind-the-scenes look at the European sector.

The Vicksburg crew—Elmer Johnson, Alfred Dillard, Michel Fedell, Theo Phelps, L.V. Dixon, Shedrick Johnson and Rose Tribble—for invaluable help in confirming details of the early years.

The Chicago crew—Baby Doo Caston, Malcolm Chisholm, Ron Malo, Dick Lapalm, Jimmy Rogers, David Meyers, Buddy Guy, Al Duncan, Phil Upchurch, Koko Taylor and Marshall Chess—for sharing memories of the Chess and Cobra era.

The English crew—Tony Russell, Bruce Bastin, Tony Burke, Bob Laughton—for discographical assistance. Also Brian L. Smith in England and Jonas Bernholm in Sweden for help with photos.

Acknowledgements

Andy McKaie at Chess/MCA for general assistance and access to the Ruppli discography of Chess Records.

Mary Katherine Aldin for supplying all the pertinent early discographical information.

Peter Golkin for volunteering use of his manuscript on Chess Records and supplying information on film/television material.

Suzanne Steel at the Center of Southern Culture's Blues Archives at the University of Mississippi for assistance and advice.

Jim O'Neal, founder of *Living Blues* magazine, for assistance and advice.

Gordon Cotton and staff at the Old Courthouse Museum in Vicksburg, Mississippi for assistance.

Toni Castonie at the DuSable Museum of Afro-American History in Chicago for assistance on basic Chicago history.

Donna Cline for doing the map.

Judy Reynolds for typing the manuscript.

Numero uno for foiling the Coyote Police.

Hoochie Coochie Music is solely owned by Willie Dixon and administered world-wide by Bug Music.

All photos are courtesy of Willie Dixon except as otherwise indicated. Mike Leadbitter photo courtesy of Brian Smith. Best efforts have been made to contact the photographers whose images are used.

While the Blues Heaven Foundation searches for a permanent location in Chicago, information can be obtained from P.O. Box 6926, Burbank, CA 91506.

The italicized sections beginning each chapter were written to provide background and context for Willie Dixon's life story. Unless otherwise indicated, the first passages following the italics are the words of Willie Dixon.

Don Snowden,
Los Angeles, 1990

INTRODUCTION

I am the blues
I am the blues
The whole world knows
I've been mistreated and misused

I'm the moans of suffering women
I'm the groans of dying men
I'm the last one to the start
And the first one to the end

I'm a thousand generations
Of poverty and starvation
I'm the dog
Of the United Nations
I am the blues
I am the blues

I'm the last one hired
And I'm the first one fired
I'm the only man
That has never been satisfied
I am the blues
I am the blues

My name is Willie Dixon and frankly, I come from blues country.

All of my life I've had blues but at one time I had the type of blues that had me feeling insecure. As I grew up through life and began to see things and as my people explained things to me of the past and their experience, it gave me a more secure feeling about the blues. This secure feeling made me know that if I understood the blues for what they actually are, it would give me a better understanding not only of me and my folks but the rest of the world. It made me know I had a job to do as long as I lived about trying to educate the world about these blues.

According to Biblical history and all of the history of the world, the blues was built in man from the beginning. The first thing that came out of man is the blues because, according to the Scriptures, when God made man, man was lonesome and blue. God decided to take a rib out and make the woman because the first thing a man seeks when he's become lonesome and blue is companionship.

This woman, according to the Scriptures, was made for a helpmate and the companionship of a woman either can straighten his situation out or make it worse. To a certain extent, she had kind of a corner on this blues situation as far as the feeling of the individual is concerned. She can give him the blues or take it away from him.

The whole of life itself expresses the blues. That's why I always say the blues are the true facts of life expressed in words and song, inspiration, feeling and understanding.

The blues can be about anything pertaining to the facts of life. The blues call on God as much as a spiritual song do. The blues calls on love as much as a love song do. The blues call on happiness and understanding. The blues calls on the sadness as much as prayer do. The blues calls on working—even working on the railroad and chopping cotton, they could always build a rhythm up to this that made it the blues.

A guy was asking me one day, "Since you feel all blues songs are related to the facts of life, can you tell me what a line like, 'Blues jumped a rabbit and rode it for a solid mile,' would mean?"

The dog jumping the rabbit in the morning meant a great thing. Everybody knew if you jump a rabbit in one place, he's going to make a circle and come right back across the same place. A lot of times, we didn't have a shotgun but we had clubs waiting on him when he came back. I remember many days that if my old man hadn't shot a squirrel or killed a rabbit that morning, we wouldn't have had anything to eat.

It didn't mean nothing to people that lived in cities because they had plenty of meat and didn't eat rabbit. The average individual can't understand that because he wasn't living in the past to know what was happening in the corn fields, cotton fields and on the plantations.

But when you go to talking about the things of today, the average individual can relate them with the things of today. If you don't know about yesterday and today, you don't have the least idea of what you think can happen tomorrow. By knowing about yesterday, how things came along and are still advancing, it can give you a greater idea of what the future could be. This is why the blues represents the past, present and future.

It's necessary for people to know all the various parts of the blues and the various things that have happened in the blues so they won't make the mistakes in the future that have been made in the past. I feel people have neglected the ideas that the blues have given them. They've got blues books out there that tell a little bit about everybody—his name and what songs he sang—but they don't have none of the actual blues experience involved.

Ninety-nine percent of the people that wrote stories about the blues gave people phony ideas and this gave the blues a bad reputation. They had people believing the blues was a low-down type of music and underestimating the blues one hundred percent. The majority of people have been taught to stay away from the blues because the world didn't actually want you to understand what the blues want. To brainwash people, they have to make you think that things that are good for you are against you.

The majority of the blues have been documented through time with the various people involved with the blues. All of this is unwritten facts about the blues because these blues have been documented but not written—documented in the minds of various men with these various songs since the first black man set foot on the American shore.

My old man was singing the blues in the field all the time. He used to talk so much about blues and the difference between the music and all like that until he got me interested in it real early. My old man would explain it all so we accepted his philosophy more than we did anybody else's because it made sense.

My old man used to explain that the reason they called it blues was that the people that sung 'em was blue and lonesome and they wanted to tell their troubles to the world. Everybody called anything that wasn't spiritual music a "reel."

When Little Brother Montgomery would be singing "Vicksburg Blues," the old folks would say that it's a "reel" song but one group of people was calling it "reel" because it was the real facts of life, talking about going up Clay Street and coming down on Vine in the city of Vicksburg. Those were the things people were doing at the time. Other people were calling them "reels" because it certainly wasn't about Christianity and going to get to heaven.

My father said when you talked about "reel" music, it meant the type of music that was talking about the real things of life. He always said your god is your forefathers. He taught all of us them songs about going down to the River Jordan because these are the songs that people made to go back to their country.

That song, "Swing Low, Sweet Chariot/Coming For To Carry Me Home," he said "home" was Africa at that time. When the slaves, years ago, would sing, "On Jordan's stormy bank side" or "Going home, going home/If I never see you no more," they were thinking about going back to Africa.

All the blues songs actually related back to Africa or some of the African heritage things. All of these songs came from the original tom toms of Africa, the rhythms of Africa. They were doing code systems with rhythm long before America and these code systems were the talking drums all over Africa delivering messages.

Music today is nothing but the old original beat, only they're making it with musical instruments instead of the drum. And the African people did always tell stories. That's where most of the Biblical stories come from.

The delivering of messages in a song is the blues, but today, people don't look into the song to get information. They just sing the song for the musical quality or rhythm quality and they never get the actual reason of the song.

People have lost the original blues and the blues itself by the other creations that surround it. That's the reason I always say about music, the blues are the roots and the other musics are the fruits. Without the roots, you have no fruits so it's better keeping the roots alive because it means better fruits from now on. That's why I say the blues will always be because the blues are the roots of all American music.

As long as American music survives, so will the blues because there has been nothing different from the blues in America. It's just different arrangements of the blues that people have renamed to commercialize it and make money. You can take any 12 bar blues pattern—me and Memphis Slim used to do this all the time—and any song you can sing, you can play a 12 bar blues right along with it and it blends.

They call it the old 12 bar blues because people like Little Brother Montgomery and other guys started putting a left hand boogie beat to 'em. In those days, if the beat wasn't uptempo, they called it "barrelhouse" and if it was uptempo, they called it "Dudlow" or "Dudlow Joe." They would call this left hand putting the dudlow to the blues.

After people got wise enough to commercialize it, somebody said, "Well, we'll call this boogie-woogie." That gave everybody a chance to say, "This is my boogie and that's his boogie." If they kept calling boogie-woogie "dudlow," then it would have been based on black folks' music. When they began calling it boogie-woogie, it creates the feeling of a certain thing anybody can do.

Most of the blues artists today, they have a type of pushing spirit to tell you what's going on. They don't ask very many questions—they tell you their expression and feeling. The story of the facts of life is a helluva thing. You can't tell it in the same mood all the time.

1

The gypsy woman told my mother
Before I was born
You got a boy child comin'
He's gonna be a son of a gun
He's gonna make pretty women
Jump and shout
Then the world want to know
What this was all about

Chorus: But you know I'm here
Everybody knows I'm here
Well, you know I'm a hoochie coochie man
Everybody knows I'm here

I got a black cat bone
I got a mojo, too
I got the John the Conqueror
I'm gonna mess with you
I'm gonna make you, pretty girl
Lead me by the hand
Then the world will know
The hoochie coochie man

On the seventh hour
On the seventh day
On the seventh month
The seventh doctor say

He was born for good luck
And that you'll see
I got seven hundred dollars
Don't you mess with me

Willie Dixon was born on July 1, 1915 in Vicksburg, Mississippi, the seventh of 14 children born to Daisy Dixon (nee McKenzie). Only seven survived—sisters Johnnie, Katie and Rose and brother Curtis preceded Willie into the world while brothers Louis (L.V.) and Arthur (now Kabar) followed.

Charlie Dixon had married Daisy McKenzie in 1903 (the marriage certificate reads Charlie Dixon and Daisy McKinsie) but nine years later filed for divorce on grounds of adultery. The final divorce was granted in 1913 and another man began to figure prominently in Daisy Dixon's life—Anderson (A.D.) Bell, who, in all likelihood, was Willie Dixon's actual father. Dixon is referring to Bell when he speaks of his father in this chapter.

At the time, Vicksburg was the second largest city in Mississippi, a bustling port town and railroad transportation hub located halfway between Memphis and New Orleans and the key stopover point in the Mississippi River boat trade between those cities. Historically famous as the site of a major Civil War siege and battle, Vicksburg sat on the southwestern edge of the Mississippi Delta region that spawned many major blues performers. Guitarist Charlie Patton, a major influence on Dixon's later associate Howlin' Wolf, called Vicksburg home but piano players and Dixieland-style bands were the order of the day when Dixon was growing up in the early 1920s.

Willie was big enough, apparently, to be accepted into classes at Cherry Street School two years ahead of schedule. Known to his friends in Vicksburg as W.J., the bulk of his early childhood centered around the restaurant Daisy Dixon ran in the Jackson Street/Oakwood Street/Locust Street triangle in what was then the northern edge of Vicksburg. It was an integrated neighborhood, a mixture of blacks

*and immigrant whites, filled with small shops and food stores which
catered to the farmers who came in from the countryside to load up
with supplies on the weekends.*

ROSE TRIBBLE: Willie Dixon's older sister.

L.V. DIXON: Willie Dixon's younger brother. He died in 1988.

*MICHEL FEDELL: a childhood friend of Willie Dixon's who still lives in
Vicksburg. He spent 20 years distributing blues records to jukeboxes in
Mississippi before opening a record store in Vicksburg.*

My mother's maiden name was McKenzie and my father's name was
Dixon but I had a stepfather named Bell. It was me, L.V. and Arthur
who were supposed to have been Bells, according to what other
people said, but my mother always said we were Dixons. I never saw
Charlie Dixon unless I went out to his house. Since my other sisters
and brothers were always running up to him hollering, "papa, papa,"
we got into calling him "papa, papa," too.

At that time, they didn't even care whether they registered any of the
black people or not. Those midwives would come in and most of
them couldn't read or write themselves. They didn't know what
county or what state or what city they were in.

When I was a youngster, my father worked at W.W. Lassiter's
warehouse in Vicksburg and most of the time at the Anderson-Tully
Sawmill north of Vicksburg. You probably saw him about as much as I
did, which was very, very seldom. He had nothing to offer because he
wasn't making no money. I don't think my old man was making but $7
a week at the sawmill. If we got five cents from him once in a while, we
were lucky.

Every time my old man came by the house, he always had a lot of
stories to tell about different parts of his life. Any time they got to
discussing the facts of life he would always have to tell Mama where to
get off because he felt like she had been too well brainwashed to
understand what was going on. They always said my old man was on
the wrong side of the tracks but he felt like he was on the right side
because he hadn't been brainwashed with what he called white
psychology.

My father and grandfather never believed in any parts of slavery and never believed in being hampered in any form. My father told me many stories about his father running off and how they punished him. My grandfather would tell them about various things they shouldn't be like. They'd be living in the woods being thieves but my mother was a dedicated Christian and believed that everything the preacher said was right. This enabled me to grow up between those two ideas.

When my father was a young man, these trotting horses were a great thing. He had a horse and buggy that had all the latest fashions and everybody would turn their heads when he came through town with his buggy shined up and his horse doing these steps. He always wore a big, wide hat and he was kind of a showpiece around there. Little Brother Montgomery was always telling me about my father.

Everybody liked him and he'd get off the buggy and demonstrate his gun shooting because he was a helluva marksman. Everybody was afraid of him because he didn't know how to miss. That's the way he'd always tell it, "The old man don't know how to miss. If he can see it, he can hit it." I know several old friends of his who said the same thing.

He had kind of a rough reputation around there because he was one of the guys who never pulled off his gun. He always wore two guns in plain sight. Nobody could make him get them off, even in the South when they didn't allow guns. He'd be lollygagging around there and they'd say, "Do you ever take your guns off?"

"When my skin comes off, my guns come off."

L. V. DIXON: My father was the type of person that was afraid to throw a brick in the schoolyard because he might hit one of his kids. Every now and then, we would run up on a girl that we liked and loved so well and he'd say, "Who was that girl you were with? That's no girl for you. You find another girl." We found out a lot of the girls we used to like would have been our half-sisters.

WD: My father used to talk about Victoria Spivey quite a bit. I think he was down in Texas or Louisiana at that time and knew about her as a good singer but didn't play a very good instrument. When I was a kid, we had one of them wind-up gramophones and we used to play Victoria Spivey's record on there. She was singing "Black Snake Blues," the first blues I think I ever heard.

9

My old man knew Jim Nelson and he used to take me up to his place. Jim Nelson was one of those old men that's supposed to know everything, one of those guys they called hoodoo doctors. He had snakes in jars, cooled with alcohol or something. He had a place right across from the jailhouse and he would jive the folks around there like he could tell fortunes and all this kind of stuff.

Him and my old man was real hip to everything. My old man didn't believe in nothing and Jim Nelson didn't either. Jim Nelson was kind of a big, fat man and he and my father would always get into a lot of arguments. My old man would say, "You're doing wrong." Nelson would say, "I'm doin' right. I'm making a living, ain't I? I ain't out there working and you're out there working every day."

My old man felt Jim Nelson was leading the people astray because he was telling that crap about fortunes. Jim Nelson used to tell my old man, "I'm gonna put some bad luck on you."

"You'll get my foot in your butt."

Whenever I'd see my old man, I'd catch him out at the mill or on his way to Jim Nelson's. Jim Nelson was his buddy but Mama didn't want us to go down to Jim Nelson's corner. She felt he was one of those rascal-lous guys.

They used to tell a story about my father coming home and some insurance man had his foot up in my mother's chair. My mama told him to get his foot out and just as my old man was coming in the gate, this guy slapped my mama. My old man pulled up at him and he shot my old man in the jaw. My old man shot him and killed him. My old man had a scar right along his jaw, the bullet came in his mouth and he spit it out. Nobody messed with him—they were half-scared of him down there.

I guess that's one of the reasons Mama didn't want him around because he didn't believe in nothing but his gun. He had shot several white people around there and everybody said he was crazy. He died the first time I was in Chicago, when I was 13 years old. He was working at the sawmill and a log got off the roller and mashed him.

All my life, my mother had been schooling me about different things because when I was there with her, she was talking about different things about life and the things you had to learn. It made me always want to go and see what was happening. She used to talk about Africa, what they did in slavery, what they did to her full parents.

My mother always said, "The smaller the writing, the more important it is." That's like the recording business, you know, with contracts and everything. Most of the time, I read the subject and the next thing I look for the smallest writing on there. In those days, the people felt the reason they wrote the smaller things on the contract was because most black people couldn't read and when they would start, the first thing was to read the biggest thing they could see.

My mother had all kinds of books and she tried to make us study them but, hell, we didn't want to read. A lot of times, when people would throw out their garbage, we'd be rambling through the garbage and find these books. Mama would say, "That's a good book. You should read that."

Had I been knowledgeable enough to read some of those books as a young child, I'd be the smartest man in the world. She had a lot of big law books and a Bible, one of the first of the King James version. It had all black pictures all the way through it.

L. V. DIXON: Willie and I knew the Bible backwards and forwards. My mother was the type that everything she would say she'd try to make it rhyme. Willie got in the habit of listening to her and whatever would come up he'd always make it rhyme. He got that gift from our mother.

She ended up writing two or three books of her poems. A lot of times Willie would look in her new book of poems and say, "I like that—I think I'm going to change the words around on that." "People talking about the seventh son," I think that's one of the pieces he wrote when she wrote something about somebody being lucky with seven this and seven that and talking about the cat had nine lives.

WD: As kids, my brother and I used to sit down and make poems out of anything. He'd call a name with something and I would say all the things that sounds close to it and made sense. We'd do this all the time and once in a while, we'd call out something being funny and try to make poems to criticize each other. It was just a funny thing we had with trying to use words, some that existed and some that never existed, some meant something and some didn't mean nothing.

I was in about the fourth grade in school and there was a boy called Eddie Cooper who was a natural cartoonist. This guy used to get on the blackboard when the teacher would walk out and make funny pictures of animals.

Because I was fat, he'd say, "Hey, Dixon, this is you," a big fat elephant sitting over there. "Hey, this is T.W. Gray, he's a monkey," and he would always make up a story where the animals were fighting.

This particular day, the teacher went out and when she came back, everybody was screaming, hollering, laughing, jumping up and running all over the damn place. Eddie Cooper was explaining the Signifying Monkey and everybody was laughing so the teacher gave everybody a whipping when she came in. When I got home, my mother gave me a whipping again.

Every day Eddie Cooper would have something he drew in the back of his tablet and we'd go off to recess and talk about the Signifying Monkey. We began to call Eddie the monkey and because he had named different kids different animals, we'd call each other those names. Every time we got to thinking about this damned thing, we'd get to laughing.

This went on a long time so one day at home . . . we had one of those outside toilets in the back yard. I'm sitting out there trying to draw one of these monkeys and I started to write a little story. I was giggling to myself about this and my brother joined in and we started to make it longer and longer. Eventually, I made a poem about the Signifying Monkey.

I had poem books when I was a kid but when my mother moved to Chicago from down South, they left a bunch of them down there. We never thought anything of 'em, you know, just writing in a book. My mother wasn't really well educated but she taught all of us to read and write real well even before we went to school. I think she only went to the fifth grade of school.

I was born over on 1631 Crawford St. Bottom off of Clay Street in Vicksburg. The first thing I remember is hunting for some Easter eggs and I was too small to know what I found. They were putting them right in front of me but I couldn't see them. I was too small to do anything but step on them, I guess.

They didn't have all-black areas in the South. The whites and the blacks all lived pretty close together most of the time. The neighborhood had a bunch of raggedy houses. The white people's houses was much better than ours; black people lived in little shotgun houses.

The house we lived in on Third and Fayette Street was kind of a bungalow type house. There were about six steps up to the front porch and we had a swing there. When my brother L.V. was about a year old, I had a string around his neck swinging him in the swing, cutting his neck with the string and I didn't know it. He was screaming and hollering and I was swinging him backwards and forwards. I wasn't but about three years old.

When I was about four, my mama had a little restaurant up on Jackson about seven or eight blocks from where we lived. It was just called Daisy Dixon's restaurant. I ran away from home and ran up to the restaurant. Mama didn't believe I came there by myself but I knew the way up there.

My mother always wanted to teach us a speech as soon as we was big enough to walk on the stage. I was so small I couldn't even get up on a one-step platform to say the speech. They had to help me up there and the speech I said was, "Here I stand on two little chips/Please come kiss my sweet little lips." She taught me that when I was about four years old. The first thing I ever learned to say on my own was a poem so this could have been starting me towards getting poem ideas. I like that little poem, you know.

We lived right on the outskirts of Vicksburg. The street car stopped one block from my house. The pavement stopped where the street car line stopped and we only had dirt and mud from there on. We were considered as in the city because we were on the street but it was all country after that. We used to live on Jackson Road and Locust Street. All the places we lived were right in the city but we had to do country work, picking cotton.

We were damned lucky to have a thing to eat. A "For Rent" sign stayed up on the side of the house all the time—we wasn't paying but $5 a month but we didn't have that $5.

We were burning down the house two doors down because we couldn't get wood. It still had a "For Rent" sign on the front of it. Somebody said the rent man came there to inspect the house and hit it on the door. The whole front just fell back because all the back was gone. Everybody in the neighborhood was burning off that house.

We always raised a garden and used to go up and down through the city of Vicksburg, hustling garbage remains for the pigs. When we didn't have enough food to eat at home, we'd eat the same damn thing the pigs ate, right out of the garbage can. At that time, we was afraid to say anything about it because we thought it was shameful and a lot of other people were doing the same thing but they didn't want anybody to know.

I hadn't been exposed to music except in church. They used to have me singing a solo when I was five years old: "I came to the garden in long velvet/The dew is still on the rose/And the voice I hear/Is calling in my ear..." It was a song all the Sunday schools used to sing and I'd get up there and I thought I was raising hell.

My mother used to clean up the church so we'd be down there every night to clean up. They had a piano there that we could pump on but the only thing we knew how to play was blues songs and they didn't want none of them. We would go in there and play "How long, how long is that evening train?" My mother would go, "Get off that piano, boy."

L.V. DIXON: How Willie got to be a bluesman, I don't know because even when you was out in the mud and had to wipe your feet on the floor mat, you had to keep one foot on the floor. Otherwise they'd say you was dancing. My mother was the janitor for the church and she'd always send some of the kids over there to do the cleaning for her because she had other chores to do, like washing and ironing for people. That was before she got the restaurant.

We had to go to church all day Sunday but church wasn't anything but fun. We went so often we knew the prayers of the five deacons there word for word. One deacon we knew was going to pray a long time so we just crawled underneath the benches right on out the back door. Nobody would miss us so once something else happened we'd slip back in the church.

ROSE TRIBBLE: Willie would leave home, go down the street and play ball with the other children. He was kind of a mischievous boy and they used to leave me there with him. When I was 12 or 13 years old and Willie was about four, the neighbor called the police. He was real fat and I was small but my mother had given me permission to whip him if he didn't mind me. I got a peach tree switch and he hollered so loud till the people thought I was whipping him unmercifully.

My mother's restaurant had tables and a counter around it. It wasn't a great big place but they had some nice business sometimes because Mama was a really good cook. People used to come there and buy lunch and carry it home. She was there from morning until night. When we got large enough she would let us go over there and work and she'd go home and rest.

Willie helped a little with the restaurant. Sometimes he'd bring in wood or coal for us to burn in the stove. We had a fire in a furnace and burned charcoal in it. We'd cook on the furnace and fry fish and chicken on it, like you barbecue things.

WD: I was about five when we moved off of Fayette Street and moved right up behind the restaurant on Jackson Street. There was a little yard between the back of our house and the back of the restaurant. One was on Jackson Street and one on Jackson Road. Jackson Road was really Oakwood Street but they called it Jackson Road because the street was a V shape. Jackson Road and Jackson Street would run into each other at the corner.

The different little businesses along there were run by Syrians, Jews, some by black people. There was a barrelhouse next door to our restaurant and his name was Mr. Curley. In front of this barrelhouse was a fella that shined shoes and he could pop the rag real well. Nobody ever knew his name but we all called him "come here" because he would pop the rag and make it sound like somebody tap dancing. Everybody would come round there and let him shine their shoes.

Judge Halford was a justice of the peace who had a little place and he would give trials for different weekend things. My mother was cooking at the restaurant and sent his food across the street by one of us. He didn't do a damn thing but gamble and smoke cigars and pipes. I'd hate to go in there because it smelled so bad. Right in front of him was a guy called Hunt Davis who had a pressing shop. On the corner, Camarato's grocery store had a lot of fruits and stuff.

On another corner was Frank McCoy's grocery store and across the street was Wade Miles' Corn and next to that was a meat shop with a guy in there called Red. Then they had some Syrian people named Fedell and we was all raised together, Michel and Junior and Mary Fedell. We were there when they paved Jackson Road because it was all a dirt street then.

I was raised with Italian kids, Syrian kids, Chinese kids, black kids and white kids. As a kid, you could go all through white people's houses. Certain white people, those so-called big shots, wouldn't want you to come to their front door and like that but those that had children, we went everywhere their children went—front door, back door, played on the floor, just like their kids.

The Fedells were friends of mine and we ran around and played out there in schoolyards together all the time. We'd come to school together and play all the way home and I didn't even think about they went to one school and we went to another. Anything they had to eat and I wanted it, "Hey, I'll take some of that." If they stuck their hands into ice cream or jello, I stuck mine in, too. That's the way it was.

MICHEL FEDELL: My father ran a dry goods store and Willie's mother lived right across the street. My brother Junior used to play with his brother Arthur. We were rowdybouts, go down by the Christ Church and play, jump under the house. We were always in some kind of trouble, just a bunch of boys. When we would get a whipping, his mama whipped him, whipped me, whipped all of us.

Miss Camarato down on the corner had the prettiest red hair and we used to call her "Redhead"—"Hey, you been down to Redhead to get your Coca Cola or your ice cream?" They couldn't hardly speak English, couldn't hardly understand anything. My folks came from the old country, Lebanon, and they didn't know too much English. Jim Huston who had the furniture store used to take me and Willie—all of us—and teach us to read a book by Baby Ray.

We had a lot of good times back in those days. We'd go down into Glass Bayou swimming naked and the ladies passing by across the bayou wouldn't pay any attention to us. It was black and white and all of us played together.

When we'd get sick, I'd cross the bayou and they were all black up in there. When you'd get sick, they would take herbs off the earth and prepare it for you and you'd get well.

WD: My mama used to make some hog hooves' tea. You barely take a drink of that and you start running. When you quit running, you were all right. Boy, I hated that stuff because I'd see her cook it and say, "Now, what the hell is Mama fixing to do now?"

I'd feel like I was doing all right—"Mama, I ain't sick."

"Yes, you are. Come here."

Sometimes you didn't want to take it and she'd tell me to hold my nose and there it goes. Sure enough, it wouldn't hardly hit the bottom of your stomach before you was on the run and the next day you forgot you was ever sick.

My mama at that time knew every root in the field. She'd go out there and say, "Hold it," and start digging. "Hey, Mama, what's that stuff?" "It's ginseng root." They used to make hog hooves' tea, ginseng tea, sage tea and used to have aspidium bags on your chest.

I was always the largest one in the family. My mother and father were both pretty good sized. My mother always weighed over 200 pounds and she was around 5 feet 8 or 9 inches tall. When I was a kid, they used to call me "Fat Papa" because I was always fat. Then I grew up and started getting taller but at one time way later I was weighing about 380 pounds.

I always thought I was stronger and I tried to show it, you know. I always ate twice as much, too. I always felt that I had to do more, felt like I had to be strong, felt like I had to accomplish more. I felt like I had to know more because people had always felt that if a kid was bigger than the other, they felt like I was influencing him because I was the biggest.

If anything happened with a bunch of kids, I was always in fault because I was the biggest, even if a little guy was the oldest and would influence me. Being big you always fall victim to those kind of things but after a while, you grow accustomed to it.

A lot of times you'll say, "Well, instead of this big argument, I'll just knock the hell out of him and get it over with." They're going to blame you for it, anyway. That's the way a lot of people felt about being black, you know. If they see you running, the others are going to blame you for it anyway so you just stay there and get involved.

L.V. DIXON: By Willie being such a big boy, he was always the best of everything around there—the best ball player, the best wrestler, the best boxer, the best swimmer. Nobody could out-run him, big as he was. When everybody else would go picking berries with a pail, he'd have a tub and fill it. Go fishing the same thing, he'd come back with a ton of fish, never a little line or something like that. He wasn't afraid of anything, ever.

WD: We used to get Prince Albert tobacco cans and make rhythms and sing songs. If we had a meaning we wanted to express, we could play these Prince Albert tin cans— *clickety lick a lick a lick a lick*—to attract the attention and say everything we wanted together.

The biggest thing around Curley's Barrelhouse at that time would be piano players. You could hear Little Brother Montgomery's tunes there and "Black Snake Blues." Charlie Patton came from Vicksburg and a whole bunch of piano players used to come around there.

I wasn't able to go to a lot of functions and parties when I was young. Little Brother would play out in the Southside Park club down at Marcus Bottom and up in Waterville at the Rock House. Those were the two main places. I used to follow Brother around everywhere he went. He was one of my greatest influences because he was a little guy then and we thought he wasn't older than we was.

Little Brother was always the friendly one. He'd come and shake the hands of the little kids around there and I used to think that was a great thing because he shook my hand. Little Brother used to come around to see my sister Johnnie once in a while. We would be glad to see him because Mama didn't allow my sister into the Barrelhouse but Little Brother would go in there and play the piano and we'd hear him on the outside.

When I was seven or eight years old, I was just runnin' up and down the damn street seeing Little Brother play and get my butt beat just about every night. I would be running bare-footed with cut-off pants on and my shirt all open, just following them from corner to corner and listening at 'em. I remember the band they had—Little Brother played piano, Charlie Page played the trap drum, Lit Rose played clarinet and another guy, Blind Joe, played a banjo. A guy would talk and sing through a megaphone because they didn't have electric instruments.

They used to come through the city. They would advertise during the week by coming down Washington Street and up Jackson Street where the people was. Sometimes they would have a wagon bed with two mules hitched to it and one time they had an old T-Model Ford with a flatbed truck on it. They'd play on this corner, go a couple of blocks away and the guy with the megaphone would be telling them where the dance was going to be on the weekend.

My mother didn't want me to be following none of that stuff. Some times she'd think I was at school and I would be, part of the day, but every day around noon, about the time the school kids get out, they would come down there and start playing that music because they knew all the kids would draw a crowd. When the bell rang, some of the kids would go back into the school. I was always one of the ones that wouldn't go back.

Then they were playing at a place called the Bell Cafe down on South Washington Street. We used to go out in the back of Bell's Cafe and when they opened the doors, you could hear the music coming out and these guys would be playing in there. I always liked it and I always followed it after then.

My mother had taught me how to do everything she could do—washing, ironing, cooking and sewing. The first actual money I ever earned at a job I got working at Lindy's pressing club. He had a little place where he cleaned and pressed clothes and I worked there about two or three weeks. I was getting about $3 a week.

I was about 10 or 11 and after that, I got a job working at a Chinaman's laundry. It was $2½–$3 a week and I had to take the money home for the family every week. This Chinese guy didn't know I could iron and he went away one day. I ironed up a lot of shirts and he thought I had burned up people's shirts. He was just fussin', looking at the shirts because I had folded 'em so well and he started laughing and patting me on the back. He gave me a raise to $4 a week.

At that time, I thought I wanted to be a preacher or a cowboy. The first movie I ever saw was my own self in a movie. I must have been about 11 and some fellows came down there with a movie camera and they had me and Norman Kincaid run backward and forward across the street. They made my mother come to the back door with my brother in her arms.

These fellows had a bunch of my sisters getting on a train because they said there was a movement where all the black people were moving to Chicago and all the other northern cities. My mother got paid something for it. They gave us all tickets and we went down to the Almo Theater and saw this picture. Every time I'd look up and see myself, I would start screaming and hollering, "There I go!

There I go!" It was a silent—I think it was just like a newsreel.

When I was real small, I was pretty happy but after I got old enough to understand the race situation that existed, I began to get unhappy. This started mostly when I was going to Cherry Street School. When we would be coming home from school, a bunch of white kids would be chasing us with rocks and throwing bricks at us.

I used to hear my parents talk about it but you know how kids are, they pay no attention to this. After they started chasing me with the rocks and things, I began paying attention.

I tell people about things that happened when I was a kid and they go, "Oh, Dixon, man, cut that. People don't act that way." When I was a kid, we were living on Jackson and Locust Street and the Ku Kluxers marched by our house, dragging some black guy up to the school, tarrin' and featherin' and all that kind of stuff. You couldn't do nothing about these things.

The black man had to be a complete coward. Babe Harmon was the sheriff down in Vicksburg and he was going with a black woman that lived right across the street from us when we were on Locust Street. He'd go there any time of day or night and when he went to the house, her old man would have to run off the back porch. She got to the place where she'd get out there and say, "Hell, if that so-and-so comes back here . . ." and she was talking about her own husband.

They said that they were gonna keep everybody in what was considered their rightful place. All the people in the neighborhood, you knew 'em and everything would be okay, but when you'd get strangers walking down the streets, a lot of times they would look at you as if they wanted to tell you to get off it.

When you wasn't in your own neighborhood, a lot of times you'd have to walk out in the street rather than on the sidewalk when you'd see a bunch of younger white people coming along. The older ones, it didn't matter too much but the younger ones would get at you. They would always be casting slanderous remarks. That's when I started to get uneasy and unhappy so that's why I ran off the first time when I was 11 years old.

I ran out in the country to a place 11 miles from home called Bovina, Mississippi. People used to come in to my mama's restaurant from the country on weekends and buy bowls of soup for a dime. I met a lot of the country kids and they'd tell me about the fun they had out there. I thought they were having it better than us because they'd be sitting around counting their money after they'd sell their charcoal and vegetables.

I made up my mind—my mother sent me to go down to my sister's house so I just walked all the way out there on Jackson Road. I didn't know how to find the Tribbles but I thought I had walked to the end of the world and I hadn't gone 10 miles yet.

The first night it got dark and I didn't know where to stay. I went to this lady's house and slept on the porch and I didn't know she had these big old dogs in there until morning. She let those dogs out and scared the hell out of me. I walked down on this little old road until a man came along on a wagon and took me on down to Mr. Tribble's house. They were surprised, asked me how I had got there.

It was nothing like I expected—man, you're talking about a shack. I thought our house was raggedy but they had an old cistern on the side of the house where they run the gulleys from the side of the house so that when it rained, the water would go down in the cistern. You could draw water out of that cistern and how in hell people lived, I don't know. That water had wiggle-tails by the thousands in there—wiggle-tails is little young mosquitos—and those guys would be drinking the water and throwing back the wiggle-tails.

The house they lived in had great big holes in the floor. You could see the hogs and chickens running around under the house. They had bunk beds that were nailed upside the wall with hay on the bottom and a sheet or cotton sack or something. You could lay in the bed and see the stars outside and if you wanted to urinate, you'd get right out of the bed or stay in the bunk bed and urinate through the floor under the house on the chickens and pigs. They had a tin top on this house. It was always hot but when that rain would come, it would sound like a real storm and it would hardly be drizzling.

These youngsters were going to show me how to make a charcoal kiln and a little charcoal. I knew they'd come in on the weekend and bring charcoal and sell it for about 25 cents a lard can. I figured I was gonna make charcoal and make a whole lot of money. I had never worked like that before in my life—these guys were used to handling mules and I wasn't.

First they get upside of a bend in the river and start cutting down these trees that were roughly a foot through the middle in diameter.

Some of them were long enough so they'd cut 'em into logs, eight to ten feet long. They made this bed for the fire and started cutting these little trees and putting them along the end.

Those little trees was heavy because they were green and the sap and water were running out of them. A lady would bring us some dinner—a bucket with some beans and cornbread in it and a piece of sowbelly on top. We'd eat and go right back to work.

It took us about three days building this damned thing so we had all kinds of logs stacked up around there. After we got it set on fire, then we'd take the dirt from this hillside on top so it would smother down and punch air holes in there to keep it going to make this charcoal.

I was figuring it would be over by tomorrow but hell, that damn thing was burning a week. Then we had to haul barrels of water all the way from the creek so we had six or eight barrels of water sitting there. When the smoke turned white, the charcoal was supposed to be ready.

Sometimes, in the middle of the night, they'd have to go down there and sleep. I had never lived in the country before and we'd be going down through hills bare-footed. These guys would stop and say, "Hey, see that snake?" and kill a snake right in the road in front of me and I hadn't even seen the snake yet.

One night, we must have stayed too long but the damned thing caught afire and burned up most of the coal. They got me out of bed in the middle of the night and I'm damned if I can see them. We saved about three barrels of coal—selling it by the can like that, I guess we'd get about $3 out of it.

The country people who came into my mother's restaurant on Saturdays naturally told her where I was. When my mama was coming to get me, I was so glad I didn't know what to do.

She thought they lived in a better place, too, because she had never been out in the country that far. She brought me some clothes because I had worn my shoes out completely, my pants was all rags and I was in horrible shape. I thought I was going to get a whipping but she sat down and talked to me. "If you wanted to go, you could have said so but you didn't have to sneak off like that."

I was so happy to get back. I didn't know there was so much hard work in the world.

2

Now everybody's talkin' about the seventh son
In the whole round world, there is only one
I'm the one, yes, I'm the one
I'm the one they call the seventh son

Now I can tell your future before it comes to pass
I can do things for you that'll make your heart feel glad
I can look at the skies and predict the rain
I can tell when a woman's got another man

I can hold you close and squeeze you tight
I can make you cry for me both day and night
I can heal the sick and raise the dead
I can make you little girls talk out of your head

I can talk these words that sound so sweet
Makin' love with me, your heart will skip a beat
I can take you, baby, hold you in my arms
And make the flesh quiver on your lovely bones

*The Bovina escapade didn't cure Willie Dixon of his wandering ways.
Vicksburg would remain his home base until he headed to Chicago but*

his stay in Mississippi from 1926–36 was punctuated by frequent jaunts through hobo jungles to New York City and all over the South.

Some of his travels were involuntary. Dixon was arrested for stealing plumbing fixtures from an abandoned house in Vicksburg when he was 12 and sent to the Ball Ground County Farm north of the city. In 1929, he was arrested for hoboing near Clarksdale, Mississippi and sentenced to 30 days at the Harvey Allen County Farm before escaping and making his way north by mule and train to his sister's home in Chicago. Following a New York excursion, it was back home to Vicksburg and other occasional sidetrips—from inadvertently winding up on a boat headed to Hawaii to a more planned stint with the Civilian Conservation Corps at camps in Morton, Mississippi and Pensacola, Florida.

Part of the appeal was pure adventure, but another was the more practical one of survival—it was the onset of the Great Depression and Dixon was one of millions riding the rails in search of work. His size stood him in good stead around Vicksburg when it came to manual labor . . . be it loading coal at Dan Parker's coal yard, working as a roustabout loading and unloading boats on the riverfront, chopping wood or briefly working for the government.

And Dixon was already taking his first steps toward a musical career when he was home in Vicksburg, converting the poems in his poem books into songs and hustling some to hillbilly/country & western groups there. Later, a printer printed up paper strips with Dixon's words to "The Signifying Monkey" and he began selling those around town.

Dixon acquired his first formal musical experience singing bass with a local gospel quartet named the Union Jubilee Singers. The group was popular enough to tour in Mississippi outside the Vicksburg city limits and broadcast a 15-minute radio show every Friday from the WQBC studios on the eighth floor of the Vicksburg Hotel during the early and middle 1930s.

Another lure was boxing. Toughened by years of hard work, Dixon was a rock solid 200-pounder in his late teens who received a bit of training and began seriously considering a career as a fighter. And when that happened his eyes inevitably turned north, away from the limited opportunities in the South, to Chicago. In 1936, Dixon headed upriver towards the city that would be his home for the next 45 years.

SHEDRICK JOHNSON: a schooldays buddy of Willie Dixon in Vicksburg.

THEO PHELPS: the leader of the Union Jubilee Singers in Vicksburg and the man who taught Willie Dixon the principles of harmony singing.

I got up to be a pretty good size and I began to hear the kind of blues they sang on a county farm. They put me on a county farm, a place they called Ball Ground about 15 miles north of Vicksburg. This was the first time I had ever been in jail and I must have been about 12 years old. Me and Shedrick Johnson and Leroy Wilson got put in jail for a year for going into an old doctor's house. We got some old pipes and things that they had torn down.

That's when I really learned about the blues. I had heard 'em with the music and took 'em to be an enjoyable thing but after I heard these guys down there moaning and groaning these really down-to-earth blues, I began to inquire about 'em. I would ask guys why they sang these tunes and what does it mean and various ones would tell me. They were in prison for different things and at that particular time, I didn't know what it meant to fall victim of circumstance, although I was a victim of circumstance myself.

I really began to find out what the blues meant to black people, how it gave them consolation to be able to think these things over and sing them to themselves or let other people know what they had in mind and how they resented various things in life. I guess it kind of rubbed off on me because after you see guys die and everybody living in hopes . . .

The first time I made it with a woman was during the time I was in prison at Ball Ground Farm. The fat lady forced me. I used to see her messing around with different guys. She come along there and almost pick out the ones she'd want—"Hey, send me that big old nigger that was down yonder picking cotton on the end. I want him to clean out the barn."

She'd take 'em in the house or sometimes out in the corn crib and say, "I want you to do this." They had to do it all, just the way she wanted it. She could have hollered rape any time and from what I had heard, this woman had had other men killed.

It was humiliating. It really turned me against all that for a while. She was just a filthy woman and I really thought that all the women were like that.

I stayed a year and then I ran north. I got caught up there on a bigger county farm for riding the freight train. I hoboed up there with Shedrick, Robert Murray and Leroy.

The trains would be loaded, hobos from everywhere. It was the Depression and everybody was looking for jobs. We called ourselves heading up to Chicago and got caught there in Clarksdale, Mississippi. Me and Shedrick were walking along the highway right behind the rest of the guys. All of a sudden, the police come along and didn't do a thing to anybody else but they stopped us.

"Hey, where you guys going?"

"We're going to Memphis."

"Did you get off that train back there?"

"Yeah, same as everybody else did."

The next thing I know, them guys put cuffs on us and put us in the back of this damn little truck. They locked us up all night, picked up five or six other guys and all of them was black. We kinda began to realize and talk about that. The guys came the next day and said: "We're givin' you 30 days out on the Harvey Allen County Farm."

"For what?"

"Hoboing."

"But everybody else was hoboing."

"That's none of your business. We caught you."

They took us out there and they had a thing called the Cage, where everybody's supposed to count in at night and they put stripes on you and shackles on your leg. You'd have to learn how to put on your stripes with your chains on your legs. Most of the guys slept with them on.

They'd haul us out there to work and put us on a great big ditch dig. I had never seen a ditch that big and everybody jumped off the truck and was down there cutting weeds and singing. We were on top cutting and all of a sudden I hear somebody screaming: "Oh, Lawdy! Oh, Lawdy, captain, please stop doing it. Stop doing it."

That scared the hell out of me and my partner. I dropped the hoe I had and I run over there peepin'. Boy, they've got five guys on this one guy, one sitting on his head, one on each arm and each leg and this guy sitting up on the hill—they called him Captain Crush—has got a strap about eight inches wide. It's leather, about five or six inches long, a handle on it about two feet long and holes in the end of this strap about as big as a quarter. They called it Black Annie.

He's up on a mule and every time he hits this guy, flesh and blood actually came off this cat. He only hit him two or three times after he got to hollering and the guys holding him down could turn him loose after three licks because it would damn near paralyze him. He was out and they were still beating him.

We were standing there wide-eyed looking—you know how a bunch of kids is. I was only 13 years old then.

"Hey, come here," he called me.

"Me?"

"Yeah, you."

I go down there and this guy took that damn strap and hit me upside the head and I stayed deaf for almost four years. He knocked this big patch of skin off my face and I didn't even know what the hell was up. He hollered at me and I was laying there like a damned worm. I couldn't even get up. The guys dragged me into the wagon and drove me to the nurse. The next morning, when it was time to go, the guys had to snatch me out there with the rest of them.

SHEDRICK JOHNSON: I was involved when Dixon got arrested in Clarksdale and went to that little county farm around Clarksdale. I was a couple of years younger than he was and the age didn't make any difference. They'd pick you up during the harvesting season and throw you on the farms for so many days and get that free labor. They had straps and would whip you on the rump with a strap. That's the kind of deal it was back in that time.

WD: This Captain Crush that was running the farm didn't have no mercy—you talk about mean, ignorant, evil, stupid and crazy. He fouled up many a man's life. There was a preacher down there and this was the first time I saw a man beat to death. To hear a man screamin' and cryin' and begging God and everybody else to have mercy, this is a helluva thing in a young person's life. He never really gets over it, you know, because you'll always see it until the day you die.

They beat this guy until blood was running out of his mouth at the Cage. He died right there in his own blood and that dirt would be so hot and that dust so thick it would burn your feet through your shoes. After they beat him, they drug him over to the side and a little breath was still left in him. Where he had been bleeding out of his mouth and nose, you could see a little, bloody-colored bubble coming up from where he was breathing there. After awhile, you didn't see them no more and they'd tell you, "Go bury this nigger."

The word nigger means ignorance on the part of the individual who uses it. The people who use it are narrow-minded and stupid enough to want to harm somebody else in a way of speaking. When I hear blacks or whites use it, that's the only thing it means to me. If I don't know his name, why should I call him something that would make him feel bad?

The word nigger was created in slavery times when they claimed they were using the word nigger because people came from the Niger River. But common sense will tell you you don't name nobody by the river. If that was the case, everybody born along the Mississippi River would be called Mississippi. The word Negro is the same as nigger as far as I'm concerned because it's nothing but a nickname to try and embarrass somebody else.

It must have been about 15 days after Crush beat me when they said, "Look, you're going to be the water boy." I had to get these big barrels, go down to pump the water and then bring it up.

This went on until I knew my 30 days was up. I asked, "Hey, man, my 30 days, I know they're up now." A guy told me, "Hell, ain't nobody get away after 30 days. You'll be here until the day you die."

This kept running through my mind and every day I'd hear the train blowing. I knew they'd always be shooting or beating somebody to death there. There was another guy, a youngster—"Hey, you can run fast. We want to train the dogs so we want you to go up way over yonder. We'll let the dogs stay here until you get over there and up in one of those trees and then we'll turn the dogs loose."

They'd let the guy get way out in the middle of the field where they'd know damn well he couldn't get to the woods in time and they'd turn loose 15 or 20 bloodhounds. You'd hear him fighting or hollering for a little while and the dogs fighting and raising hell over him. These dogs would come back all bloody and sticky. They'd say to us, "Go out there and wash them off." Them dogs would be biting and every damn thing else and you're out there trying to wash them off with pump water.

I had been there maybe two months and one day I went to pick up a barrel of water about three o'clock. I made sure it was one of those days the dogs had been running a lot because they'd come back tired and lazy and hungry. They wouldn't be wanting to go out any more. I went down to a place where there was a mule and I got on and started riding.

I went by an old house that was way up there on the plantation and this old lady had some clothes hanging on the line. I figured I'd get some of those clothes but the minute I got off that mule, that old lady started saying, "Oh, no, son, please don't head over here. They killed my son, they killed my son."

"Well, I've got to have them clothes."

"Here, I'll throw you some," and she got up and throws me a pair of pants and says, "Don't get off him. Go on somewhere else."

I didn't think a mule had this much sense but this sonuvagun, knowing I'm trying to get away, started coming right back around these trees. I went to the Yazoo River and made him swim to the other side. That sucker had made a great big circle and was coming back to the police. He got up on a hill and started to hollering so I got a club and hit that mule upside his head and he fell out.

You get out there in those little country towns and you don't know where the hell you're going. You wouldn't know he was circling because you're trying to keep to the sides of the road and you're tired as hell. If I hadn't seen some of the buildings and places we worked before, I wouldn't have known.

It's close to 60 miles from Clarksdale to Memphis but the Allen Farm was 16 miles south of Clarksdale, right next to Parchman Farm. All you know is wide open spaces and woods. You knew the train was going north and south all the time so if you're walking along the edge of the woods, as long as you can see the smokestack and hear the trains blowing, you can go a certain direction. In the day time, you've got to get back in the wooded areas but a lot of times people have houses in them. It's a helluva job trying to duck all this stuff.

They didn't catch me and we went on farther by going along the railroad part of the way up. It had to be three or four days to get from that farm to Memphis. In the South, people had potato pumps. You get some corn stalks, stack 'em together, put sweet potatoes under there to keep during winter time. If I could find somebody's potato pump, I'd hang around there until I could get close to their houses some way and take a bunch of potatoes out of there. I ate fish, crawfish on the river bank, things like that. I lost so damned much weight on that one trip, you wouldn't believe it.

We came almost into the Nonconnah Yards and that's where I went north. I got on the freight train and came from Nonconnah Yards into the south yard of Chicago in Harvey, Illinois. I was afraid to contact my sister in Chicago so I got a job out there pulling onion bunches for six cents a bushel. An old man had a place over in an open field. Two or three guys were living there and they started telling me: 'Man, you crazy to be around here pulling onion bunches. You ain't gonna make no money."

"Well, what are you guys doing?" I thought I was doing pretty good making a dollar a day or something like that.

"Man, we go out and steal things."

"Like what?"

"Oh, clothing, shoes, different things."

Early one morning, I'm sleeping and this guy wakes me up: "Come on, we're going and I want you to be real quiet."

I didn't know anything in Harvey, Illinois, but this old guy's house, but we're cutting around these houses and I'm scared as hell. I can hardly see in the dark and this guy goes to a house and peers right through the window and sees another guy asleep. He goes up to another window and opens the window and said, "Get in here. I'll open the back door and I'll hand the stuff to you."

Sure enough, this guy goes in there and I'm tippy toein' around the back porch. Well, I didn't know about all these milk bottles that people leave out. I get up on the porch and sure enough, I open the damn door and hit all these goddamn milk bottles.

Somebody in the house yelled, "Hey, somebody's in here," and these cats come out through the door and we go running down the alley like hell. We must have run six or eight blocks and I don't know whether the police came or not. This cat was older and he had left his shoes there so he just took my shoes. It was two or three days before he came up with a pair of shoes for me.

Finally, I went on into Chicago. That was 1929 because I was 13 years old. It was the time of the Depression but I didn't feel it because my brother-in-law was working and so was my sister. They had just gotten there and both of them had good jobs. We were living at 4716 Forestville.

I didn't do nothing but sit around there for a while until my brother-in-law got me a job with him, you know. There wasn't any place to go but out there in the park. As a young man, I'd go to the park, go to where my brother-in-law worked and go to the movies and see Tarzan. They used to have all these different shows like Tarzan— they'd show one part today, another part tomorrow. The movie theater was right at 47th and Forestville.

The Metropolitan and Regal Theater was going good. That's when it had all these chorus girls and I remember Louis Armstrong's band was top notch—Pops was a young man and he was blowing his heartstring out. I knew some of the chorus girls at the Regal because some of them knew my sister. I used to see Cab Calloway's band there and he had on his long white tails.

That's what I had to look forward to other than trying to learn how to read and write better. They insisted on that. My sister used to make me read the paper. She said, "You don't know what's going on in Chicago. You've got to read the paper to me."

I got a job working on the L&M ice wagon. The L&M ice wagon was on State and 44th Street and I was making about $15 a week. There was a big old horse called Dan that would pull the wagon with the ice and a cover on the top of it and you'd be going down the alley selling ice. I was the one doing the work and the guy that started me off every morning was going off some place gambling and once in a while he'd come around and take my money. Carrying those hundred pounds of ice up to the fourth floor when you're 13 was nothing to laugh at.

I was involved in a lot of things as a youngster running around through Chicago. I didn't really know where I was or what the hell I was going to do, just prowlin', trying to learn. I was just a kid and I really didn't know nothing but work, go to school once in a while and work. Then the city started to get at me about going to school so I got a freight train and got the hell out of town.

I wanted to know what's in the world in different places ever since I was a kid. Naturally, I liked geography because it told me about a lot of places I wanted to see. Every time somebody said they had a chance to go somewhere, the moment they turned I was ready to go because I hadn't seen it and wanted to know about it.

I went to Midland, Pennsylvania and lived with a youngster about my age called Lawrence Lacy. I had met a guy from Chicago going back home and he was trying to find his way to Midland but he was fixing to catch the wrong train. We sat in a little hobo jungle for a while and I told him, "I ain't got nothing to do. I'll go over there with you."

Lawrence Lacy had a little garden with apple trees and I learned how to juggle apples and fool around like that. I stayed there a little while until I remembered a boy named Dumas Baker that left Vicksburg when I was a kid and moved to New York. I hoboed all the way to New York and got lost, didn't know east from west and north from south.

When I got to Brooklyn I was laying out in a little old park where all the rest of the hobos were sleeping. I lay down to get some sleep and somebody stole my shoes. I finally found Dumas and this northern boy, Scott, that had gone to school with my brother working fixing cash registers in a place that wasn't but half a block away from the park. He'd take me over where he worked so I could get some sleep and found me some shoes.

I stayed around for two or three weeks. We'd go to this really big marketplace and get packages of things they were throwing out, take them back down to the hobo jungle and fix some Mulligan stew. I stayed there until I went back to Vicksburg. I was telling all kids back there about how I had been different places but nobody believed it.

I always said that when I was grown I would do a lot of things. Naturally, when a boat would come up the river, I'd go down there when I was about 14 years old and haul sacks of whatever they had on the boat—cotton, oats, corn, everything. We would unload the barges for a dollar a day and they call that a roustabout.

We could hear the boats blow and tell what boat it was coming up the river. Everybody knew which boat it was by the way it blows— "Hey, man, that's the *George Henry Miller*"—and then everybody would run down and try to get hired for that boat.

A lot of people depended on these boats to live and when a boat would come up the river from New Orleans or Memphis, people would get on the boats. The guy would say we're gonna be gone so many days and sometimes the people would be in bad shape waiting for the man to come back with the money.

If a man went up the river and a woman didn't have no way to survive, sometimes she'd come down every day hoping to hear a boat blowing and coming back in. You take these facts of life and make them into songs. That song was "Somebody Tell That Woman" and Peter, Paul & Mary did it as "Big Boat Up The River."

I used to work at this coal yard when I was around the same age. They'd pay us ten or 15 cents a load for the amount of coal we would haul down to the railroad in one of those big railroad cars back out to where the coal yard was. They'd pay us 25 cents for each load but the driver got 15 cents and the helper ten cents. We'd make seven or eight loads a day and that was enough to eat off of.

We'd work like hell, hard all day long picking up these little lumps of coal from seven in the morning until you couldn't see at night. You'd come home, dirt smudging everything and the only bathtub we had was done with three little tubs, get the water and pour it over each other and like that. Every time we spit, it was all black as a miner. I was working for Dan Parker, the only black guy that had a coal yard at that time and he was treating the guys good.

There was this girl Elizabeth Martin that I liked. I met her when I was in the South as a youngster, around 16 or 17, and I was all bashful, shame-faced and everything. She was practically trying to put herself on me but I was bashful and didn't understand exactly what it was all about so she started messing around with a guy who was supposed to be her godfather.

One day I went down there spyin' on 'em, peepin' under the windowsill, and saw 'em in action. I was mad. I busted in the damn door there and just started cryin' and going on because I was hurt.

Sometimes I sold songs to traveling country & western groups just so I could get my name on a record. I knew one of the fellows named Tom and he used to play on the WQBC radio station down there in Vicksburg. A bunch of the fellows would be sittin' out there on a porch on Ryan Street off Belmont playing fiddles and guitars and singing. I would come up with these various songs and write it out and tell him how I thought it would go. They'd jump up, sing it and pay me.

Eventually they ended up on records but I don't know with what company. I remember some of the songs—"The Laundry Man," "The West Ain't Wild No More" and "Sweet Louise." Nothing happened with those songs but they recorded them. A record at that time must have cost 75 cents or a dollar and I didn't ever have that.

I was singing harmony in a five-piece musical thing with a carpenter down South named Theo Phelps. We used to work with him on carpenter's jobs and we'd go up to his house at night and he was teaching me and these other fellas named Willie Adams and Aaron Johnson how to sing. Every night you'd have to go over there by his piano and learn these beautiful harmony chords. I could play and sing all the parts—one time he'd have me singing the lead part, then the third, the tenor and the baritone and I wound up singing the bass all the time. I didn't play bass until I got to Chicago.

Me, Melvin Short, Willie Allen, Alonzo and Theo Phelps were the Union Jubilee Singers. The group would change because when one of the guys would quit coming to rehearsals, Phelps wouldn't use them in the group any more. Alonzo was another bass singer so whenever I would sing baritone, he would take the bass. I learned a lot of songs from this Gospel Pearl book that was a regular Sunday school and church book in the South.

We would hit all the little country churches and all the city churches. We'd have contests down there singing with different groups and we got to be pretty good. They had some tough quartets back then, like these guys out of Utica Institute that went all over the world singing. We went as far as Jackson, Utica, Greenwood and Greenville down in Mississippi.

We got a job broadcasting with WQBC on Fridays. There was a guy called W.T. Farley who had a clothing store and this clothing store gave all four of us a suit of clothes for advertising W.T. Farley. Boy, you couldn't tell us nothing. That was a big thing, you know—they didn't have but a very few radios and people would be walking for miles just to go to somebody's house, sit on the porch and listen to the radio.

We'd be going down to broadcast and hear people getting out of the neighborhood to go places where there was a radio. The guy at the filling station had a radio, Dan Parker at the coal yard and Curley's Barrelhouse had a radio. I was 17 or 18 then. There was no way to record it but I do remember they used to have a little disc recorder that would fit in a suitcase and boy, it was real high-priced.

THEO PHELPS: Me and Dixon met when times were tight. That was during Hoover's time, during that Depression. I had come out of school in '26—I went to Tuskegee Institute in Alabama—and I used to sing in the choir. I got a group of boys and we started to hang around and sing a lot in Dan Parker's coal yard. Dan Parker had a house there. He was a bachelor and a pretty good tenor singer so he would fall in and help us out occasionally.

We didn't have nothing else to do so we started to doing that quite a bit—sing in the night and go to all types of little parties. We were good, I tell you the truth. We'd hear a gramophone record and if it was good, we'd pick that record up and sing it just exactly like we heard it.

Old Dixon could sing more bass. I used to talk about him regular— "Man, we had a fellow with us who used to sing bass"—and he had so much body on it. Dixon was really good on that bass. It was in him and we just helped to get some of it out of him. Our favorite song was "Vicksburg Boys Are We."

WD: And "One Day When I Was Walking Down The Lonesome Road." What I liked about Theo Phelps, he was so rough on us with that harmony situation. Any time you harmonized with him, every note had to be perfect. We could get them chords to harmonize and blend so beautiful, boy, I hated to turn the chord loose. That harmony is sweet and it makes you feel the music and gives you inspiration. Anybody can holler but you don't feel it.

During that time, I went to Hawaii because I got on a boat that was supposed to be traveling from place to place loading and unloading stuff. They changed the cargo because the boat that was going up and down the Mississippi couldn't take the seas. I got on the boat they unloaded on and that's how I went to Hawaii.

It was a work boat and they had all kinds of people on there, everybody talking everything but English. They was hauling animals— cattle and that kind of stuff—and that was a nasty, sloppy, filthy job. I was probably out at sea three or four months.

That boat was scaring the hell out of me skippin' and dodgin'. Boy, that's the damnedest feeling in the world, going out on the ocean and getting caught in one of them storms. The waves are so deep that when the boat goes down, it looks like the waves is going to come right over the top of the boat and all of a sudden you shoot up and it's on top and you're lookin' way out across the waters. The next second you're back down—and gettin' seasick.

I met an old boy on there called Barney Phillips. He come from my hometown but I didn't know him there. He used to sing this "La Paloma" in Spanish. In the middle of the night, when the waves had calmed down and you could hear the old boat chugging, this cat would get up there on the deck. The other guys would sit around—some of 'em would be sleeping out on the deck—and this cat would get to singing this song all in Spanish in a very high tenor voice. That would sound so good to me. When we got back, I had him try and sing with the little group we had there but he couldn't stay long because he'd been running on those damn boats all his life.

One time I got a job working for the government experiment station. They had a place where they had a pattern of how all the different rivers in America run. They were trying to keep the floods away because a flood down there in 1928 had flooded all the Delta. The government was experimenting with these rivers and they'd have to make sand and dirt models to show where the water would be rising out so they would build levees along the highway.

The government at that time was a helluva good job—$60 a month. We had four black guys that was loading and eight white guys that would load this other truck.

They didn't allow us to stop. We'd have to keep shoveling and as soon as one truck got through, the next truck would roll in. We had to load twice as many as the white guys so we worked like hell. They'd give you a salt pill to take and them other guys wouldn't even be sweating.

Some wise guys said, "Look, we don't really have to go this fast," so we slowed down.

The boss found out. "Hey, what the hell's going on over here?"

"We're working."

"Yeah, but you ain't workin' at the speed you're supposed to. If you guys can't do better, I'll have to let you go."

The other guys had told me that if we're starting this thing, we're just gonna quit. I said, "It's gonna be hard for me to quit because there ain't nobody working in my family but me." But I jumped and quit and another guy quit, too.

The boss goes over to the last two guys.

"What's happened here?"

"We feel like we're working too damned hard."

"All right, you either work like you been working or you fired, too." The guys picked up their shovels and went back to work and we couldn't go back because there were about 30 guys waiting on the job. When I didn't get up to go to work the next morning, my mama cried, losing a good job like that.

Then I went to a Civilian Conservation Corps camp that they had out in Morton, Mississippi. They were building parks and planting trees in the South and they had laid out little log cabins. I already knew how to drill a little bit because of playing soldier with the boys at home and I was a big, strong healthy boy, so they named me a sergeant. I didn't have to do anything but see that the other guys do the work.

That's where I developed the idea that I wanted to be a fighter. There was an old boy at a white camp over there who was supposed to have been a professional fighter, number seven among the heavyweights. I used to go over and train with him and that guy used to beat the living hell out of me. He must have thought I was the champion of the world but I wouldn't stop because I didn't want my men to feel like I couldn't take it.

I got to a place messing with him that I could fight a little bit but that guy damned near stopped me from being a fighter. I was trying to be a rassler, too. There was a whole bunch of them around Vicksburg and I thought, because I was a big youngster, I'll go out there and rassle with these cats because they'd pay you to come out and tussle with them in this place in the park outside Vicksburg.

I would whip all the boys around there and they thought I was a great fighter and I thought I was a helluva fighter, too. I'd been working so hard, hauling logs and timber, and I was really pretty tough. The average guy couldn't hurt me.

I used to let the guys hit me in the chest, the stomach, anywhere but my face, for a nickel all the time from when I was a kid to until I got to Chicago. I'd have a stack of nickels everyday from guys who think they're going to do me some damage. A guy called Louis Carroll called himself a prizefighter. This guy swung and hit me in the stomach and broke his arm and the word got out. On the weekend, men would come from everywhere. Some of the guys would hit me and knock me down but it didn't mean nothing because I was in good shape in the stomach.

The average person doesn't know, in a whole lifetime, what it means to be in real shape. We used to be out just trying to see who could out-man each other, who could pick up logs, how far can you throw a stone, just playing around because we had nothing else to do.

When the time came to work, all of them was trying to outwork each other. They were paying $1.25 for a cord of wood—a cord was about four feet tall—and we'd be trying to see who could cut the most wood. We'd be out there working and sweating like hell. Guys were cutting two or three cords of wood a day and sometimes if two of us got together, we could cut four cords. Sometimes we're sawing down trees five or six feet in the butt end, cutting 'em up and stacking 'em into cords.

If we cut four cords, that was $5 between the two of us and most of the people around there wasn't making but a dollar a day. Nobody complained about nothing because you were doing something all the time. You didn't have to worry about getting fat when you were working like that every day all day. You'd get hard as a rock.

I had some fights down there that weren't anything. They had a big old platform on the outskirts of Vicksburg with no ropes around it and they'd have two or three of these country guys knock the hell out of each other. They'd give 'em two or three dollars and I used to go there. You fought with your fists and one of those boys would hit you with his natural fist and knock you cold.

I fought out there two or three times and was lucky enough to get away winnin'. There weren't any ropes there so you could duck to a certain extent but when you go to duckin' and there ain't no ropes, the other guy would fall right off that damned stage into somebody's arms. They'd throw him right back up there.

All those things was great experience when I was young. At the same time, trying to fit this Biblical situation that my mother and father had been teaching me into all this was a hard job. Then I got involved in a few historical ideas, reading here and there and talking with different ones around the world.

You'd be surprised at some of those old guys down in that neck of the woods. Even today, you look at them and say, "He don't know his way out of a shower of rain," and he knows a lot about the history of black people. A lot of 'em don't care to discuss it because they've been discouraged about it so much. Everybody wrote books on black history but the people that knew about it.

They didn't play blues on the radio then. The only way you would hear a blues is go by the Barrelhouse because they were playing it there on records. You could hear some of the piano players that were around there singing or guys out in the field singing blues. A very few people had a gramophone that you could wind up.

My brother L.V. was working in a little radio place there. They didn't have nothing but little crystal radios with these big antennas. L.V. made the first portable radio they had down in that part of the country. He had a little antenna on the front of his bike that could pick up everything.

When he came out with his little box on the front of his bicycle, people used to come from everywhere to stand around and see him play that radio and get different programs from different places. On Friday night, there was a station that used to come out of Chicago all night—it was on 40th and South Park—with Fatha Hines on. You'd hear Cab Calloway advertise on there.

They'd pick up that station from Chicago down in Kentucky and the Kentucky one would carry it on down to Memphis and Memphis to Jackson, Mississippi. People in each area would hear it and we'd come out every Friday night just to hear Fatha Hines comin' on. We'd be talking and a lot of us built it up in our minds that we'd be going to Chicago.

The Union Jubilee Singers were still going good. We'd go out of town places and people would be hanging all in and out the windows trying to get into the place just to hear us sing. But there was no money in it in church so me and Marion Short ran off to New Orleans.

We came damn near to starving to death and if it wasn't for a few banana cars down there we would have starved to death. We ate bananas every damned day—I didn't know you could eat so many bananas and lose weight. Finally, I got a job down there unloading barges on the wharves and that would give us something but it wasn't enough.

We was living with a lady and I think she knew we were hungry because we had a little room right next to the kitchen. She and the other ladies would be in there talking and we'd be laying there with the smell of onions cooking.

One day I was in the tub and Marion always tried to look down but we looked at each other's face and he said, "Dixon, goddamn it! I'm gonna pawn my last pair of pants."

He jumps up and grabs these gray trousers and ends up going down the street to the pawnshop, both of us so hungry we don't know what to do. He goes in and throws the pants up there. "I want to get $5 on these pants."

"Five dollars? Hell, man, we don't give $5 on a suit of clothes. It's generally a buck, a couple of bucks, maybe."

"But they're good looking, beautiful pants."

The guy laid 'em out, raised one leg and there's two big holes right in the seat of the pants. "What the hell you think I am, a damn fool? You guys get out of here!"

Marion said, "Man, I didn't know those holes was in there. What are we going to do?"

Back to the banana car. We sat down and actually cried, eating them bananas and actually crying. Most of 'em were green. They had two long lines of banana cars there. Finally, I got a job down at the wharf and they paid off every night. At this time, they had fish places where they'd sell you four or five fish for a dime. We went in there and ordered so much fish the man stopped the fire and started looking at us.

Marion finally got a job cooking on the railroad and lucky thing he was, because I was about starving to death. Before anybody else came in there, I went down and knocked myself out. That was the first time I'd had a good meal in God knows when.

Then I got a job on the *Steamer Capitol* excursion boat shoveling coal and came all the way in to Rock Island, Illinois. It was time to get involved in anything, you know. I was tired of just laying around there down South doing nothing because whatever you did, you weren't gonna get pay worth a damn and there was no way to advance. I went on to Chicago and stayed with my sister and her husband at 4837 Prarie.

3

I'm ready
Ready as anybody can be
I'm ready
Ready as anybody can be
I'm ready for you
I hope you're ready for me

I gotta axe handle pistol
On a graveyard frame
That shoots tombstone bullets
Wearing balls and chain
I'm drinkin' TNT
Smokin' dynamite
I hope some screwball
Start a fight

Chorus: Because I'm ready
Ready as anybody can be
I'm ready for you
I hope you're ready for me

All you pretty little chicks
With your curly hair
I know you feel
Like I ain't nowhere
But, stop what you're doing
Baby come over here

I'll prove to you baby
That I ain't no square

I've been drinking gin
Like never before
I feel so good
I want you to know
One more drink
I wish you would
It takes a whole lot of loving
To make me feel good

Chicago. The Windy City, the end of the Illinois Central railroad line that moved from New Orleans through Mississippi, Memphis and St. Louis to Chicago, home of the most popular black newspaper in the country, the Chicago Defender.

In the 1880s, the stretch along South Parkway (usually referred to as South Park and now renamed Martin Luther King Drive) had been home to the creme de la creme of Chicago society. By 1900, it had turned into the high-tone district for the black elite. Following the World War I era northward migration of blacks from the South (who detrained at Union Station at 12th and Michigan after it was completed in 1924), a substantial portion of the area south of the downtown loop became predominantly black.

On the northwestern edge of that area, creating a buffer zone between the city's burgeoning black population and its white neighborhoods, was "Jewtown," a district first populated largely by Jewish immigrants who arrived in Chicago in the late 1800s and later by the expanding black community. The centerpiece of Jewtown was Maxwell Street, the mile-long strip of street merchants which became a central part of Chicago blues lore as the open-air location where Mississippi transplants made their stab at survival by plugging in their instruments and passing the hat on the weekends.

Dixon's boxing plans started off well enough as he won the Illinois heavyweight Golden Gloves championship (novice division), sparred with the legendary heavyweight Joe Louis and turned pro. His pro career ended abruptly after four fights when he was suspended for a brawl in the boxing commissioner's office but Dixon had kept his hand in, musically, by singing in various groups. One, including his brother Arthur and nephew Lionel Turner, sang spirituals on Sunday morning on the WSBC radio show of Jack L. Cooper, the first major black deejay in Chicago.

More importantly, Dixon hooked up with Leonard "Baby Doo" Caston, the man who persuaded him to abandon boxing for a musical career and made Dixon his first instrument—a one string, tin-can bass. The pair entered the hustle and bustle of the Chicago music world, working on the streets of Chicago, going into clubs and passing the hat. Dixon got his first recording experience with the Bumpin' Boys, serving as an unofficial vocal coach when the group went into the studio for Chicago producer J. Mayo Williams around 1938.

Nothing came of those sessions but Dixon did eventually make it onto wax with the first serious group he formed with Caston circa 1939, the Five Breezes. In November, 1940, the Five Breezes cut eight tracks that were released on RCA's race records subsidiary Bluebird.

But it was not an easy time to break into the Chicago music world. The city's position as a major recording center had eroded following a 14-month ban on recording by the local musicians' union headed by James C. Petrillo running through 1936–37. And it was never an easy time for black artists to break into a record business which had established the separate "race music" market for their recordings.

Several companies developed race record subsidiary labels for their black artists—Vocalion with Brunswick in the 1920s and early thirties, OKeh with Columbia, Bluebird with RCA and Mercury with Decca. Race records—also known as sepia or ebony—usually sold for half the price of releases on the mainline pop labels, meaning that a 78 went for something like 35 cents, with a corresponding decrease in artist or songwriting royalties . . . if royalties were even paid for a recording.

And, of course, they usually weren't. Producers and record companies operated on a straight cash basis for sessions, and those one-shot payments became the foundation for the continuing charges *of exploitation that would surface in later years. Most black artists had no knowledge of the intricacies of copyrighting their material and producers and record companies often didn't see any long-range value for those songs. Many famous blues tunes wound up in public domain because no one figured that the money to be made by copyrighting them would amount to anything substantial.*

Race records were a marginal sideline for large record companies and that left a few individuals as major power-brokers who controlled the recording careers of early blues performers. By the start of World War II in Chicago, it had largely boiled down to two men, J. Mayo Williams at Decca/Mercury and Lester Melrose at Bluebird, Vocalion and later OKeh.

But even Melrose and Williams couldn't get around the ban on recording declared by American Federation of Musicians Union president Petrillo in an attempt to keep the jukebox business from putting live musicians out of work by demanding a royalty payment from record labels. Coupled with wartime rationing of shellac, an essential ingredient in making 78s, that effectively shut down studio action from 1942–44.

Dixon's musical career had already been derailed late in 1941 when Chicago police arrested him onstage for evading the draft. Apparently, after several months' worth of trials and imprisonment, Dixon was released, classified 5-F and barred from any sort of defense work in 1942.

He formed the Four Jumps of Jive shortly after his release, played around Chicago and ultimately the group made it into the studio in 1945 to cut four sides for the fledgling Mercury label. Dixon's army problems prevented him from joining Caston when the latter backed vocalist Alberta Hunter on a USO tour overseas but when Baby Doo returned, they joined forces again and formed the Big Three Trio.

LEONARD "BABY DOO" CASTON: persuaded Willie Dixon to abandon boxing for music, made him his first bass and taught him how to play. Caston performed with Dixon in the Five Breezes and Big Three Trio and remained Dixon's close friend until his death in 1987.

When I first came to Chicago, the area of 31st up to 55th and Cottage

Grove on the east to Halsted on the west was the area most black people lived in. They had a smaller area over on the West Side, around 14th Street to a little north of Madison. It extended from downtown all the way out to Western Avenue. They had a few nightclubs on the West Side but the main featured nightclubs, like the Club DeLisa, were on the South Side.

The Club DeLisa had been there for years and they would bring in entertainment from everywhere around the world. Every old timer who was considered anybody big worked there. They were on the south side of the street at 55th, which is Garfield Avenue, and State, but they moved across the street to a great big place that could probably seat 1,000 or more.

Early Sunday morning is when they featured the big thing and everybody would come from everywhere to put on their show. You'd have to reserve your table because everybody knew it was going to be full. If you were an entertainer, anybody in the area with a name and they knew you, you could walk in for nothing. If you weren't, you'd have to pay as much as $5-$6.

There was another club later on that Joe Louis had—the Hurricane —on 55th but up by South Park or Prarie. There was a little section there that had four or five different places of entertainment. This was right down a wide boulevard and on the other side were hotels and chicken shacks.

Everybody was busier than hell, moving all the time. Every four or five minutes there was a streetcar and all of them would be full in the morning and late in the evening with people going back and forth to work. It was the same thing on the elevated and everybody would be running up and down the main street selling fruit, vegetables or some gimmick, a doll or this barking dog.

Where I came from, I didn't know that many people was in the world. It was really beautiful but you can't imagine that after you see it today unless somebody would show you a picture. It would be nothing to see a guy coming down the street with a tall hat on or tails because he'd probably been working somewhere and walking home.

It was a great thing for a man to wear a derby. Very few had caps back then. Most everybody, I thought, smoked. If a guy didn't smoke, he was just a country guy, probably. It seemed like the country people would talk and act a little different. They would act real careful about things. They was more courteous than the average city person, and you'll find that today.

People used to think it meant something if they had a squirrel tail on their car. A lot of guys on the South Side would have his hat broke down across his eyes and stand up beside his automobile posing, squirrel tails fallin' in front of 'em and all these different emblems on the radiator cap—a horse or dog or somebody's face or a statue on the front of the car.

I was young and strong so I jumped in the fighting game. I started training at Eddie Nichols' gym down on 49th Street. The guys there could fight good but it just seemed they weren't hitting hard.

I didn't know people had to go through all the training in order to fight. One guy took me down to the gymnasium just to see the guys train and I was lookin' at 'em laughing. I was running around the blocks and I felt that was unnecessary because I had been hauling logs and everything in the South. I was hard as a rock—a guy wasn't going to hurt me unless he hit me in the eye or something.

When I fought the Golden Gloves, I didn't have any training. I just knocked out every damn body and that was it—I won the Golden Gloves for Illinois in the heavyweight division in 1937. I fought at the Chicago Stadium; they had some guy there they were trying to bill as the White Bomber out of Germany. I won that fight and didn't even hit the guy. I hit at him and missed, he fell and the manager jumped over the ropes saying, "Hell, I'm not going to let that sonuvabitch hit my boy."

I was fighting under the name James Dixon at the time. I told them Willie James Dixon but they got information from my sister. She always called me W.J. and they asked her what does W.J. stand for. She said Willie and James so they started to writing it up under James Dixon.

I got the Golden Glove and one of the medals. Things got kind of rough and I had to pawn the Golden Glove two or three years later right there on 47th Street.

I turned pro and won two or three pretty good fights. My managers were talking about how I was going to get some money but the thirty or forty dollars I was fighting for wasn't very much.

We went down to the commissioner's office in Chicago, Joe Trainor's office. I was discussing the situation with the commissioner and he said, "I think you're doing pretty good." He had a fellow look in the files and come out with the contracts. I came to find out the fights I hadn't been getting were for more money and they were having me fight for less.

The first fight, they gave me $50 and that was supposed to have been a $200 fight. The second one, I think they gave me $100 and that was a $300 or $400 fight. The third fight I was supposed to have got $1,000 and I think I got $200 and it had to be cut up between my managers and trainer and everything else.

We were discussing it when my managers came in and we got to scuffling up there in the boxing commissioner's office. Me and my manager knocked over a gang of things and tore up the office pretty bad. They sent us a letter expelling me from the fight game for six months and they expelled them for keeps.

When I first came to Chicago, there was a fellow named Brother Ratliff and we had a little group. Jack L. Cooper was one of the first black radio announcers and we used to broadcast out of Chicago at Jack L. Cooper's station at 45th and Indiana on the top floor. We used to go up there to sing with the Spiritual Quartet. I was doing spirituals with one group, singing pop tunes with another group and blues with another at the same time.

But Brother Ratliff, he and I and Bernardo Dennis—the same one that was in the Big Three Trio, I was living in Bernardo Dennis' house at 39th and Dearborn—and Bernardo's little brother would go up to Jack L. Cooper's station every Sunday morning. We started singing kind of popular stuff and then Bernardo's little brother got involved in some trouble and that broke up the group. Baby Doo Caston found me after that.

During that time I was just laying around and training, Baby Doo came in the gym there playing guitar and singing. We'd sit on the side of the ring and I'd sing with him because I had been singing harmony in those gospel groups in the South and I knew the bass line to just about everything.

In school, I used to sing bass all the time. I used to specialize in those bass songs like "Ole Man River" and "Sweet River Of Peace." I had been practicing bass singing so long until I knew the basic backgrounds of the average song because, like it's taught in harmony, it would be the I–III–IV tones that make the chord. A lot of bass singers go over real strong in organizations, particularly in harmony groups, because he can make the whole chord change and sound so much different by a half tone.

If you decide you want to lower the third, you can make a minor tone out of the whole chord just by lowering the third chord a half tone. It's just like playing a piano or any instrument—you want to design your chord system and it doesn't take but one note to make another whole chord.

LEONARD CASTON: Dixon was singing with his brother Arthur and I and his nephew Lionel Turner and another fella named Paul had a group called the Bumpin' Boys. We used to go around the gym and watch him work out. He wasn't getting too many fights so I told him, "Look, man, why don't you try it with us? With your talent you probably could get something going."

WD: Me and Baby Doo hit it off right from there. I've been real lucky about things like that. I never fall out with anybody. One thing is I have never had time enough—when people were talking about something that I didn't feel was interesting enough, I just couldn't get with it.

Once you call yourself a singer, you never saw any singers that didn't get along until they started making money. Most singers, especially group singers, if you hear a couple of guys out there harmonizing and you think you can sing, you're gonna rush right over there and get your little bit in there. It always comes out sooner or later.

By Baby Doo being around there all the time, he didn't have anything else to do but practice and they liked the idea of my harmony with the group's. He'd come up with a different outfit every day but he got this Bumpin' Boys group together and I was kinda instructing them a little bit.

They liked that and they were so glad when I got the chance to get out there and get with them. I didn't actually play with the Bumpin' Boys. I was just singing bass and I used to try and imitate the Mills Brothers where they had this bass you'd do with your mouth.

We did some things with J. Mayo Williams when he was working for Decca. J. Mayo Williams had an office on Hubbard Street. The Bumpin' Boys was my nephew Lionel, my brother Arthur, another boy called

Paul, and Eugene Gilmore, and we used to go out there, sit around all day and eat. When the Bumpin' Boys went into the studio, Baby Doo was in there because he was playing the guitar.

I'd made a song called "Beat Her Out, Bumpin' Boys" and, at that time, they didn't have tapes. They had those great big thick waxes they used to cut on. If you ruined one, they had a shaver that would shave the thing down and get it level again. They'd make another cut on the same wax and when they got the better takes, you could press it right off that wax. Those big old thick waxes was expensive and by the time we ruined a couple, hell, they was about ready to get rid of us, anyway.

LEONARD CASTON: Later, we got together and formed this group called the Five Breezes in 1939. There was a fella named Cool Breeze, Dixon, Willie Hawthorne, Eugene Gilmore and me.

This guy Cool Breeze was named Freddie Walker and he was the MC and frontman. He was a fairly decent singer and we were practicing harmonizing together without any instruments. In those days, the Mills Brothers, Ink Spots and Cats and Fiddles were very popular and they were singing this four and five part harmony stuff.

We tried to develop a style of our own but, in order to get recognition from people, we had to do some of their stuff. Dixon always wanted to be original. He used to tell me, "A mockingbird can always imitate other birds singing but he don't have a tune of his own," when I was figuring I had to play like other people.

WD: I was playing this big, tin-can bass that Baby Doo made. He took an oil can, put one string on it and I could play that thing pretty good. We were working at Martin's Corner on the West Side of Chicago. Jim Martin was a big politician over there. He had a gambling casino on Lake Street.

LEONARD CASTON: The Five Breezes used to go around from place to place and pass the hat. We went into Jim Martin's dirty and ragged, didn't look like nothin', but we had good harmony. Mrs. Martin and Joe Louis' wife, Marva Louis, heard us and they called us back. We went in there that night and the next day, too, passing around the hat.

Jim Martin called and they hired us. We went in there with an old guitar and Willie had an oil-drum bass. Martin saw that we needed some instruments so he called the Chicago Music Company store and told 'em, "I'm sending some kids down there. Give 'em what they want." I got my first electric guitar and Dixon got an upright bass that was tall but not oversize. We stayed at Martin's Corner for almost a year.

WD: We could have stayed there as long as we wanted but we wanted to move around. The Five Breezes got a job at the Pink Poodle at 502 South State Street and these two gangsters, Louie and Joe, ran it. They had one of those B-joints where all the chicks would walk around on the stage half-naked and sing and talk trash and con the public.

Some guys came in from Springfield, Illinois and hired us to go down there and by this time we had our thing together pretty good. We would perform in a church in the daytime, play spirituals and things, and play blues, swing and popular music at the club at night.

But the guys we had been dealing with in Chicago sent these two guys down to where we was working in Springfield and told the owners there that Joe and Louie wanted us back at the Pink Poodle the next Tuesday. The guy in Springfield was afraid to keep us so we had to go back.

LEONARD CASTON: We were there on a Friday night and that Sunday, he took us to the railroad station and we rode the Abraham Lincoln train Sunday morning. We got back in Chicago and called this guy at the Pink Poodle, told him we was in town and we went to work that Sunday night. In fact, we had to break up in order to get out of there. But he was paying us $35 a week apiece and that was good money in 1941.

WD: That was better than everybody else was making. My brother-in-law was a board-cutter in a place called the Inn Tag Ink company. They made printing ink for papers and things. He got me a job but it wasn't paying but $25 a week and I was there for about a year steady. Everybody thought that was a great job but I quit to come back to singing with Caston.

We made more in tips. Jewtown was the best place to go, especially on the weekends. Sunday morning early people came from everywhere to sell their goods. Garage sale stuff, they'd have it in the streets all over the place. If you gave a guy a decent price for anything, he wouldn't refuse it.

Everybody knew it was a bargaining thing. Guys would raise their price so they could bargain and cut down. I could get ten pairs of good socks for $3, take them to another street and sell them for $1 a pair. They'd sell these hot dogs and things, cook 'em out in the open, hamburgers and chops, onions and hot peppers; you could smell it cookin' a ways away.

We'd go to Jewtown and set up and man, the people would come and give us so many pennies and dimes and nickels, we'd just have a bucketful of them. We wouldn't even count 'em. We'd just put 'em in three piles and everybody would take a pile. I remember many times when we used to come home with $50 apiece and that was more than the average guy was making as a salary. I was working at the stockyards and I wasn't making but $30 a week.

I was working in the freezer there most of the time, luggin' beef or pushing beef around on rollers or taking 'em from one place to the other on your shoulder. You didn't have a long ways to carry it because they kept the boxcars as close to the freezer as they could, but you had to pick it up off the rails and put it on the other rails in the boxcar. Some of it would weigh 3–400 pounds if you had a whole half of beef. That's heavy work but you get accustomed to it like everything else.

I could always get a job, being young and strong. Anywhere they needed somebody to do any kind of labor they'd look up and see me. I'd work every place they'd let me work for a while and sooner or later, they'd fire me.

One of the reasons I never did hold too many jobs too long is that when they get a big guy that's young and healthy, they think he should do all the heavy work. Every time they get ready with something heavy to be hauled or lifted up, they'll have you come by 40 of the little guys that ain't doing a damn thing. My salary was the same and a lot of times, I'd just say the hell with it and quit.

I worked at a beauty parlor down there on 47th and South Park, too. They call it Martin Luther King Drive now. They had me cleaning up around this beauty parlor and if you have ever had respect for women, don't work in a beauty parlor. Every woman in there was trying to show her behind to you or they'd have you shining shoes and they wouldn't have on panties. I saw most of those women's butts more than I saw their faces.

I got into women after I came back to Chicago. I had some little old girl I would play around with down South. I was dying to be a fighter and I told her that when I went to Chicago and won the Golden Gloves, I was going to marry her. Well, I came to Chicago, I won the Golden Gloves, but I didn't marry her.

Her mother and her came up there to see me in Chicago—her name was Mary Hunter and I guess we stayed together for a year or so. She ran to go to other places and see more. I was real jealous of her and like that. She told me to give up that bass fiddle for her and I couldn't afford to give it up.

She called my bass fiddle the starvation box. She said, "One of us has to go. You either give up that starvation box or me." We had things pretty rough when we were youngsters and it was hard but I gave her up and kept the starvation box. I've met her on several occasions since then. She said, "That old starvation box paid off, huh?"

When we weren't doing anything, I used to just go up and down the street giggin' with the bass by itself. This is one of the ways I learned to play the melodies of all the songs from anything. I could play the melody on the song, sing a little bit of the melody, dance around the fiddle, get the people clapping their hands and I'd be going into my act with the fiddle and I could make money.

Me and a guy called Irving Spencer got into a place where the guy wanted to put on a show and didn't have a piano, so we just put on a show right on Madison Street with just a bass and guitar. You come up with a couple of girls that can kick their legs up high and dance and that's enough.

When I got to Chicago, I was selling "The Signifying Monkey" for ten cents and 15 cents or two for a quarter everywhere. I'd have 'em made up in large bundles and sell it to several different guys who could sell it for me in the street. They'd go into beauty parlors and nightclubs and barber shops and just up and down the street talking about the Signifying Monkey: "The monkey turned around on a bright summer day/There's a bad so-and-so right down the way." They'd go through it and people got to laughing at it and they'd sell it to them, you know. I must have sold 30–40,000 of the things.

I used to sell song sheets on the streets of Chicago. Me and Cool

Breeze used to stand in front of a place called South Center that was like a big shopping center down on 47th and South Park and sell these song sheets for ten cents or 25 cents. A lot of people would make them on their own and a lot would make them for recording companies.

They had the Big Ten popular songs and the songs that black people did they called race songs. Every month they'd come out with a new list of songs. When a song comes out, they put them all on song sheets and sell 'em. You could buy the song sheets over in Jewtown.

I made up a little thing they called the "Song Title Jive." I'd get these song sheets that had the different songs and I'd take the different song titles and say 'em all together: "Hello, there, Miss Feeling Fine/Tell me your name, I'll tell you mine/Under the shade of the old apple tree/I want some brown girl to rock it for me/Ooh wee, baby, you sure look good to me." All these are the names of songs and when I stopped, I'd tell about this song on the hit parade. I'd always have my "Signifying Monkey" in my other pocket in a little roll by itself and sell it separate from the others.

Then I'd say, "Now, I got this special for you. Did you ever hear of the Signifying Monkey?" Then I'd go to telling it: "Said the monkey to the lion on a bright sunny day/There's a big bad mother living right down your way/Talking about goats and elephants and a lot of other things I'm afraid to say/The lion jumped up all full of rage/Like a Harlem cat that's full of gage/He chased the elephant under the tree/And said, Hey, big boy, it's you or me/But the elephant looked at it from the corner of his eye/Sayin' you better find somebody to fight your size/So the lion jumped up and made a fancy pass/And the elephant knocked him on his hairy ass." I was using all the bad terms and it was rough.

Then the war broke out and everybody started adding to it. After I got involved in music, I decided to clean it up and put it on record. When you cleaned it up, it didn't sell as well. A lot of times they called it "The Jungle King" because we recorded it as "The Jungle King" with the Big Three Trio when we first made it as a song in 1946.

The army had been sending me a personnel notice off and on for a long time but I made up my mind I wasn't going no damn where. They came on the stage down at the Pink Poodle when the Five Breezes were playing one night, when we came back the second time. This was during the time that Japan bombed Pearl Harbor and they picked

me up and put me in jail. I told them I was a conscientious objector
and that I wasn't gonna fight for nobody.

They started my trial and I told them I didn't feel I had to go because
of the conditions that existed among my people. I explained to 'em
that I didn't feel it was justified according to the laws of the
government because of the way they were treating black people. I
explained to them in several court cases, "Why should I go to work to
fight to save somebody that's killing me and my people?"

I said I wasn't a citizen, I was a subject. I was telling them about the
14th and 15th Amendment. A lot of people in Chicago felt like this,
you know. Under the conditions that existed at that particular time,
what the hell did you have to fight for? They were mistreating every
damn body all over the world, especially our people.

I just stayed in jail, about ten months off-and-on. They put me on
bread and water for a while there but I just wouldn't go. After I got in
jail, I started explaining to people why I wasn't going. Some of 'em
were mad with me and some were glad. It was creating arguments and
making a disturbance so they were glad to get me out of there because
I was working up too damn many people.

They started telling me, "Well, you were born in the United States."
Hell, that doesn't make you anything. All my folks were born here but
they never had papers or anything. I told the judge one time, "An egg
can be hatched in a stove but that doesn't make it a biscuit just because
it came out of the stove."

They must have had me come to court 30 or 40 times trying to pass a
decision. Every time they'd bring me to court, I'd tell them about the
Congressional Record I had read that Senator Bilbo from Mississippi
had a bill that was stating any African descendant that rebelled against
the United States government would be henceforth and forever more
free to return to Africa and go to the Liberian government that America
had set up for the free slaves of America. I created such a helluva
commotion in the courts about this thing until they were afraid to let
me out and afraid to leave me in jail because they said I was
influencing the black people's mind about going into the army.

They claimed I must have been educated somewhere else and all
like this but the only education I had was from the actual experience
up and down the highway. They got to the place where they wouldn't
even let black newspaper reporters come in and find out what was

going on. They even wrote my mother down South telling her about what it meant if I didn't go in the army.

When they started talking about Muhammad Ali not going into the army, all my family knew I had done this back in 1942. If the country had treated me right, I would have been glad to go. I feel more like going today than I did then because I received and experienced some of these rights and my opportunities in court have become better.

They put it in the paper that I was getting five years and a $10,000 fine and the next morning they turned me out. "You sign this piece of paper here. We don't want you in our armed forces because you would be bad medicine for the rest of the people." If I kept my mouth shut and didn't work around factories where I could sabotage anything, they gave me a classification as a 5-F. I don't know what that meant and nobody else did, either.

I can't remember exactly the words of the thing I had signed but I was skeptical about signing it because you sign a piece of paper for anything and they leave this wide open space between your signature and the end of the agreement. I was afraid they might add something else in between there pertaining to me going into the army. I remember signing it close to where the agreement was. The guy said, "Man, you don't even trust the government." I said, "No, the government don't trust me."

I don't know why they let me out. I guess they must have felt like I would be better off for them on the outside because I'd have to hustle like hell for a living. I went back to work playing music and writing songs. That's when I formed the Four Jumps of Jive. We went to work at Libby's on the northwest side, and I stayed over there a long time, almost two years. We recorded some of the first stuff Mercury ever recorded with the Four Jumps of Jive.

My mother didn't care too much when I started playing music in Chicago because I was working all the time, too, always in-between. You know how people always felt like if you're working, that's it, but I always had a thing against that. My old man used to make it known to me, "You know, they brought you here just to work and you doing exactly what they want you to do."

He even stressed that if you want to be boss, you've got to get something to be boss of 'cause you're the boss of nothin' to start with. I always wanted to be the boss of something. I figured if I could get a little band, not only could I understand a little bit about it but then I could start seeking more and more information about the whole music thing.

I never was a nightlife person. I didn't know nothing about musicians until the 1940s. We'd get out there with the Five Breezes and run around all night and get up and go to our jobs the next morning, if we wanted to or not. I didn't even join the musicians' union until the 1940s. Baby Doo had joined a USO tour and went to Europe but after he came back to the States, we formed the Big Three Trio.

LEONARD CASTON: I had got a job in the army stockyards driving a forklift. Ollie Crawford and Alfred Elkins and myself, we had formed this trio called the Rhythm Rascals and we were playing in a place called Cafe Society on 55th and Garfield. This guy from the USO who was out looking for talent to go entertain the soldiers overseas came in, heard of us and called us over. He explained they were paying $110 a week plus expenses and the soldier in the regular army wasn't getting but $50 a month so we jumped for it.

They sent us to New York, getting ready to be shipped overseas, and they put us with Alberta Hunter. That's where this group called Rhythm & Blues Unit 47 was organized. Our first shipping was to India and we went from there to China, Burma, Calcutta, Bombay, Karachi, Cairo, Egypt and then Casablanca. We were on our way back home but they had the papers there to induct us into the army so we re-joined in Casablanca.

We went all over Paris, France, Reims and then Eisenhower heard about Alberta Hunter and this group in that theater. They had a big meeting in Frankfurt, Germany and he sent a plane down to bring us to do a show for him and Marshal Zhukov from Russia and this German general.

It was a big meeting, all brass; nothing under a captain was there. This was the thrill of my life—I had the opportunity to do the show for Mr. Eisenhower, got his autograph. We came back home after the Japanese surrendered and we got the Big Three organized with me, Willie and Bernardo Dennis playing guitar.

4

See you watchin' me like a hawk
I don't mind the way you talk
But let me tell you, somethin's got to give
I live the life I love and I love the life I live

So if you see me and you think I'm wrong
Don't worry 'bout me, just let me alone
My sweet life ain't nothin' but a thrill
I live the life I love and I love the life I live

My diamond ring and my money too
Tomorrow night they may belong to you
Because you and me (ain't that well)
I live the life I love and I love the life I live

I may get a thousand on a bet this time
One minute later I can't cover your dime
Tomorrow night I could be over the hill
I just want you to know, baby, the way I feel

Well, I'm rockin' when you pass me by
Don't talk to me, 'cause I could be high
Please forgive me if you will
I live the life I love and I love the life I live

It was a much different music scene that Dixon and Caston returned to.

The biggest change was in the nature of the record industry. Fed up with inattention from major labels, the black listening audience began turning towards a spate of small, independent companies formed by hustling entrepreneurs who realized there was a substantial audience waiting to be satisfied in the immediate post-war era.

And the sound of blues that drove the race records market had changed dramatically—the older style of artists recorded by Chicago powerbrokers like Williams and Melrose were falling out of favor. The West Coast jump blues style—an outgrowth of economic factors which forced the territorial big bands popular during the war years to scale down to rhythm section plus horns supporting a singer belting the blues—was the happening sound in the mid-1940s as artists like Louis Jordan, T-Bone Walker, Roy Brown, Wynonie Harris, Roy Milton, Amos Milburn and the occasional suave balladeer a la Nat "King" Cole and Charles Brown came to the fore.

When the established record labels failed to recognize the shift, in stepped the independents—Modern, Imperial, Aladdin and Specialty out of Los Angeles, King in Cincinnati, Savoy in Newark, New Jersey, Duke/Peacock out of Houston, Chess and VeeJay in Chicago, Apollo and Atlantic in New York . . . and a host of other small operations which sprang up in the mid-1940s through the early 1950s catering to the burgeoning blues and R&B market.

But black artists remained largely shut out of the wider musical picture. The American Society of Composers, Authors and Publishers (ASCAP), the dominant performance rights organization monitoring payments in the music world, was still a closed door society that only legitimized composers, artists and publishers working in mainstream popular music of the day. Its fledgling rival, Broadcast Music Inc. (BMI), was founded in 1939 with a policy of signing the creative talents ignored by ASCAP—be they black blues and jazz artists or white country (then known as hillbilly) performers—as long as they were making valid, profitable music.

The Big Three Trio (named after the wartime Big Three—Roosevelt, Churchill, Stalin) formed in the first half of 1946 with Dixon, Caston now on piano and Bernardo Dennis playing guitar. The latter only lasted a year before Caston's Rhythm Rascals cohort Ollie Crawford replaced him.

The Big Three were neither a hard Chicago blues band nor representative of the jump blues sound. Their models were the popular black vocal groups of the era—the Mills Brothers and the Ink Spots and Chicago outfits like Cats and Fiddles—and their repertoire consisted of pop standards and blues sung in harmony instead of deep down-home blues. Their sound was light, swinging and jazz-tinged, their stage presentation slick and rooted in the tradition of the professional entertainer.

Caston and Dixon had been hanging around Tampa Red's house, a center for the old-time blues musicians who were recording for Lester Melrose. They began working as session musicians on some Melrose productions and ultimately Melrose recorded the Big Three and sold those first recordings to the independent Bullet label out of Nashville.

"Lonely Roamin'" was a regional hit in the South and "Signifying Monkey" hit the national race records chart in 1946. In 1947, the Big Three signed with Columbia and earned another chart hit with their treatment of a song written by Art Tatum and Big Joe Turner, "Wee Wee Baby, You Sure Look Good To Me."

But changes were brewing, too, as new players and sounds emerged in the late 1940s from the tough blues bars on Chicago's South Side. Those developments didn't immediately affect the Big Three and the other blues performers who were frequently booked into downtown Chicago clubs that catered to white audiences.

Muddy Waters, Little Walter and the other artists who would permanently put modern Chicago blues on the map were working largely to black audiences at hole-in-the-wall neighborhood joints. The division reflected a split in the structure of black entertainment at the time; deep down home blues were largely looked down upon as disreputable by the tastemakers within the black community.

Nationally, the Big Three and others were being booked into show clubs seating 3–500 people where featured artists would perform two or three week engagements rather than the endless string of one-nighters that became synonymous with paying blues dues. The Big Three were regional favorites but their strongholds weren't the blues circuit of the deep South or the major East Coast cities. Instead they worked a midwestern network which regularly took them to white clubs in Montana, Minnesota, and cities like Omaha, Nebraska, Denver, Colorado and Cheyenne, Wyoming, interspersed with performances before black audiences in midwestern towns and cities.

Even as the group continued touring, Dixon was branching out. He had never stopped writing songs and Big Three recording sessions gave him a first outlet for his material . . . and first source of frustration as Caston and Crawford turned down originals that would later crop up as Chess hits for safer, pop-oriented sounds with guaranteed audience appeal.

Dixon had ballooned up to 330 pounds, met Elenora Franklin at a Big Three gig in Chicago and became a family man by the end of the decade. His studio experience with Melrose piqued the interest of the brothers Chess, who checked him out at jam sessions held at the Macamba club they ran on the South Side.

They began calling him in off the road to play on sessions for their fledgling Aristocrat label whenever his schedule with the Big Three permitted. That studio work—the first one on a Robert Nighthawk session in November, 1948—began moving Dixon towards the day he became a linchpin of the Chess operation.

BOB KOESTER: the owner of Delmark Records in Chicago who worked closely with many of the city's older blues musicians.

BABY DOO CASTON: see Chapter 3.

JIMMY ROGERS: the rhythm guitarist for the Muddy Waters Band in the late 1940s through the mid-1950s. His own recordings included the 1950 hit "That's All Right" and he played in Howlin' Wolf's band in the late 1950s. Rogers remains an active musician today.

I used to go down to Tampa Red's house on 35th and State. That's where Lester Melrose hung out and Lester Melrose was the go-between man between the blues artists and the recording company— the old ones like Memphis Minnie, Tampa Red, Leroy Carr, Big Bill Broonzy, Washboard Sam, Son Joe. Very few black artists at that time had a contract with the company. They had to have their contract with the go-between man.

Baby Doo was around up to Tampa's house before I was. He knew

Tampa Red and all the other blues artists, Leroy Carr and them guys. He introduced me to them when we first went there and he knew Lester Melrose. By me hanging around Melrose and them, that's where I began to get quite a bit of knowledge about recording before I went to Chess.

We'd sit down there at Tampa Red's house on 35th and State right up over a pawnshop. I would go up there and Baby Doo would sometimes play piano and I would play tin-can bass with different artists and we'd have jam sessions in the back room. Tampa Red's house was a madhouse with old-time musicians. Lester Melrose would be drinking all the time and Tampa Red's wife would be cooking chicken and we'd be having a ball.

BOB KOESTER: Everybody who came to town hung around Tampa Red's house if they were well-known artists and even if they weren't. Tampa Red's house seems to have been a combination rehearsal hall and storage room. There was a piano in the kitchen and another one in the front room and a guitar player could play anywhere. Next door was a bank they called the "Melrose Bank" and some of the artists apparently thought Lester Melrose owned it. It was a place where the guys could cash their checks so 35th and State was the center of all this activity.

WD: We'd go down and play at recording sessions for Melrose and we would never get the union scale. At that time, we weren't even in the union ourselves but he could always get the thing done through the company one way or the other and we'd get $25 or $30 or whatever he wanted to give us. With RCA Victor, I recorded on several things playing an upright tin can with one string, including the first Sonny Boy Williamson, John Lee, that song about "Elevate Me, Mama," ["Elevator Woman"] and that great big number, "In The Dark" that Lil Green had.

There were three of us bass players—me and Big Crawford and Ransom Knowling. A lot of people didn't know one of us from the other so, in the books, they had me doing some things with the first Sonny Boy that I wasn't doing and someone else on the things I was doing with him. That "Elevate Me, Mama" I did all that stuff and the books had Ransom Knowling. They really wasn't giving a damn about who was on the record in those days. They'd put anybody's name on there they thought was popular enough to sell the record.

Most of Melrose's things was 12 bar blues music. The artists were what they considered older types and all these guys had a straight 12 bar pattern with a punchline and I couldn't get any of them to use introductions or melodic lines for their music. Melrose wanted all those things to sound alike and we would have quite a few arguments about it.

I used to tell him, "Every damn thing you make sounds exactly the same, just a different verse to the old melody, you know?" He'd get drunk and say, "Go to hell, Willie, you don't make no damn difference anyway." Melrose and them had electric instruments but were keeping 'em turned down to sound acoustic-style. I couldn't even get them to put the harp electric.

Melrose's music was done for a lot of different labels. During the time the musicians' strike was on during the war, we was recording like hell and I don't know where half of them went. Sometimes he wouldn't give it to the label he said he was going to give it to and it would wind up on another label. I know my groups wound up on Bullet, Decca, several different labels.

Everybody wrote so many songs around then and would sell 'em to Melrose for whatever he'd give them. A lot of times we'd get the songs mixed up but Melrose would give you $15, $20, or $25 for a song and we would take it. I learned quite a bit about the recording business fooling around with Melrose but I didn't learn anything about the business parts and the business part was where he was taking all the money.

Back there with Melrose I wrote that song about "Big Boat Up The River" but we called it "Somebody Tell That Woman" when we recorded it with the Big Three Trio. I wrote another song "Lonely Woman/Roamin' Blues" and the Big Three Trio recorded a song that Art Tatum and Joe Turner wrote called "Wee Wee Baby, You Sure Look Good To Me," and made that tune popular.

LEONARD CASTON: When we got the Big Three together, we recorded "You Sure Look Good To Me" for Jim Bulleit and we were going into World Studio in the Wrigley Building on Michigan Street in Chicago.

They were just beginning tape then and that was taped. The Columbia recording was at the World Theater.

Me and Dixon were the very first organization to start singing blues in harmony. In those days, the Ink Spots were singing popular songs like "If I Didn't Care" and they were harmonizing behind. The Mills Brothers were singing "Glow Worm" in harmony and then they'd do the changes imitating instruments with their mouths.

WD: That's what made the Big Three Trio very popular because we could sing the whole tune like "Wee Wee Baby" and all the riffs and everything. Columbia recorded it in 1948 and our record must have sold about 80–90,000 and that was definitely a hit in those days. Everybody was buying it, both white and black.

Melrose would always call us up and give us the statement but it was a second-hand royalty statement and he would sometimes have Columbia paper to put it on. We always owed him because we were borrowing $50, $25 from him at a time and when royalty statements time came, we didn't have nothing coming.

LEONARD CASTON: If he gave you a statement, it would be from Wabash Music Incorporated and we would be recording for Columbia. "You Sure Look Good To Me," I got one check for $1100 for the whole Trio.

WD: Melrose's brother had a publishing company in St. Louis so these guys had their own set-up. That's what they used to do with those publishing companies. When I talked to Art Tatum, he hadn't gotten any money on "You Sure Look Good To Me," either.

When I started out, there was no BMI. It was ASCAP and at the time, they didn't want black artists involved in it. When I would send them a song, they would say they wouldn't publish a tune until you had three hits. Now how could I get three hits if no one would publish my songs? Over and over again I wrote 'em and I had to get my songs out there anywhere I could.

I made the first songs Memphis Slim made in Chicago for Miracle Records in 1947—"Darlin' I Miss You," "Kilroy Was Here," "Lend Me Your Lovin'," and "Rockin' The House." Memphis Slim had Alex Atkins and Ernest Cotton who had a very smooth sense of harmony. Just two horns can make a beautiful harmony that blended with

Memphis Slim's piano. When Memphis Slim recorded, I was playing bass and he didn't have drums.

"Rockin' The House" was the one that put him over. Right after he started it off, I took the first solo on bass. I was using it as a drum by slapping it at the same time, getting the bass quality of the tone and kind of a drummer slap sound to give it a beat. Everybody from all over everywhere wanted to know who was playing that bass because they didn't know a bass could make triplets like that. That was one of the biggest songs Slim ever had in his life.

Little Brother was actually my influence about a lot of things. He had such a wide variety of material and could play so many different things that other people just couldn't play. He was always telling us about music, about way back when he was a kid that he heard other guys play that never got a chance to play on radio or television. There wasn't even a way of recording.

I liked the idea he could play so many different types of music because he had variations. The type of thing he had going for himself always out-stood the rest of 'em. Some of those things were so hard to play, the average guy in the blues wouldn't fool with them anyway. He'd have bass lines going one way and he's going the other and you can't find that today. I was never influenced by any bass players at all.

I was, at that particular time, one of the most flashy bass players around. I wasn't playing what the media was callin' correct bass but I was the flashiest bass player and the loudest one. Years ago, when a guy played the bass, nine times out of ten you couldn't hear him. I always did tell people, "I don't care what you're playing, give me a solo. When it comes my time, I want to be seen and heard."

I could always sell the bass with a solo. I could put on a good show with the bass. I used to be spinning the bass around, laying all down on the floor with the bass, ride it like a horse. I had all kinds of gimmicks with it so it didn't take the Big Three Trio long to catch on wherever we went.

When we first started, we were working at a place called the Sky Club over on North Harlem Avenue on the West Side of Chicago. We worked there off and on for a long time. In the Sky Club, there was a fellow who used to come in there from one of those big oil companies, the Standard Oil company. Every time this guy came in, he'd give everybody in the place $100.

He'd walk in the door giving out hundred dollar bills and all we had to do was sit there and play and sing his songs. We could order anything we wanted to and like that. Sometimes we'd wind up with a couple hundred dollars in one night apiece.

There was a doctor who used to give us a lot of money, too. I don't think the guy was really a doctor but they called him "Doc." Every time Doc walked out, you can bet we had over $100 apiece but every time this guy from Standard came there we knew we would have $200 apiece.

Everybody would give a dollar or something but after you get spoiled to the big money, you don't like it when the whole band winds up with $200. That was big money at first but after we got spoiled with Doc and the Standard man, we got to the place where we felt like that other money wasn't much but it was enough to keep us buying clothes with.

Back then, we started wearing real loud colors—red and green, yellow and purple suits and sharp, you know. It was helping us get a lot of jobs. People feel like because you're on the stage entertaining you're making more than what you're really making because you have to fly false colors by wearing flashy clothes and like this. Everybody thought these guys must be cleaning up and most of the time we couldn't pay for the suits we had on.

We had good publicity and our pictures were always in the paper when we were working downtown in Chicago. There was a tailor called Skeet (Scotty Piper) who specialized in extravagant styles of anything that was different and he wanted the publicity, too. He was about the sharpest cat you've ever seen.

Every time you'd see him, he was putting on airs and posing. He'd tell us that if we let him use our picture for advertisements, he could give us a better deal on the clothes. And he would, because I know what he was charging other people, he wasn't charging us.

We would take all our tip money and always pool it together to put down on the suits. We had a running debt with Skeet all the time and he'd make us some extravagant clothes. We had on a great big suit and the zoot suits and reet pleats and big shoulders and odd colors and that was attractive. We'd get on the street car or the elevated back then with that stuff on and people would be pointing there looking at us.

Sometimes we'd all have our uniforms alike and sometimes three loud uniforms, different, because Skeet made us two or three suits at a time of the same color. After we'd get two or three, Baby Doo would have on a loud red, I'd have a loud green and Ollie would wear a loud yellow. Sometimes we'd change them around, wear a loud red coat with loud green pants and just switch them around. Purple and checks—anything we could think of that was different, all we had to do was tell Skeet about it.

He had a little tailor shop on Prarie and 43rd Street. Every time he got an odd-colored piece of cloth, he'd call—"Hey, Dixon, come right here. Imagine having a suit like this." Later on, he started making two tone, two color clothes. Half a suit would be one color and the other half another. The trousers would be blue on the right half and red on the left half and the left side of the coat would be blue to match and the right side of the coat red to match.

We had purple and gray and he had the suit with great big purple patch pockets on a gray suit. He made some two tone things for Sonny Boy Williamson. Sonny Boy had one suit, I think, half of it was white and half blue. He'd take pictures, turn around on the stage—"Hey, take me in my white suit"—and then turn around—"Hey, take me in my blue suit."

Most of the entertainers went to a fellow called Fox on Roosevelt Road. Fox had a wholesale place there plus they had damned good tailors that could make a suit lay on you just like a vine. Skeet was dealing with the guys that he could but the big timers went over to Fox.

I met Elenora during the time I had the Big Three Trio. We were at Smitty's Corner in 1946 or 1947 and we started having kids about 1948 or 1949. I had seven kids by Elenora but I was never married to her because she didn't want to get married. She was influenced by the idea that some fortune teller in the South had told her that she was going to marry a rich man and she didn't want to get married to me. We stayed together a good long while.

We were working on the near North Side and downtown with the Big Three and we was doing mostly the Top Ten tunes. On the South Side, they weren't caring about the Top Ten tunes so when we'd get off at night, we'd go out there with Muddy. He hadn't been long come from the South and he was working down on Wentworth around 35th or 36th, not too far from the White Sox baseball park [Comiskey Park].

We'd get off work downtown at the Brass Rail or some other place, come out to Wentworth Avenue and have jam sessions with Muddy Waters, Little Walter, Jimmy Rogers and Robert Jr. Lockwood. They was working one side of the city and we was working the other because we always worked mostly for white people and they worked mostly for the black.

JIMMY ROGERS: I saw the Big Three Trio play at a couple of clubs, the Blue Flame over at 3020 Indiana and a club downtown called Frosty's Corner on the North Side. After Muddy and I got pretty popular in the area, they didn't play the clubs that we was playing. They would mostly play jazz clubs and they played at the Brass Rail. Little Brother Montgomery was downtown, a Brass Rail man, and they were all hanging in the downtown area, the Old Town area.

We were playing further south where places were swinging and the blues were big. We would get off at two—on Saturday it would be three—but Dixon and the downtown guys had short hours. Most times they'd start at nine and they was off at one and they'd come out in the neighborhood where we were and get a chance to sit in. Baby Doo loved to come around and sit in on piano and then he'd play Muddy's guitar, crack a few jokes.

Dixon wasn't as frequent coming out as Baby Doo. You wouldn't see him around those clubs too much because he was trying to write but he would pop by occasionally when he had something going. He and Memphis Slim used to hang around together a lot.

LEONARD CASTON: Back in the 1930s and 1940s, you just didn't go to the elite places and play blues. The Class A places wouldn't accept it. If it was the blues, not Tin Pan Alley, then back to the juke joints.

WD: We started traveling all over but we couldn't make the blues circuit because of all the popular material we did. We could make all the big clubs but they couldn't hire us on the blues circuit because we were asking . . . hell, we started off making about $375 a week so we had over $100 a man after we paid the agent. That was big money in those days.

A guy called Joe Musse was booking us out of the ABC agency. We felt like we weren't getting as much money as we should because we would go places and ask for more money and folks would gladly give it to us.

We went to a little place just north of Chicago and told the owner, "Look, man, we know we ain't making enough money. Book us two weeks and if you don't feel like we're worth it, we'll get another job. If you like it, we want a $50 raise." Sure enough, the guy was giving us the extra money and the agent that was booking us didn't know.

When he found out that we had worked our salary up close to $1,000 he was complaining that we should pay him a commission on it because he was only getting commission on what he had booked us in there for, $375. He had another job lined up that was paying about $500 but we were making more than that and didn't want him to know it.

Finally, the agent came to where we were working and was talking about taking us out of there. The man that owned the place said, "Hell, no! I'm payin' 'em too much money." That's when the agent found out what we were doing him for.

We didn't care where we went. We'd play in all the white places and they accepted our songs but we didn't play too many of the real bluesy blues. When we recorded "Wee Wee Baby," everybody played it on damn near all the stations. They knew it was a blues but when we started singing in harmony, people didn't know whether to call it a blues or something else.

Everybody liked it and everywhere we went, that song was requested. Up in Minnesota, where I know they didn't like nothing but polkas, we'd be up there playing a polka and hear, "Hey, man, sing 'Wee Wee Baby.'" We'd be jamming with these polka players, everybody singing "Wee Wee Baby," and boy, a polka band can mess up a blues worse than anything in the world.

LEONARD CASTON: We'd go out for two weeks with options. We was versatile and proved that we were a fairly decent trio. We just couldn't make no money and they kept us everywhere but the right spots. They kept us out of Chicago and we never did get to the East Coast or the big Southern cities and these were the places our record "Wee Wee Baby" was selling.

We were working in St. Louis in a place called Melby's Show Bar at Claremont and Taylor. People would come hear us play and didn't realize who we were. My wife—we had just gotten together—was with us at least three or four months before she recognized that she was with the Big Three Trio.

Charles Brown came into town and we went down to see him play at the Union Club. He announced, "We've got the Big Three Trio here and I'm going to do one of their big hits." When they found out that was us in there, the people went wild.

WD: We worked practically all night long. Most people would start entertaining around nine o'clock and went up until two. We'd get off at two at night and go some place where you could lay around, eat and talk trash and then go home to sleep. It was very seldom that we was working any one-nighters like they do now. Everybody stayed two or three weeks. Most of the time when you had those kind of jobs, you wouldn't have a day off.

We'd put on a little show set with the Trio and then we'd have a dance set. Most of the time, we'd do three sets, two dance sets and one show set. Sometimes we'd just play the show set all the time. It all depended on what the guy wanted. He had a lot of props and things sometimes and sometimes it was just the music. We got a chance to add a couple of them wild old songs—"Cigarettes, Whisky And Wild Women," things like that, drivin' them people nuts.

LEONARD CASTON: Ollie and I used to ignore some of the things he would come up with. We was thinkin', "Ain't nothing we can do with Dixon." After he got with Chess then we found that these were the tunes he was trying to get us to do. We were thinking that we shouldn't be playing the roots, play some other halfway jazzy songs which most people were liking at that time.

He always said, "Get something of your own." He had a lot of tunes he used to bring to us to do but truthfully speaking we would just ignore some of the good songs that he had. When we turned around and somebody else was doing 'em, then we knew what we had bypassed.

WD: Most of the songs I'm playing now, even up to the present day, are songs I made back around the Big Three Trio days or before that. "Violent Love" and "My Love Will Never Die" were songs of mine I made way back there and recorded with the Big Three and nobody paid attention to it.

The first time I met Leonard and Phil Chess, we were working at a club called the El Casino at 39th right off Cottage Grove. The Chess brothers had one right on 39th and Cottage Grove, a quite lively joint called the Macamba. When we'd get off from working at the El Casino, we'd go around to the Macamba and listen to Tom Archaia and the band play. Different people would come in and jam and once in a while, I'd bring my bass in there and jam with them so they found out I was a pretty good bass player.

Meantime, we noticed Chess had a little recording thing. I remember when they said they was first going to have a recording company and this singer Andrew Tibbs was involved. Leonard Chess was talking about getting me to work with them and I couldn't because the Big Three was on the road.

I don't remember the first one I played on with Muddy but it was the same time I was playing for the Robert Nighthawk things. Chess said, "I'll pay you for this session" and I didn't even belong to the union. It took him about a month to come up with the session money but he finally sent the money in a check one day and said, "Well, this is for two sessions in one." At that time, you were getting about $35 for a recording session for each man so I got a $60 check.

Different guys would call me in off the road and have Chess talk to me. We'd made some kind of deal financially and if I could catch my day off I'd come in and record and go back out on my job wherever I worked. I made two or three different trips out of Omaha because we were playing at the Dundee Dell there and I did that out of Denver, too. We played 60 miles from Omaha and then we played across the river in Council Bluffs and other places, too, Sioux City, Iowa.

LEONARD CASTON: We used to go there every year. We'd leave Chicago and our first stop would be Omaha, Nebraska at the Dundee Dell, right on the edge of town. We would leave there, go to Denver, then Cheyenne and we came back the last time to Dubuque and Sioux City.

I used to love to drive . . . I could sit at the wheel and drive from Chicago to Omaha, about 500 miles, rest three hours and drive to Denver. In those days, there weren't no freeways and no speed limits so we'd do 70–75 miles an hour.

One night we had been up in Hibbing, Minnesota and you couldn't stop at Kentucky Fried Chicken or McDonald's, wasn't no such thing. We'd stop at a drug store, get us some lunch meat, some crackers or a loaf of bread, just about 15 cents then. We'd have our lunch in the car with two or three bottles of milk.

Dixon was driving that night and I was sitting in the back seat. We had the bass across the top of the seats and Ollie was sitting over on the other side in front. I was going to relax and eat me a bologna sandwich and milk.

Ollie had his window cracked and Dixon used to have this two toned whistle and he used to whistle that way all the time to keep himself alert. When the bottle of milk was empty, I thought his window was down so I just hauled off and hit that glass with it. When it hit that glass, Dixon jumped and his head hit the ceiling. He didn't know what the hell it was.

WD: It was so cold one time we were up there in Mankato, Minnesota. I think the temperature was 58 below zero. They had all these old people that had never been in a nightclub before lining up outside our place. There was ice and snow all over everything and ice on the inside of people's houses that was an inch thick. Boy, you're talking about COLD. I never did go back.

The next time we went out west, we played Great Falls, Montana. Some guys that had come from Alaska was paying us real pieces of gold. I wore this gold nugget on my neck for a long time till somebody stole it.

LEONARD CASTON: When we were in Great Falls, Willie was up there playing his bass fiddle and these people had silver dollars, okay? They'd be throwing the money up there trying to throw it in the F-hole. He'd be sitting there playing and one would hit the fiddle—"*BERRKK*."

I was wondering what that sound was and I heard the money hit the floor. Then I saw these guys sitting around the bar like they were throwing darts. They had this bass fiddle trashed up bad.

WD: I didn't like them scratching up my fiddle but, boy, we had a lot of those silver dollars.

When some guys got loaded, you'd have a better show than if you had hired entertainers. I worked down in Springfield, Illinois and this guy was supposed to be the strong man with the circus. We went in this little restaurant down there to eat and this guy came along and was gonna put us out of the restaurant. We were standing at the counter and he comes in.

"Hey! Where I come from they don't allow niggers in here."

We just kept on and after a while, he grabbed Ollie, the littlest in the band, and I reached over and pulled Ollie loose. This guy was going to hit me but the minute before he was able to hit me, I caught the cat and knocked him over the tables. They had a long table, there was tile on the floor and this big old table goes way up front and bang! out goes the window.

In no time the police came and were going to put us in jail. The owners said, "These guys were tending to their business. This guy started the fight." We finally worked it out where the guys made me pay for putting the window in.

The next night, the same guy came in to the place we worked at. I didn't know who this guy was because he looked like an Egyptian mummy with all this stuff around his head.

He said, "You don't know me, do you?"

"Am I supposed to know you?"

"I'm the one you hit last night."

I was half afraid of this cat because I was thinkin' he was going to do something to me. But that guy followed us everywhere, buying drinks and everything for the guys.

We'd be playing a dance down South and it was supposed to be a colored dance and the white ones would come in. When they got places where they let the white ones come in, they'd put a rope between the two, colored on one side and white on the other. When the ball got going good, occasionally somebody would cut the damned rope and the big dance is on.

Down in Kentucky and southern Illinois, they'd have a guard sitting up there. He'd be raisin' hell about somebody cut the rope and the kids would be dancing all over the place. Sometimes they would stop the dances because somebody cut the rope.

There were times going places where you couldn't get a place to sleep and couldn't eat in the places. They said, "We'll give you something out the back door." We'd make arrangements for hotels in front and when we'd get there and they found we was black, we couldn't stay there. Many times we'd have to just sleep in the car and all like this.

We went to filling stations and they'd sell you some gas but that was all. If you broke down on the road, you didn't wait for somebody who would come along and help you until some other black person came to pull you in or push you in. You couldn't get assistance out of a farmer.

If you wasn't on the job on time, you didn't get your money and I got people right now that owe me money from way back when. In those days, they didn't have laundromats so we'd go down to the river and wash the clothes, hang 'em out and they would dry.

But when most people know you're an entertainer, they try to give you a little more respect than they would have the average person. We were working in those types of joints where they'd respect you to the utmost because they thought we were kind of heavy. We always got that certain note of respect but sometimes when we went places where they didn't know us, there could be a problem.

We lived good in Cheyenne, Wyoming. We damn near were controlling the whole city of Cheyenne then. We came in there, went to this little old hotel to stay and this lady came out. We weren't dressed up like entertainers and we wanted two rooms. "I can give you the rooms but I've got to have $7 a week in advance and if you want to eat, you're gonna get it for a dollar." We paid, walked down the stairs that night and boy, she must have had a seven-course dinner for a dollar.

That evening our picture came out in the paper, saying this is the Big Three Trio, they're going to play at the Cheyenne Nightclub and they had a reputation. When they saw that picture, they said, "Hey, why didn't you tell us who you was? We've got much better rooms and it won't cost you more." We said we like the rooms we got but went downstairs the next afternoon and she sold us the same identical meal for $3.

We had some beautiful shows out there because we were broadcasting every week, sometimes two or three days a week at the Cheyenne Nightclub. They used to have a wake-up program out there and I used to go down and jam with a bunch of cowboys. The

Cheyenne Nightclub was up on a hill, right on the outskirts of town. Everybody would come up to the club on horses and wagons with beautiful riding saddles, buggies, and beat-up cars.

This fellow called Miles Kline at the Cheyenne Nightclub, he taught me how to sing in Hebrew and English, saying, "Yiddisher Mama." Every time they had a Jewish affair anywhere they would call for us to go out and sing "Yiddisher Mama."

We used to jam with the Sons of the Pioneers back in the last of the 1940s there. I didn't know they were the Sons of the Pioneers at first because we used to go to a place called "The Summit" and we'd meet different guys up there.

Every time we'd come to Denver, we'd go to Cheyenne. When we was in Denver, we worked at the Five Point club there. We did that twice a year, three years in a row. They'd always hold us over, sometimes for a week or two.

One night we had just got off the Five Point club. We walked out and there was a guy standing there. They had a lot of Indians in that territory and any time you could see them with one of them blankets wrapped around themselves. He said, "I like you guys' music" and then this other guy got out of the car, a white fella, kinda bald-headed.

"You guys are musicians. I'd like you to play for us. We got a little place up in the hills there. What are you charging?"

I don't know how much I said but I figured, "Okay, we'll play but it's gonna cost you $500 a night." That was big money in those days.

He said, "Okay, we'll pay. What about tomorrow night?"

"Tomorrow?"

"Yeah, we'll be here to pick you up."

"But we got to have a contract."

"I'll give you the money now."

I thought he was kidding but he give us half the money and said he'll give us the other half tomorrow night when he would come by to pick us up. None of us knew it was a nudist colony.

The next day we got in the automobile. It was warm out there and this guy Bob was sitting in the front seat and we were sitting in the back seat—me, Ollie and Baby Doo. We had the fiddle cocked up there one-sided in this little station wagon-like thing.

The guy leaned back and said, "You ever played at a nudist camp before?"

"No."

"Well, when you're at the nudist camp, don't get excited."

Me and Ollie nudged each other and laughed about it. Sure enough, we were traveling around in the woods up there and all of a sudden we saw the lights back there and this guy's standing up at the gate buck naked. Then we really nudged each other. We started laughing and the guy sitting up front laughed.

Just about the time we got there, this little place that's got a dim light over it and here come some kids streaking across the yard naked and then the grown folks come around there naked. They said, "You guys want to join us?"

"Yeah, but with our clothes."

"Well, you just want to get comfortable."

"I can't get comfortable and be naked, man."

We had a lot of jokes and laughs about it. We finally pulled off our shirts and like that. I think by the time I left there, we had gotten down to our underclothes but that was as far as we could go. We had a good time out there.

I just couldn't picture eating with a bunch of naked folks and they had everything to eat, man. I was hungrier than hell but I just couldn't picture eating with somebody serving food with a damned apron on and nothing under there but the apron. We made jokes about this for years.

Another time we were out in Boulder, Colorado. This guy in an Oldsmobile come up and say he wanted us to play something in the woods and would give us $5,000. This was after I had the Big Three and I just went out there with a band that had Billy Boy Arnold playing harmonica. I told this guy I wanted $5,000 for this thing . . . no trouble.

I thought he was kidding but we went up there in the mountains and played. That was the quickest $5,000 I ever made in my life and I split it with all the guys. We went back to work that night. Those people out there were giving us a lot of money, anyway. They were giving us a hundred dollar bill as tips.

Another time we had been working up in Grand Forks, North Dakota. Baby Doo and them decided they were going to leave and I wanted to stay up there because I fell in love with the waterfalls and a lot of fish all out in there. I hung around up there because I thought I was going to get involved in something. This was the time when Baby

Doo was afraid to advertise where we were going to be because his old lady could catch up with him.

I went up to Alaska. It got cold up there at this little club in Fairbanks but this woman called Jo Evil I was playing with was the ugliest chick in the world and she had every bag of miners' gold there. At that time, women up there was as scarce as chicken teeth and every man was after her.

In 1951, the Big Three Trio had to give up the road because Baby Doo had matrimonial troubles. He and his wife was having a big thing and everywhere we would go, the police would come and pull him off the stage. They came down to the Brass Rail in Chicago and took him off and in Denver and Omaha, too. He wasn't paying his alimony or something.

His first wife seemed to have been very extravagant with what little he was gettin'. We were working in places and wasn't making the amount of money he was trying to send her. He was begging and getting money from everybody in the band to send to his family and we didn't have it, either. He had to cut out and that left us stranded for a while.

Baby Doo introduced me to Lafayette Leake and I was trying to get the Big Three Trio working again with Lafayette Leake playing piano and working for Chess at the same time. By then, all these different artists started coming up with Chess and I got into that part of it.

5

Chorus: I am the back door man
I am the back door man
Well, the men don't know
But the little girls understand

When everybody is trying to sleep
I'm somewhere making a midnight creep
And every morning when the rooster crow
He's telling me you got to go

They took me to the doctor
Shot full of holes
And the nurses cried
Please save his soul

I was accused of murder
In the first degree
The judge's wife plead
Let the man go free

The cop's wife cried
Don't take him down
I'd rather you give me
Six feet of ground

When you come home
You can eat pork and beans

I eats more chicken
Than any man's seen

Some people have called Leonard and Phil Chess visionaries who recognized the potential in the visceral blues of post-World War II Chicago. A far greater number have branded the Chess brothers as exploiters who systematically took advantage of the artists who created that music, but they were indisputably instrumental figures in the development of Chicago blues.

That probably wasn't the future the Chess brothers envisioned when they arrived in America in 1928 from Motol, a town in western Russia right on the Polish border that was also the home of Chaim Weizmann, the first president of Israel. Born Lazer Shmuel Chez, Leonard suffered from polio and hid his leg brace when the family arrived at Ellis Island.

The Chesses moved on to Chicago to join their father, who had emigrated to America several years earlier, and settled into the Jewish section of Chicago bordering the South Side. Leonard worked at various jobs—selling newspapers and shoes, delivering milk and ultimately in his father's junkyard. Near the end of World War II, Leonard moved into the liquor store business and then ran several South Side bars featuring live music.

The first was the 708 Club on East 47th Street but the biggest was the Macamba Lounge, a nightclub on the corner of 39th and Cottage Grove where such rising young jazz stars as Billy Eckstine, Gene Ammons, Lionel Hampton, Ella Fitzgerald and Louis Armstrong were known to perform. The Macamba was located in Drexel Square, the bustling heart of Chicago's black community, and the club was reputedly a prime center for prostitution and heavy drug dealing.

When Andrew Tibbs, a local singer featured with the Macamba house band, began attracting attention from a record label talent scout, Leonard and his younger brother Phil, who missed out on the early stages of the bar business due to an army stint in World War II, decided to take a stab at the record business themselves. They founded the Aristocrat label in 1947, operating out of an office at 71st and Phillips (later 52nd and Cottage Grove), and enjoyed sporadic success with songs in the smooth, jazz-tinged style of artists like Macamba bandleader Tom Archaia and Lee Monti's Tu-Tones.

Aristocrat's first taste of success and notoriety came later that year when Tibbs recorded a 78 of "Union Man Blues/Bilbo Is Dead" backed by Dave Young's Orchestra. The record, because of its reference to the death of Mississippi's segregationist Senator Theodore Bilbo, was reportedly both banned in the South and destroyed by teamsters who objected to the sentiments of "Union Man Blues."

But pianist Sunnyland Slim and Muddy Waters were also featured on some of Aristocrat's earliest sessions and with the latter's second release for the label, the Chess brothers stumbled across the sound that became their bread and butter for the next 20 years. Not that they immediately recognized what they had—during the rehearsals of "I Can't Be Satisfied," Leonard Chess reportedly asked, "What's he singing? I can't understand what he's singing." But when the song sold out its initial pressing within 12 hours of its release in April of 1948, the Chess brothers began shifting their musical focus to zero in on that untapped audience.

The Chess brothers were the first to gamble on recording the new style and classic Chicago blues became so thoroughly identified with the label bearing their name it was often described as "the Chess sound." It was a rough-and-tumble roar of guitars, harmonica and drums, rooted in the country blues of the Mississippi Delta but heavily amplified to slice through the din of Windy City nightclubs.

In 1950, the Chess brothers bought out their partners in Aristocrat, folded that company, and began releasing records on the label bearing their name. The first Chess single, "My Foolish Heart" by Jazz saxophonist Gene Ammons, cracked the R&B Top Ten and both Muddy's "Honey Bee" and "That's All Right" by his rhythm guitarist Jimmy Rogers kept the label viable during the first year.

The Chess brothers worked hard to keep it afloat—distributing records from the trunk of a car in the early days to the porters and Pullman conductors, barber shop and beauty store owners who made up their sales network on the South Side. Leonard Chess made frequent scouting expeditions lugging a wire recorder through the South in the early 1950s, looking for new artists and establishing contacts with other small-scale producers working with blues performers. One was Sam Phillips, who secured his place in the Rock 'n' Roll Hall of Fame with the Sun rockabilly stable of Elvis Presley, Jerry Lee Lewis and Carl Perkins a few years later.

Phillips leased Jackie Brentson's "Rocket 88," a number frequently cited as the first bona-fide rock 'n' roll song, to Chess and that song gave the company its initial number one record on the R&B charts in May, 1951. Another 1951 hit courtesy of Phillips was "How Many More Years," the first Chess release by the performer who became a mainstay of the label when he moved to Chicago from Memphis two years later, Howlin' Wolf. And Muddy Waters developed into the label's most consistent hitmaker with four Top Ten R&B chart entries.

By 1954, Chess was solidly entrenched in the record business as a viable label. Its music publishing wing, Arc Music, had started up the year before, and virtually every release by Muddy Waters and harmonica wizard Little Walter placed high on the R&B charts. Pianist Willie Mabon's "I Don't Know" and "I'm Mad" had already joined "Rocket 88" and Walter's 1952 instrumental "Juke" as R&B chart-toppers for the label.

Their success in awakening the "sleeping giant" of the blues made Chess a magnet for aspiring black musicians who came knocking at their door, instruments in hand and dreams of a hit record dancing in their hearts. Not everyone came to sing the blues. A 1951 session with the Evangelist Singers of Alabama marked the label's first foray into the gospel market, which became a rock-steady foundation of the Chess operation.

Back on the secular plane, vocal groups started figuring prominently in the label's releases circa 1953; the Moonglows' 1954 hit "Sincerely" set the standards for vocal group harmonizing and served as the soundtrack for countless teenage passion plays. In 1955, Chuck Berry and Bo Diddley arrived to blur the boundaries between the blues tradition and the emerging rock 'n' roll sound.

Chess had already moved from its original cramped quarters in a storefront at 49th and Cottage Grove to larger offices a block north. The extra room allowed for a rehearsal studio that would occasionally be used for recording after, according to Dixon, the installation of studio equipment purchased in 1954 through the Reverend C.L. Franklin. The Detroit gospel preacher, whose recorded sermons cemented Chess' gospel base, was the father of future soul queen Aretha, who cut an album's worth of gospel standards for Chess in 1956 when she was 14.

The label also initiated two subsidiaries. Designed as the Chess operation's R&B label, Checker debuted in 1952 and Argo was created four years later to handle the jazz side (although those clear-cut distinctions soon became muddied). There was a practical reason for the additional labels—most R&B radio deejays would only include a set number of records per label on their playlist. More labels offered more chance of getting more songs played on the air and hence generated more record sales.

By 1956, Chess and its affiliate labels had racked up 60 R&B chart hits, many destined to become the standards of the rock 'n' roll generation and the backbone of oldies but goodies radio playlists. Many 45s bearing the Chess or Checker logo had been spinning regularly on the radio shows of pioneering deejays like Alan Freed, programs bringing the popular black music of the day within earshot of a sizeable white audience for the first time.

Following the dissolution of the Big Three Trio, Willie Dixon had become an integral part of the Chess operation, the in-house music man who helped to whip the material of the label's artists into shape. Dixon was a full-time employee after 1951—producing, arranging, running the studio band and playing bass on "everybody's everything." His role was so crucial that Leonard Chess would later describe him as "my right arm."

His first listed Chess (as distinguished from Aristocrat) session was Jimmy Rogers' "Back Door Friend" in 1952. The real breakthrough arrived in January, 1954 when Muddy Waters stepped into the studio to record "Hoochie Coochie Man." The success of that song convinced Chess that Dixon's material would pay off commercially and for the next three years, Dixon was indispensable to Chess—dishing out tunes and working sessions with downhome bluesmen like Waters, Little Walter and Howlin' Wolf as well as slicker, more sophisticated artists like Willie Mabon, Eddie Boyd, Jimmy Witherspoon and Lowell Fulson.

In 1955, Little Walter's "My Babe" became the first Dixon song to top the R&B charts but his contributions weren't limited to the blues sphere. The El-Rays (later the Dells) did their first Chess session in 1954 backed by the Willie Dixon Orchestra; he was also in the studio for several Moonglows sessions, including "Sincerely." With the "Maybellene" session, Dixon began an association playing behind Chuck Berry in the studio that would last virtually uninterrupted until the early 1960s.

But storm clouds were on the horizon. Dixon's move to Chess effectively meant the end of his recording and performing career during that time. He recorded a few songs for Chess under his name but only one, "Walking The Blues," received much exposure.

The demands of providing for a growing family and the reluctance of the Chess brothers to fork out money or let their artists record more of the songs he had stockpiled left Dixon increasingly frustrated and financially pressed. Near the end of 1956, he parted company with Chess.

MALCOLM CHISHOLM: engineered on sessions for Chess at Universal Studios from 1955–8 and served as the chief engineer at the Chess studio at 2120 South Michigan Avenue from 1958–60. He returned to work at the label from 1966–8 and 1970–3.

JIMMY ROGERS: see Chapter 4.

Chess gave me a contract and this contract didn't have too much of a stipulation on it. They insisted that I assist them in everything they'd do. At that time, the Chess company was on the northwest corner at 49th and Cottage Grove. Then they moved down to a bigger place at 48th and Cottage Grove.

When I first met the Chess brothers, I thought this was going to be a beautiful thing for me to execute some of what I thought I knew. They let me have a free run with just about everything because Leonard used to admit that he didn't know as much about it as he thought I did. He treated me with respect, about as much as the average black folks was getting and that wasn't too much anywhere.

My job was to assist. I did everything from packing records to sweeping the floor to answering the telephone to making out orders but they weren't giving me much of a pay thing. They promised to give me so much a week against my royalties and then every week, I'd have to damn near fight or beg for the money.

I recorded some things for Chess but they only released one record on Checker, "Walking The Blues," in 1955. Jack Dupree wrote that and he had it out on another label. It was me singing and playing the bass, Lafayette Leake on piano and Fred Below was walking on some boards down there at Bill Putnam's studio down on Ontario Street. They found out that if they released songs on me, I'd have to be running up and down the road behind them. I couldn't watch the company, too, so they had me stay in the studio.

We were doing "Violent Love" with the Big Three Trio. The only reason we recorded it with Chess back then was that Chess was trying to hook me to get me to stay there and help 'em with the other artists. We used to do "29 Ways" with the Big Three Trio, too, but we never recorded it until I did it with Chess in 1956.

"This Pain In My Heart" is with me and Lafayette Leake in 1951, when Leake started playing with me. That was one of the first things I ever did for Chess—me and Leake and Ollie Crawford right after we broke up the Big Three. We started this other thing with hopes that we were going to keep it with Chess but Chess wasn't interested in nothing but me, to tell the truth. When Chess found out the Big Three Trio was going to break up, he said he was going to record me and he told a lie that we was going to release those things on me.

"This Pain In My Heart" was one of the first songs I wrote when I must have been around 14 or 15. I couldn't get nobody to play it with me then but I would be everywhere singing that all the time. Theo Phelps wanted to sing spirituals and I'd always come up with "This Pain In My Heart" and he didn't like that. It was just one of the sor gs I remembered real well from down South.

I had told Leonard Chess I had quite a few songs but he never wanted too many of them at first. A couple of years after I started working there, I told him about this particular song, "Hoochie Coochie Man."

"Man, Muddy can do this number," I said.

"Well, if Muddy likes it, give it to him," he said, and told me where Muddy was working. Muddy and I had talked about the song on a couple of occasions. I had sung "Hoochie Coochie Man" out there where we used to go out and meet him and play on the South Side when I had the Big Three Trio.

I went over there to the Club Zanzibar at 14th Street and Ashland. At intermission, I had Muddy come off the stage and I was telling him, "Man, this song is a natural for you."

"Well, it'll take me a little while to learn it," Muddy said.

"No, this is right down your alley. I got an idea for a little riff that anybody can play."

You know how it is, a lot of guys feel like if you made a song complicated, it would do more. I always tried to explain that the simpler a thing is, the easier it can get across with the public.

He and I talked about it and I said, "Get your guitar." We went and stood right in the front of the bathroom by the door. People were walking by us all the time and I said, "Now, here's your riff: 'Da-da-da-da-Da.'"

"Oh, Dixon, ain't nothing to that."

"Now remember this: The gypsy woman told my mother/Da-da-da-da-Da/Before I was born/Da-da-da-da-Da/You got a boy child coming/Da-da-da-da-Da/He's gonna be a sonuvagun."

He could remember those words because they were the type of words anybody can remember easily. All through the history of mankind, there have been people who were supposed to be able to tell the future before it came to pass. People always felt it would be great to be one of these people: "This guy is a hoodoo man, this lady is a witch, this other guy's a hoochie coochie man, she's some kind of voodoo person."

In the South, the gypsies would come around and tell fortunes. When I was a little boy, you'd see a covered wagon coming along and these women with their great big dresses—doggone knows how many dresses they'd have on—and all of them would have pockets up under them. I didn't know some of them would steal, you know. Nobody's paying attention to a little kid like me walking around there and these gypsies would take little gadgets from rooms.

Naturally, if somebody who wants your money and wants to use you is going to tell you a story, they have to tell you something you want to hear. If the gypsies come up to some lady's house and she's pregnant, the first thing they'd say is, "Ooh, you're going to have a fine fat boy. He's gonna be able to tell the future before it comes to pass."

The average person wants to brag about themselves because it makes that individual feel big. "The gypsy woman told my mother/Before I was born"—that shows I was smart from the beginning. "Got a boy child coming/Gonna be a sonuvagun"—now I'm here. These songs make people want to feel like that because they feel like that at heart, anyway. They just haven't said it so you say it for them.

Like the song, "I Just Wanna Make Love To You," a lot of times people say this in their minds or think it. You don't have to say it but everybody knows that's the way you feel anyway because that's how the other fella feels. You know how you feel so you figure the other fella feels the same way because his life is just like yours.

To know the blues is to know a feeling and understanding within people that puts you in the position of other people by feeling and understanding the plight that they're involved in. You don't always get the experience in the blues from the life you live because sometimes these things are built into a certain individual.

A man don't have to be starving to know how it feels to starve. All he's got to do is know how it feels to miss one or two meals and he knows that other fella is in much worse shape. But if a person don't have no feeling, no imagination or understanding, you can't create a feeling with him because he doesn't hear what you say.

We fooled around with "Hoochie Coochie Man" there in the washroom for 15 or 20 minutes. Muddy said, "I'm going to do this song first so I don't forget it." He went right up onstage that first night and taught the band the little riff I showed him. He did it first shot and, sure enough, the people went wild over it. He was doing that song until the day he died.

JIMMY ROGERS: This "Hoochie Coochie Man" thing, Dixon came to the club and he would hum it to Muddy and wrote the lyrics out. Muddy would work them around for a while until he got it down where he could understand it and fool around with it. He would be onstage and try it out, do a few licks of it. We were building the arrangement, that's what we were really doing; it wasn't like the snatch and grab of today.

WD: I really wasn't well known as a songwriter until "Hoochie Coochie Man." I must have had 150 songs, a whole bagful, when I went there but I couldn't get 'em out. There was no market for this type of thing. Chess was the first to take the chance. "Hoochie Coochie Man" was selling so good Leonard wanted me to come up with another one right away. We did this "Make Love To Me" ["I Just Want To Make Love To You"] and then I told him about "I'm Ready" so we went with that and it got to going pretty good.

I had been trying to do patterns like I was using with Chess before, when I worked for Lester Melrose, but I didn't have enough authority with Melrose. When I got a chance to do it with Chess, I could clue the guys, like on that "Third Degree" I did with Eddie Boyd. Eddie didn't want it at first but after he was saying, "Dixon, give me a part of yourself. I don't mind playing it but hell, I don't want to take no chances." I had to change it back but it turned out to be a very big song for him.

Eddie Boyd never was a helluva of a piano player but he could sing pretty good. Eddie was one of those guys that got into the blues because he'd sing blues things that reminded him of different things in his life. He'd get drunk and come in there crying and get back there on the piano. Everybody got excited and Leonard would say, "Call the musicians, man. This cat is ready."

I'd start calling different guys and sometimes we'd get something halfway decent and sometimes we wouldn't. After they found out he was that kind of person, I think a bunch of 'em would try to get him drunk on purpose, just trying to get a recording session.

Willie Mabon talked different from the average blues artist because he carried longer phrases than the average person. The first song he made himself—Chess bought it from Al Benson—was "I Don't Know." That was a real good number for him but Chess and Mabon always had fights in the financial department. I think they may have given $5,000 to Al Benson but Mabon didn't get any of it.

Willie Mabon made several sessions that would have been great sellers but he and the Chess company had some kind of complicated situation and never actually released that many songs. I know several songs of mine were never released. I found out what was happening when other people were coming up with these songs I had intended Mabon to do.

I made a song called "Would You, Baby?"—"There's you and I face to face/Nothing between us but silk and lace/And you thought it wasn't no disgrace/Would you, baby?"—that turned out to be a big one. "The Seventh Son" was one I gave Mabon, too, and everybody else did it their way but him and he was the one who asked for it.

The Seventh Son is kind of a historical idea. In New Orleans and Algiers, Louisiana, they have these people calling themselves born for good luck because they're the seventh sister or seventh brother or the seventh child. The world has made a pattern out of this seven as a lucky number. Most people think the seventh child has the extra wisdom and knowledge to influence other people.

I wrote "Tollin' Bells" for Lowell Fulson and the idea was like in New Orleans, when they'd have a funeral, guys would be marching for the funeral with the church bells tolling. The idea was to make these horns blend in a minor tone, with the minor against the major. I was using the horns to play two parts of a minor chord and the piano playing the other. The idea was to do something with a different harmony blend but a good blend.

Chess had quite a few different artists that he was fooling around there with and a lot of 'em, after he played the record one or two times, he just put it down. When Jimmy Witherspoon came in there, I had this song all ready when he got there. I made this song about "Great God Almighty, when the lights go out," and that was a big number for him and "Big Daddy" also.

After awhile Chess got to the place where they would always depend on me to have a song when somebody else ran short of a song. I'd write for any artist that Chess had come in and a lot of times I was doing a little sidetrackin' stuff with other companies.

I was recording for Peacock and Duke and Chess and United all at the same time. Each one didn't want me to work for the other ones but I had to do that to keep a little income coming in because nobody wanted to pay me every week.

I wrote for Shakey Horton and quite a few songs for Leonard Allen at United Records on 51st and Cottage Grove. I was writing for several different people and some I was putting other names to because I didn't want the Chess company to take all of my songs.

I did a lot on the sly but a lot of times they could catch it anyway— "Man, that sounds just like some of Dixon's music or Dixon's writing." They'd come up and have a way of saying: "Man, you're supposed to have been writing for us. I think you should let us hear about these things before you let anyone else."

I've been real lucky about writing people songs but a lot of times, if I picked the song, the guys didn't want the song for himself. Muddy didn't want the ones I was giving him and Howlin' Wolf didn't want the ones I was givin' him. The one Wolf hated most of all was "Wang Dang Doodle." He hated that "Tell Automatic Slim and Razor-Toting Jim." He'd say, "Man, that's too old-timey, sound like some old levee camp number."

I wrote several songs for Muddy but after that first one, I didn't have to convince him very much about a song. I had been trying to give Little Walter "My Babe" because of his style of doing things but it took damn near two years for him to record it.

Whenever I work with an artist or group, I like to hear them and get a feeling about the style that people like to hear them sing. I could make a song on the spot sometimes that would fit the individual just by watching his action. There are certain ways people act and music just fits what they're doing.

The average blues song must have a feeling or the world won't accept it. You have to have a lot of inspiration and you have to be able to sell that inspiration to the other fellow. If the artist can express the song with inspiration, it inspires the public because music has that generating thing. If it touches you and you can feel it, you can inspire someone else. It's just like electricity going from one to the other.

Feeling has a lot to do with it all the time. If some guy calls you a dirty name, you know when the guy means it and when he's just kidding. Dusty Fletcher was a comedian who used to do the "Open the door, Richard" routine onstage everywhere. He would come on at the Regal Theater in Chicago and cuss and raise hell and talk more bad talk onstage and everybody would be crying they laughed so much. Somebody else says "damn" onstage and everybody's insulted.

I felt Little Walter had the feeling for this "My Babe" song. He was the type of fellow who wanted to brag about some chick, somebody he loved, something he was doing or getting away with. He fought it for two long years and I wasn't going to give the song to nobody but him.

He said many times he just didn't like it but, by 1955, the Chess people had gained confidence enough in me that they felt if I wanted him to do it, it must be his type of thing. The minute he did it, BOOM! she went right to the top of the charts.

All the time I had at Chess was spent working with the artists. The artists would come in and the first thing, they would be sent to me: "See Willie and what he thinks about it." They told me if I thought it was a good thing to let them know and get it together and they would decide whether they would record it or not.

They were going to do what they wanted to, anyway, but I would kind of approve them first. I was doing a pretty good job at it but you had a lot of yes men around then. If I didn't like it, I'd say I didn't and they didn't like me because I would speak frank.

If it sounded close to someone the Chess brothers knew, they didn't want to record it. I found Otis Rush down on 47th Street and I knew he was a good artist but Leonard Chess thought he sounded too close to Muddy Waters. They couldn't see the difference.

There was a lot of fellows I was intending to get into Chess but Chess wouldn't accept Otis, Harold Burrage or Magic Sam at that time. Later on, he took 'em on after they had records on Cobra.

Frankly, the only reason Chess went along with the blues was because he lost out on his other recording company by not having the blues. They actually didn't know as much about the blues as people might think.

There was always a lot of artists around. Any time you open up a recording company, you don't have to worry about people coming there. They will run you crazy. You'd be surprised how much talent is out there but it's a hard job to make them understand the record company had to spend a lot of money to make you a success.

The jukebox operators wouldn't put your records on, especially a blues, unless you gave them so many free ones. The distributors wouldn't handle your record unless they had free ones to advertise with. Most of them would just sell their free ones.

No disc jockey was going to play your record then without you paying him and that was the truth. Nobody wanted to play the blues and they would only play the tunes they had the money on. They would play 'em two weeks, three times a day and that was it unless you came up with more money.

Some of the disc jockeys would play all of one company's records and there wasn't a whole lot of radio stations like there are now. A radio disc jockey would say, "Look, I can play this record and that record of yours but I have to play some by somebody else. If you wanted a third record played of yours, you have to pay for it."

That meant you paid him and that's where all the payola stuff came from. If you didn't play a song three or four times a day, it wouldn't get enough into people's ears for them to ask for the song and sell it.

A lot of times the company knew the way an artist brought a song in wouldn't sell. The Chess brothers would say, "Dixon, go over there with these folks and straighten up their thing. Get a better introduction on there. Get 'em to sing the words right and get the tune in shape to record."

I would get a few dollars because the company would want them to practice. Most of the time they'd have to rent somebody else's place or go in some tavern. We used to get in a lot of arguments with people because we didn't have a place to practice. The people are sitting around there and the first thing you would always hear after you started up was, "Hey, I want to make a request." "Sorry, man, this ain't request time."

Most of the guys at that particular time felt like the blues had to be 12 bars. When we would tell a guy about making up a different pattern, they were always wounded because they couldn't understand why theirs had to be different from somebody else's. Naturally, I would explain to them that if they all sounded the same, why should someone want their record as opposed to the other fella's?

The first time Chuck Berry came there, we knew "Maybellene" could be a crackshot hit. The minute I heard it, I knew it had that certain quality and feeling, a complete story with good understanding. The average youngster liking automobiles and racing, it had to go but Chuck had it sounding more like a country & western tune called "Ida Red." I had heard this "Ida Red" and it had the country & western pace completely but I always felt that some kind of bluesy idea or feeling that wasn't in there would make it a better song.

We discussed it pro and con for two or three days. I knew Chuck probably got angry because things weren't really going as he thought they should. I'd say, "But, man, this is too great a song to let it get away with another person's tune," because if it went over, whoever was involved with "Ida Red" would come running.

He got a lot of ideas so he went back to St. Louis and said he would call when he thought it was better. I think Chuck had to go down and sell blood to the blood bank to get money to get back to St. Louis. Sure enough, a few weeks later, he called up and sang it on the telephone. We told him, "Come on in and we'll go to work on it."

It was me and Phil Chess, Chuck and a bunch of other people who went down to Universal Studios to record it. I had a studio band that was doing most everything for Chess and we recorded most of the first stuff with him. Chuck had a guy named Johnny Johnson who was a helluva good piano player but he didn't play on the first sessions—it was Lafayette Leake.

Leonard Chess was out of town and, when he came back, "Maybellene" was playing on the air because we made a dub of it that quick. Leonard came in and said, "Man, somebody's got a record on the air that's burning up." He didn't know it was our record, his own organization.

We had so much confidence in "Maybellene." Chess would never get over 1,000 or 2,000 records on anybody but when we first cut that Chuck Berry number, I think he put 10,000 on the floor at the first shot.

Me and Lafayette Leake, Harold Ashby and Al Duncan were the first road band Chuck Berry had. Chuck was a fast driver—I always thought he was trying to prove something to Maybellene when he was out there. Just about every time we went to eat, he would order chilli. I guess that was about the best thing we'd get for the money we had.

He put on a beautiful show even in those days. Chuck was cooking because he insisted that everybody playing with him cook with him. He was very serious about his music. He wanted the musicians to play exactly like he had his ideas and sometimes we had to practice quite a bit to get it.

Most of the guys at that particular time had evolved just playing the blues but it really became a big change when Chuck started. All the rest began grabbing hold of that particular angle of sticking the electric guitar out front. A lot of people would put a few licks in here and there before then but it seemed like they was afraid that they were jive.

For my money, Chuck was the first actual rock 'n' roller. I felt that all the others took after him. The kids might have had a few of those rock ideas to a certain extent but they really weren't as deeply into it as they got after "Maybellene."

I can give you a little insight into why Bill Haley and Elvis Presley got all the credit for beginning rock 'n' roll. Chuck was in one vein of blues and some radio stations just didn't consider playing blues. At the time, the majority of people got it in their minds they didn't want the black man's music to move and blues is the black man's music.

They had plenty of big clubs in Chicago but you would seldom get a new artist out of a big club because they would get put in there by agents. The Club of Leisure, the El Casino, the Flame, the Brass Rail, they would be booking professional entertainers during that time. As a talent scout for Chess, I was looking more for neighborhood spots and weekend things. Somebody would say they got a good band at this particular place so I'd ease by there and hear 'em a little bit.

Sometimes I'd hear them in the streets or some other place playing. I heard Bo Diddley playing in the streets lots of times. He had a little band that would go from corner to corner, set up and start playing. We'd see him all over the place and one day somebody brought him into the studio. He did this song, "I'm A Man" and kept developing it.

I played bass on some of Bo Diddley's first sessions. He came there with one fellow playing bass but that guy didn't have enough firepower in his bass. I knew Bo had a very good rhythmic style and this gave him the thing to emphasize. When you hear a guy come up with a beat like "Boom da boom da boom, da boom boom," right out of nowhere, it's going to attract your attention.

The drums have always been giving messages. In slavery times, they didn't allow black people to tap or drum on wooden things because they could talk the message of rhythms. That's why Bo Diddley always carries this particular pattern. The drums are speaking and he'll tell you what the drums are saying.

What made it confusing with Bo Diddley was the group was trying to get a recording session and Billy Boy Arnold, the harmonica player out of the same band, had gone across the street to VeeJay Records. VeeJay told Billy Boy they would record him but Bo Diddley and the band was over at Chess. They both got a deal at the same time with practically the same songs in mind. Chess and VeeJay got into some kind of heated discussion over it and finally, Billy Boy went on VeeJay and Chess took Bo Diddley.

I knew Chess and Jimmy Bracken at VeeJay was threatening each other because when I'd go across the street, Jimmy thought I was coming over to try and find something out for Chess. I said, "Hell, I ain't comin' over to find out nothin'. I just got a bunch of songs to sell."

Jimmy said he wanted some and then Chess said he was going to fire me if I let Jimmy have any. I started trying to figure out how can I get certain songs to other people because from then on, Chess wanted them all.

Some of these tunes, I found out Chess was just taking the ideas and putting them with other things. I'd listen and say, "That sounds like my tune," and they'd say, "No, so-and-so wrote this tune." It was the same identical tune but with different ideas, you know.

I had heard about copyrights but I really didn't know anything about 'em. I had been trying to get into ASCAP ever since the Bumpin' Boys and when I started working with Chess, I kept talking about joining. I had heard about BMI but I figured it was just like the other one and there was no way I could get in there, you know. One day, one of the Goodman brothers came in and said he could get me in there because I had a couple of pretty good songs out with Chess. I signed the thing and didn't hear from him for a long while.

Sometime later on, he come in there to Chess and brought me a couple of checks. I didn't squawk about them, didn't know if they were right, wrong or in-between. Later on, BMI started writing me about different things and, ever since then, I started loading them up with songs.

Some of the first stuff we recorded before Chess got his own recording studio was down on Erie Street where a fellow named Bill Putnam owned Universal Studios. He moved his studio to Ontario Street a couple of blocks away and we did the Moonglows, Flamingos and a few other guys there in 1954.

The Moonglows used to work at a place called the Crown Propellor that me and Baby Doo Caston opened up. I got the Moonglows that gig. I was working night and day with them trying to get the songs together.

Old man Chess had a building around 45th and Graves. He was letting the Moonglows stay there and getting ready for the recording session. They got a lot of rehearsing done at that place and Chess wasn't charging them much rent while they were trying to get their record together.

The first record with the group was based on the side "Tempting" but they fooled around and made this tune "Sincerely" that really touched something. Everybody was saying how great "Tempting" was but some deejays turned the record over and "Sincerely" took off like a jet.

They had to go on the road and naturally they didn't have cars or money or nothing. Chess sold them his old Cadillac to hit the road with and, boy, they were tickled to death. I don't know what he sold it to them for but later on the guys were squawking that it was too much money he charged 'em.

It was right about that time when Chess bought this recording equipment second-hand from the Reverend Franklin over in Detroit. Once he got it set up over at 48th and Cottage Grove, we'd go in the studio for three hours and get three or four songs in. It all depended on what shape the guys were in and how much time we had to spend with them before we got 'em in the studio.

MALCOLM CHISHOLM: Leonard Chess had what they laughingly referred to as a studio but he wasn't such a fool as to think it was a studio. He went to one of the independent studios in town, Universal Recording, and it was run by a fellow named Bill Putnam. Bill had been running quite a high quality studio and the reputation of that studio was good with musicians.

I went to work for that studio some time in 1955 as an editor and maintenance man. I was about as technical as possible and knew something of music. Over a fairly short course of time, because the record business was growing and the staff was not, I was put on record gigs. Because of the lack of a real studio at Chess and because Bill was doing very important people like Stan Kenton, Duke Ellington and Count Basie, I caught the "other stuff." The "other stuff" consisted in large part of nobodies being recorded by Chess Records.

While Chess was not specifically a low-life company, Chess was quite specifically a very minor company. However, some of those nobodies turned out to have made Chess a major minor. I recorded a nobody named Ramsey Lewis, first LP, another one named Ahmad Jamal, first album, Chuck Berry's first sessions and came drifting by these blues gigs, which no one took with the slightest degree of seriousness.

With the assistance of Will Dixon, who was the writer and producer and bass player on an awful lot of this stuff and who would occasionally tap you on your shoulder—a sensation not to be forgotten easily—I learned about blues very rapidly. What I know of blues other than the simple musical aspect, I learned from Will.

He trained his own engineer as it were and, because of that, when I worked with Will it got to the point very quickly where our tastes in many things ran very similar. It got into an ideal situation—which doesn't happen frequently between producer, musicians and engineers—where we didn't have to talk to each other.

Will and I never had a failed session. Adventure is usually the result of incompetence and the sessions with Dixon ordinarily went very well. Will could go out on the floor and do his band work because he knew I was hearing about what he was hearing and if it wasn't what he had in mind, he'd probably like it anyway. I might do it differently but I wouldn't do it wrongly according to his concept of what he had been trying to do.

At the time, the mix was the mix and if you missed it, you missed it. Will would tell me if he wanted to hear more guitar, which is not just a matter of turning up the guitar. Music is an animal with a goodly number of legs and they all have to reach the ground. If you don't have enough of something or too much of something else and the other balances don't fit within that pattern, the animal limps.

Blues is a very dynamic medium, and for an engineer, highly dynamic music is much more difficult to handle. Will told me what the fixed balance of blues should be—that is, you carry far too much guitar and far too much voice because they need to be heard and the fill instruments are carried a little lower than one might ordinarily expect. Above all it has to be clean, especially as it is, by and large, not very well rehearsed and you get into odd balances and odd situations constantly in the blues when you have the multiple solo thing.

Blues is polyphony and you had three solos going at the same time. I got into the habit of picking one, featuring it and subordinating two others, do that for eight bars and then change over. It's difficult to know just what you should do under those circumstances so you do whatever the music allows you to do in terms of varying things. That requires a certain amount of interpretive talent and it requires working to some sort of standard. Mine are Will's because what I know I learned from him.

WD: I see recording like a painting. If you put a black picture on a white wall, the background helps the picture and the picture helps the background so you enjoy the both of them together unconsciously. This is the way about the melodic lines in music—you use them as the basic background because it beautifies the complete story. You know the background is there so you can express the words with a certain feeling. If you care to make variations, your variations won't bother the background and the background won't bother you.

The sound we got that people began to talk about as the Chess sound was based on the idea of harmony. A lot of folks didn't know anything about harmony but I could always sell it to them in that certain groove.

By me being involved with quartet harmony singing, I would stop and hum the tune that the instrument would be playing. Being able to whistle two tunes at the same time in harmony, I could do the sounds that gave the two instruments this particular blend. People branded that as the Chess sound.

JIMMY ROGERS: It wasn't hard at all to work with Dixon because he never would really stay in the way. He knows how to lay in the background. An upright bass is not very loud anyway and in the studio he wasn't really coming through to interfere with our sound. He really tried to play what we was playing.

The only thing we listened to him for was when he would be arranging a song. We would stop playing and listen to the way he would phrase the lyrics and changes, we'd get that down and practice on it until we got it straightened out.

WD: It wasn't hard to blend my acoustic bass with the electric guitars when you know how. The acoustic bass and the electric bass have two different sounds in the same note and that makes the blend a completely different thing. An acoustic bass is a feel instrument. It don't have frets and when you know your instrument, you can feel exactly where to blend it perfectly.

The studio band was me, Al Duncan, Harold Ashby and Lafayette Leake. I tried to use the little fellows. I was trying to encourage young musicians that had a pretty good thing going in preference to the guys that were already making it. Some old guys would tell you in a second, "Don't tell me how to blow my horn."

I used Harold Ashby all the time because he was a darned good horn man and he had a unique sound that the average fellow just couldn't get with the tenor sax. I remember that later I did a thing called "Sittin' And Cryin' The Blues" over at Cobra that required a "crying" type saxophone. I couldn't get anybody else to even understand what I meant but Harold did it the first time.

When I needed a good drummer, I would get Al Duncan, Fred Below or Odie Payne. Al would be the first choice because it wasn't a hard job explaining what you wanted him to do. He could handle it if it was writing or ad lib.

Lafayette Leake could read music real well and he knew his piano. Anything you wanted him to play, he could do it the first time. The guy could do miracles on piano. Quite often the Chess brothers would come in with some ideas—"Man, do this with one hand, that with that hand and this right here at the same time." A lot of times you couldn't physically do that but Leake would find a way to put that third hand in.

Little Walter was a very good player but Big Walter—we called him Shakey Horton—was a helluva harmonica player. Big Walter would be doing a lot of the harmonica backgrounds that people thought was Little Walter. He kinda taught Little Walter, Sonny Boy Williamson and all those guys.

They underestimated Big Walter because he'd stay loaded most of the time but once you'd get him in good condition, he could run rings around all of them. You couldn't whistle, sing, hum or play a rhythm of anything that he couldn't do like you wanted. There were ways he would cup the harmonica with a glass to make it sound like a horn. He'd take a beer can, cut the top out of it, cup the harmonica in there and make that sonuvagun sound like a trombone and no one could tell the difference.

Sometimes one of the guys would go off with somebody and we'd have to change men. There was a whole crew of us, that was working. A lot of the personnel things won't show up listed on the Chess record because they were doing things in many ways, most of them undercover.

We tried to keep the sessions down to business until one of the Chess brothers would come in shooting the bull with different guys and starting little arguments. They were callin' guys names, "Hey, you so-and-so. What's wrong, can't you get it right?"

I think they did that to kind of boost their morale, get them to arguing and fighting and they'd cuss him back. It didn't mean nothing. They would figure they could tantalize one of the musicians a little bit, get him halfways upset and by the time he would cuss them out, they'd go out and we'd get the song done.

I think the Chess brothers had an idea within themselves that these kinds of ideas stimulated the artist to make 'em more vigorously involved. My parents always taught me it was better to be smart and don't get mad. A lot of times that's awful hard to do but if you think about it, you can control yourself much better.

MALCOLM CHISHOLM: Leonard used to come in and screw up sessions at which point, not being dull, he would notice that my ears would turn bright red. I hated that and frequently the session would go to hell because the musicians got upset, irritable and wouldn't play very well. Sonny Boy Williamson's "You can call it your mama if you want to but the name is 'Little Village,' " after which you hear me blowing the take number, is typical of the sort of thing that occasionally went on.

WD: Most of the musicians were paid the union scale. The union required the scale to be paid to the musicians within 14 days of the session but most of the fellas wanted their money the same day they finished. A lot of times Leonard Chess would say, "Look, if you'll take half the money, I'll give it to you now."

They were paying something like $42.50 so he'd go over and say, "I'll give you $22 and we'll call it even, okay?" They'd argue for more and sometimes they'd get it, sometimes they wouldn't. Sometimes they paid 'em all off on the spot.

At that time, we didn't have any idea of the impact those early 45s were making around the world. The South Side of Chicago was mostly a bluesy area. You'd have 20 people playing their radios on the South Side and maybe one out of 20 would be something other than blues. They weren't interested in what the Top Ten was. They were interested in blues music.

Big Bill Hill, Al Benson, Jack L. Cooper and later on E. Rodney Jones and Pervis Spann were deejays who would play what was considered

South Side blues. All those guys were strictly bluesmen. Frankly, they didn't have but one main blues station during the Chess time and that was Al Benson—practically everybody on the South Side listened to Al Benson's station, WGES.

Big Bill Hill was on another station, WOPA, because I wrote a commercial for WOPA about Big Bill Hill. A man named Sounderling owned it—he owned two or three stations around there—and I was trying to get some kind of commission or royalty thing and he wanted to buy it from me outright. I got $2-300 or something like that.

Chess was selling a lot of records, too. At that time, they didn't even think about if rock 'n' roll was keeping blues from becoming popular. It was much later when they really started thinking about that because Chess was going good in 1956.

Chess got in good shape early. Andrew Tibbs recorded this tune "Bilbo Is Dead" when he had the Aristocrat label and the other side was "Union Man Blues." Bilbo was a Senator out of Mississipi that was heavily against black people.

The Chess brothers found that when they were shipping their records to Mississippi, the people didn't like it and were busting up all the records. They had all of them insured so all the other stuff they couldn't sell and were trying to get rid of—some of the records were already broken—they started sending down there.

I think Chess took advantage of everybody because I don't know anybody they gave all their money to. But I felt like you have to pay for everything you get and if you don't pay one way, you have to pay another. I knew they were getting me but I didn't have another place to go. Chess had threatened other people in recording companies like Leonard Allen with United and States Records and two or three other little companies around there that if they started recording me, they were going to have troubles out of them.

Frankly, Leonard was a maneuverer. He was dealing with people who didn't know anything about the recording business. I call it swindling but most people call it smart business when you can take advantage of someone who don't know no better. I didn't know anything about copyright laws or anything like that.

I thought I was dealing with honest people and when you trust somebody that's dishonest, you get bitten. The law can take care of it if you can get enough money to get a lawyer to get justice. They felt like if they could keep you poor enough, you wouldn't have nothing to fight with and that's the truth. I didn't have $2 a lot of times to have a copyright paper on a song sent into Congress.

Leonard Chess' wife told me one day right in front of him, "Ooh, Willie, you've got five songs in the charts at once. You're going to have a whole lot of money. You might even end up a millionaire." Leonard caught her right then, took her straight out of the room and I heard him raising hell with her about talking about how much money I was going to get. Every time I asked him about money from then on, he'd act like he was mad.

Leonard knew how to confidence certain people. Dealing with the guys he had records with, he'd talk on the phone about how he was gonna do this deal with them. When they'd get down to the office, he wouldn't be there. Before he would leave, he would load up the table with all different kinds of whiskey.

Everybody would be there but Leonard and the secretary would say, "Leonard told me to let you all in so go on back, sit down and make yourself comfortable." They'd go back into the room, open the whiskey and drink. An hour later, Leonard would call in to his secretary.

"Hey, are the guys there? What kind of shape are they in?"

"They're drinking."

After a while, Leonard would call again and say, "I'm sorry I couldn't make it. I'm just running late." But he knew what he was doing. He'd let 'em sit there and get loaded. When he came back in, the first thing he would say was, "Have a drink with me," and they've already thrown up.

Then he'd say, "Look here, this has been a long friendship but I've got to tell you. That deal I was talking to you about on the phone, there's no way I could do that. I found out it would be too much money to put this record out."

"Oh, man, you promised me $5,000."

"Well, maybe in the long run, but not right off the bat. I can give you $2,500."

They'd start maneuvering from there. A guy in those days could not wait so they'd get in a corner maneuvering, "Three thousand and pay me out later." Chess would give them the $3,000 and then they would never get together. If the guy got $3,000, he was damned lucky.

Leonard might give you $1,000 when you did a session and four or five months later he would say, "Man, I gave you a thousand dollars then." Hell, between food and bills, that thousand went with the wind. They would use up a lot of your money, too, running errands for them but they didn't want to give it back. When Leonard got sick, I had even more trouble getting money out of Phil.

Leonard went into the hospital and his brother didn't know what kind of deals I had with the company. When I tried to get money from Phil, Phil couldn't come through. Now I've got a family that's just about starving and I was running over there working every day doing everything at Chess—packing records, playing the music and writing the arrangements. I explained to them that if I couldn't get money, I had to go.

Cobra had been after me for a long time anyway because Cobra didn't have but one artist, Arbee Stidham, and he wasn't raisin' no hell selling at all. They knew that everything I had touched at Chess turned to gold, the things I'd done with Muddy, Robert Nighthawk, that guy whose wife played the drums, John Brim.

Chess would always find one way or the other to take my money. Hell, I needed money to live. It was that simple, so I left Chess and started working with Eli Toscano at Cobra. I got a chance to get more new artists involved there and get more of my songs out.

6

I can't quit you, baby
But I've got to put you down for awhile
You know I can't quit you, baby
But I've got to put you down for awhile
Well, you messed up my happy home, babe
Made me mistreat my only child

You know I love you, baby
My love for you I could never hide
Yes, you know I love you, baby
My love for you I would never hide
Yes, you know you're the onliest one, darlin'
You're just my heart's desire

Well, I'm so tired I could cry
I could just lay down and die
I'm so tired I could cry
I could just lay down and die
You know I love you, baby
You're just my heart's desire

When you hear me moanin' and groanin', baby
You know it hurts me way down inside
When you hear me moanin' and groanin', baby
You know it hurts me way down inside
Yes, when you hear me holler, baby
You know you're my heart's desire

Early Chicago blues history is littered with the remains of small, independent record companies who briefly flared up on the strength of a hit song or artist and then faded away. Several of those labels were either bought out or absorbed by Chess. The most enduring Chicago-area competitor for Chess was VeeJay, a black-owned company which lasted until the mid-1960s behind a full roster of blues, R&B and gospel artists that ranged from the brooding blues of John Lee Hooker and the sublime slow grooves of Jimmy Reed to the smooth vocal harmonies of the Dells.

One of those labels which came and went was Cobra Records. Owned by Eli Toscano, Cobra was the successor of the Abco label which released seven singles in 1955–6 and, typically, it was another record company run on little more than a wing and a prayer.

But Cobra was also the place where Willie Dixon, for the first time, had full creative control over his blues sessions. In the small homemade studio located behind Toscano's record shop on Chicago's West Side, Dixon began fully to hone his producing and arranging style, merging some of the jazz-tinged sophistication of his early work with the gutbucket punch of the increasingly guitar-oriented Chicago blues.

The Cobra interlude was crucial in another respect—the young artists on the label like Otis Rush, Buddy Guy and Magic Sam began putting on record what became known as the "West Side Sound," one that fused the Delta influence of classic Chicago blues with single-string lead guitar lines à la B.B. King. The West Side gave birth to a less traditional, more modern blues sound and the emphasis placed on the guitar as a lead instrument ultimately proved to be a vastly influential force on the British blues crew in their formative stages.

Blues wasn't the only form Dixon was involved with on the 33 singles put out by Cobra and the five records on its short-lived subsidiary, Artistic. There were unreleased gospel sessions, a few shots of R&B featuring singers like Betty Everett and Harold Burrage and the last single on both Cobra and Artistic featured Ike Turner and his Kings of Rhythm.

Cobra had gotten off to a flying start when the label's first single, the Dixon-penned "I Can't Quit You, Baby," turned into a Top Ten R&B chart hit for Otis Rush late in 1956. But Cobra had pretty much ceased to function by the time Eli Toscano was reportedly fished out of Lake

Michigan one day in 1959. Some called it a boating accident, some a murder over unpaid gambling debts, and some evidence has emerged that Toscano didn't, in fact, die until 1966.

But Dixon had already drifted away from Cobra—the issue again was money and the extra financial responsibilities that came with maintaining two households. After fathering seven children, his relationship with Elenora had grown increasingly frosty and he had met and fallen in love with Marie Booker. The first of their five children was born in 1957.

His estrangement from Chess during this period hadn't been complete—he was playing bass behind Chuck Berry on the monumental hits "Sweet Little Sixteen," "Rock 'n' Roll Music," "Johnny B. Goode," "Memphis," and "Sweet Little Rock 'n' Roller." He recorded behind the Diddley Daddy on "Hey! Bo Diddley" and frequently with Little Walter and Sonny Boy Williamson (including the infamous "Little Village" session) during 1957-8—surprisingly, more often than he did with Muddy Waters or Howlin' Wolf. By early 1959, Dixon was back full-time at Chess.

During the Cobra period, Dixon was getting more involved with different facets of the music business. He had been running the Ghana Booking Agency since the early 1950s, booking an assortment of blues artists and dancers around Chicago and elsewhere. In April 1957, he shifted the name over to his publishing company, Ghana Music, when he registered it with BMI.

But the blues were hurting in Chicago in the immediate aftermath of the rock 'n' roll explosion and that got Dixon and his old buddy Memphis Slim thinking about taking steps to change the situation. The two had begun teaming up again for duo performances around Chicago when they could find them and a new development on the music scene—the first stirrings of the folk music boom—helped open the doors to a new audience.

Not only in Chicago—Slim and Dixon started traveling, making two appearances at the Newport Folk Festival in 1957 and 1958 and hitting both the West Coast coffee house circuit and the folk clubs in major Eastern cities. It was during a 1959 East Coast jaunt that Dixon, together with Slim and some old compadres like Harold Ashby, recorded his first album as a leader, Willie's Blues, for the new Bluesville subsidiary of Prestige. The duo also made several sessions *for Verve (*The Blues Every Which Way*) and Folkways (*Live At The Village Gate*) that were released in the early 1960s.*

Slim and Dixon made their first overseas jaunt when they traveled to England in 1959 but their biggest break came when they returned home. Playing at the Gate of Horn club, they ran into an Israeli woman who wanted them to perform at her club in Haifa ... and the blues entered a new, international phase.

PHIL UPCHURCH: *a Chess sessionman in the mid-1960s who later moved to Los Angeles and recorded with George Benson, among others.*

PHILIPPE RAULT: *a French blues producer who recorded Memphis Slim. He now lives in Los Angeles and books artists for music festivals.*

Eli Toscano was the man who had the Cobra recording company. He had one artist, Arbee Stidham, and he had one record out which wasn't raising hell but it was playing over there in the black neighborhoods of Chicago.

We sat down and talked. He was telling me he was looking for some more artists because Arbee wasn't selling. I told Eli I could get him some new artists because when I was working for Chess, there were quite a few artists that I would say were good enough but the company would always find some reason to say no.

Eli let me have about $30 up front and I promised to work with him. We were going to make up a contract for me and him to be partners. Cobra was on West Roosevelt Road on the West Side of Chicago. Eli was selling records in the front and we built a studio in a big garage in the back.

When I went over to Cobra, that's when Phil Upchurch first started playing because he used to come by there. He was a youngster then and he'd come by so glad he could play this song, "Moonlight In Vermont." He'd play it for me every day: "How do you like this, Dixon?"

PHIL UPCHURCH: There was a record shop around the corner from my house in the 3300 block of Roosevelt Road and housed in that record shop was Cobra Records. They knew me as the little kid around the block who was a pretty good guitar player and they let me hang around.

They had the equipment sitting up on garbage cans and 2 x 4s. I can remember watching Willie work with people like Otis Rush and Buddy Guy when they were doing their premiere work on Cobra.

It was just a back room of a record store, everything done live. Eli was running the equipment and engineering. It was a very basic, simple set-up—come in and set up, put mikes on everybody and they'd record performances, as opposed to these days when they perform recordings.

WD: When I first met him, Eli had some recording material and called himself an engineer but he was a shyster engineer. He claimed he knew all about mikes and PA systems and by me bringing some of my things over, that put him in business. Eli didn't even have enough money to get Otis Rush an amplifier. I jumped up and bought the amplifier with $75 of my own money and I don't think I ever got my $75 back.

Eli was trying to be a gambler and a con man—he was more interested in gambling than anything else. Eli was one of them guys who wanted to be involved with something heavy. He would have thought it to be an honor to be accepted like he was with the syndicate. He was a chronic liar, too. That kind of went with most of the recording men, chronic lying. I guess they had to do that to keep things rolling.

There were sessions at Cobra whenever Eli could get one because he was trying to work off a shoestring. I ate more hot dogs over there than I ever ate in my whole life. That's all we'd have—hot dogs for breakfast and hot dogs for lunch.

I called Otis Rush first thing because Otis had been out at Chess trying to get a session there. I told Eli about Otis and he gave me car fare to go out to Otis' house. I finally got Eli out to the place Otis was playing and when he came out, Eli didn't like the songs. He didn't like nothing.

I came out to Otis' house again, sat around and talked with him when Eli wasn't there and we finally got it together. Otis was having a little trouble with his girlfriend Freddie at that time. I think she cut out on him to St. Louis and he was still in Chicago grieving about her. That's when I wrote this song, "I Can't Quit You, Baby."

That was the first one we recorded with Otis. I got Shakey Horton on the harp and it was Lafayette Leake on the piano, I was playing bass, Otis was playing guitar and I think it was Billy Stepney playing drums.

We got up there in the studio at Kimball Hall on Wabash Avenue and going through the process of recording it, I found Otis was really weak for the girl. All I had to do then was get him in the mood to talk about Freddie and he had this feeling for her. Several times we went through the motions of the song and he didn't have the right feeling but I told Eli, "Look, this is going to be a good song."

Eli was sitting in the booth shaking his head right and left. He didn't know what he was talking about because he hadn't had any experience in it. I found that most people involved in recording companies don't know a durned thing about music but they're smart enough to get people around them that do know something. That's what keeps them going.

Eli liked the blues but he couldn't understand people being all emotional over them. You can't explain nothing to someone until you've had a personal experience of getting that feeling and understanding. I told him, "One day, somebody's gonna play you a blues that's going to hit you and it's going to hit you hard. You won't be able to hide your feelings."

"No, nothing could make me get excited like that."

Eli was begging for a good-selling record. I told him, "This record will sell," because Otis was a helluva good singer with a lot of expression. We were fooling around in the studio and I figured the best idea was to dim the lights to get Otis in the mood. I told him, "When you think you got the mood, just break out with the first part of the song."

Everyone else thought that was the wrong idea but that's the way I wanted to start it. He made several attempts and all of a sudden he hit the chord and I knew the minute he hit that chord. You can feel the blues better than you can understand them and that feeling says more to you than all the words that anybody can express.

I was lookin' in the booth at Eli when everybody fell in so smooth and red pimples broke out on his face like he had smallpox or something. That must be the first time I ever saw anybody's hair stand straight up on their head. I thought that was a lie about people. The other guys were playing, watching each other and that room was sounding so good until we sung the thing down and the engineer cut it off.

Everybody looked around at Eli and nobody said a word because these pimples were sticking out on him. All of a sudden, they started to go away and everybody started laughing. Somebody said, "What's the matter, Eli?" and he was crying. I wasn't expecting him to feel it this quick, you know. We'd just talked about it a week or so before. It's got to be a natural feeling and nobody can tell you how to feel a natural feeling.

After we took that take, everything was all right. We went into a couple of other songs and put "Sit Down, Baby" on the other side. We got that record together and took the dub over to Big Bill Hill's studio on Roosevelt Road. He had a little switchboard there that could take in eight or ten calls at the same time. Eli and I walked in there and Bill Hill started raisin' hell.

"Oh, man. Here come you cats with another damned record for me to play and nobody ever comes up with no money. You know I'm going to make the record get over and you didn't bring any money."

"Man, I got no money," Eli said.

"Oh, you can get some money."

"Well look, man, if this record sells, we can let you in on the deal because I want you to play it."

"I know it ain't nothin'."

Sure enough, he put the record on and told the audience, "Here's a new record by a new artist, Otis Rush. You've never heard him but Eli says it's a good record."

The minute Otis sang, "Ooohhh, I can't quit you, baby/But I got to put you down for a little while," every light on the switchboard lit up before that record was halfway through. Bill Hill thought the switchboard was broken: "What the heck is this? They ain't never called in like this."

Everybody was saying, "Play that 'Can't Quit You, Baby' again," over and over. Everybody was asking where could they buy the record and we didn't even have a record pressed. When we finally got the records out there, it went straight into the Top Ten on the charts.

We went on the road to try and collect the money for Cobra from the distributors because you know how it is in the recording business—

until you get the second big-selling record, you don't get that first money. Everybody wanted "I Can't Quit You, Baby" and grabbed the initial order. Some of 'em would pay and some of 'em wouldn't. The second order is when they would send their checks in.

That's the way most recording companies do unless the guy's got a helluva good credit thing going but the new companies all have to do that. A new company has to have money to run on and they don't have no credit established. The next record we made was on Otis Rush again, "My Love Will Never Die" and that took off like a jet, too. Eli and I went all over Cleveland and different places trying to collect the money.

But when we come up with this Magic Sam thing, he started getting first money. Magic Sam had a different guitar sound. Where most of the guys were playing the straight 12 bar blues thing, he was doing it to a 12 bar pattern to a certain extent but the harmonies that he carried with the chords was a different thing altogether.

This particular tune about "All Your Love," he expressed with such an inspirational feeling with his high voice and this was the thing I really accepted him on. It was the way he used his voice, the variation he was using.

He and Otis Rush were about the same age and I tried to get Sam involved in some of the things with Otis Rush. It seemed like Sam had just trained himself to that particular style and couldn't move easy. This is why I used that particular style with him and it turned out to be pretty good because you could always tell him, even from his introduction to the music. I would try to wrap it up with other instruments around him but he always stuck out in the same manner.

I played some club dates with Sam sometimes, one-nighters. I never did like to get hooked into those guys' bands because they weren't making no money in the first place. I'd just get in there to help out.

Buddy Guy sounded too much like B.B. King when he got his start and he didn't go over because that was B.B.'s style. It's like this old phrase I've often said: "A mockingbird is supposed to be able to sing the tune of any bird but he's not a popular bird because he's singing all the other birds' tunes. But the birds that sing just one tune, which is their own tune, get more respect than the mockingbird because they got their own thing." This is the way it is with a musical thing. When you come up with your own thing, people respect you for it.

I got the opportunity to do more songs in the minor keys over at Cobra. A lot of people didn't understand minor keys being kind of a soulful sound. Everybody could sing and play straight harmony but knowing a 3rd chord, which made it a minor, a lot of people just couldn't adjust themselves. When you go to tell them about lowering the 3rd chord, they didn't know what the hell you was talking about.

A lot of people can hear a minor and if it's not fully covered with the harmony, they can't understand it because it sounds weird by itself, somebody trying to sing a minor note into a chord. A minor has to be in a chord more than it does in a single note and when you try to give somebody the understanding that don't know very much about music, they can't hear the minor as well. They think it's a discord. Otis Rush liked minor keys once he got involved in it. It wasn't tough to convince him after he heard the sound.

Otis has got a beautiful voice for singing the blues. We used to do that "My Love Will Never Die" when we toured down in Florida after the first time I recorded him. It was a mess. We got in six jails down there, saying we were speeding and we weren't doing but 45 miles an hour. We had Little Brother on piano, Otis Rush, Jody Williams on guitar and Tim Overton on saxophone in the band.

We had an introduction with that band that could bust the heart of a grizzly bear. I would get hold of Otis and get him all wound up. He was young and anxious to get out there, so the band would play, we'd bring Otis on and bring it down quieter than a mouse until he started. That cat would come out there and get to screamin' and hollerin', those folks would be crying and raising hell.

I had a lot of fun out there on the road because I hadn't been away from Chicago for a while. They got a guy 'round there in Florida called Guitar Shorty who used to do a lot of trick guitar playing. That was the guy Buddy Guy resembled because I was explaining to Buddy Guy about how to twist his guitar around, throw it up in the air, upside the wall, different little trickeration stuff just to excite the people. Guitar Shorty was the first one I saw with that idea and I started Buddy to playing with it.

I used to take Buddy over to Jewtown and I had an old guitar that didn't have electricity to it. I used to take him over there every Sunday morning and tell him, "Man, put some show into the guitar. Throw it up, catch it." When he got it going, boy, he turned out all the guys.

Buddy practiced it harder and he got to be a whiz, everywhere he went. All the guitar players now that do tricks with their guitars, they're either doing Chuck Berry or Buddy.

I didn't record at Cobra as an artist because they didn't have any way to expose the records. Heck, I'd just be recording them for myself. I got other artists over there and we made good records on Harold Burrage, Betty Everett and this fellow called Reverend Ballinger. I used to play with him in different places, just the two of us. He was a helluva piano player and boy, he and I would tear the place up.

People that are involved with religious things, a lot of them don't know what they got but they know they got a feeling. This guy could really hammer a piano out, Reverend Ballinger. He recorded for Peacock, Duke and Chess, too, but he never recorded too much because he was one of those fellows who felt like the world was against him.

He was a helluva guy but he was very misunderstood about a lot of things and he didn't have the ability to express himself. I played with the Reverend Ballinger a lot of times but he didn't want to play on my blues things and we were playing the blues all the time.

The first thing Freddie King ever recorded was over at Cobra but I don't think Eli ever released it. This place Freddie was working at up there was on Roosevelt Road and this particular song I named after that place—"Hideaway."

There were two or three people playing their own "Hideaway" but the guy who really wrote "Hideaway" was this guy called Irving Spencer, the one I used to play with back on Madison Street, that was on Koko Taylor's first recording. He was playing that "Hideaway" for years before anybody paid any attention to it. Other people just picked it up from him because he could play a helluva guitar but he was a slow thinkin' kind of guy.

Eli was a chronic gambler—that's the reason his business went out as fast as it did. I was supposed to be a 50% partner but he would never come up with my 50%. His wife Archie told me he was catching the mailman two blocks down before I could catch up with him.

He was always crying about money but he'd go to a convention and gamble all day and all night. He'd mess up and lose a lot of money. While we were working with Otis Rush, we had tipped the trade away from Chess but Eli told me on several occasions that he borrowed money from other recording companies, including Chess, and he had to pay them back.

Every time Eli got in bad shape, he'd run down there to Chess to sell him something or pawn something or get something one way or the other. All that Harold Burrage and even some of Otis Rush and Buddy Guy's stuff, Chess got most of it. Leonard let him have money on some terms but whatever it was, Eli wasn't being fair with me. He and I started eventually getting away from one another.

Back before then, I had met Marie on the way to work in Chicago. She worked in a drug store on 47th at Prarie. She remembered me at the second one, because she moved to another drugstore on the corner. One day I was coming from Cottage Grove on the bus and had a cup of coffee and talked to her for a while. I missed her—I went down there a couple of times and she was gone.

My brother L.V. would hang out down there and make her mad all the time. He told her I was working shows at the Regal Theater and she came there to see it.

I'd be playing there at the Regal different times with different people. A lot of times bands didn't want to haul a great big bass fiddle in the band so when they'd come in town, they wanted a bass fiddle player. First thing, someone would say, "Get Dixon."

It didn't take me long to put my bass in my car and come on down there because I didn't live but about four or five blocks from the Regal Theater at 47th and King Drive. It was adjoining the South Center. I knew just about all the songs they was doing in those days, I knew the city, and it was a one-night gig, make a few bucks, you know.

I was working at a place called the 708 Club, and her and some old girls come down there. I started talking but she didn't pay any attention.

When I came to the Regal Theater one time from this place where Howlin' Wolf was working, I found out she was working right across the street from where she was working before. When my brother told her I was his brother, she didn't believe him. She came up asked me one time if I was and I said yes. Then we got to talking from there, on and on, and that was the beginning. She and her sister had a place on 49th and I started to hang around there quite a bit.

I was looking because I was very much displeased with my first wife because she didn't have much understanding. She didn't have time to talk, didn't have time for nothing but her children and she was trying to make a show of it.

I explained to Marie about it. She said, "You married? I don't mess around with married men." She couldn't believe I wasn't married to Elenora for a long time. Finally she said, "You're not married. How come we can't get married?"

"I don't want to get married until I get in a position where I can have some kids, you know."

Marie and I had been together a year before we had Patricia. You see, most people have always tried to make it some type of disgrace because a man has more than one woman. Ever since the beginning of time, according to Biblical history, the male sex of everything on the face of the earth has always had more than one female.

According to Biblical history, the wisest men in the world had the most women. Men have always fought each other for rulership and left more women than there were men so they had to be taken care of, too.

I don't feel it's no disgrace for a man because it's 40 cows to one bull, ten hens to one rooster, one male fish to hundreds of females and if there's one tomcat in the neighborhood, he keeps everything in full bloom. If it's kings, the wisest king in the world was supposed to be King Solomon and, according to Biblical history, he had many wives. All the other kings did, too, and they were raised as great people.

I started buying Elenora and her kids a house and one for us but they got it in their mind that I was going to take care of the situation until they all got grown. Then they still felt like I should take care of the situation.

I moved to 5216½ Calumet during the time I met Marie. I bought that little house there. It was two houses on one lot, just a little old walk-in thing with nothing between the houses, you know. It was about the cheapest down payment I could get on anything and it cost as much as the rent my sister was charging me.

I was living down at my sister's place at 39th and State before and it was out of the way of all the things I was trying to do. I couldn't keep up with the gang down there, keep up with what was happening. The Musicians' Union wasn't too far from there and it was keeping such a tight schedule on everybody, trying to be sure they were involved in the union and taking all the damned money, I was trying to get away from where they could keep up with me.

J.B. Lenoir had been around Chicago making songs a good while but nothing had been happening to none of them. Folks had been recording him and they wouldn't even play his records. He was a helluva showman 'cause he had this long, tiger-striped coat with tails. We used to call it a two-tailed peter.

J.B. and I got to talking about the copyright law because none of his songs was protected. After he got a few of them together and BMI sent him a couple of checks, he got excited and wanted to get them all in. I was telling him about different publishers and I had a little thing I had just started off called the Ghana Publishing Company.

He said, "Well, I want to put all my things in your publishing company. Whatever they send you, I can check on it, because they're supposed to be giving me the same amount." We got our little thing together and I wrote a letter to BMI and told 'em to put all of his things in my publishing company.

Then, since Chess and them weren't giving me all my money and they had gotten to a place where they were checking on my songs, I figured that what I'd do was put J.B. as writer or part writer on my things and he could put it in my publishing company. I started putting a lot of different people's names on my songs to keep the Chess company from grabbing them because they felt like everything I wrote belonged to them. I put some in Ann Duconge's name, some in Lafayette Leake's name and some in my kids' names.

I didn't know at that time how to handle a publishing company like I should but I could definitely depend on BMI. The more I got interested about it, I learned how to take care of my own things. When I went overseas and found out about sub-publishing and all this kind of stuff, it helped me out too.

First, I had the Ghana Booking Agency in the early 1950s before I switched the name to the publishing. I was booking J.B. and Sunnyland Slim, Memphis Slim and Little Brother Montgomery and Steppin' Fetchit. The union gave me the authority as long as I kept my nose clean.

I was booking Koko Taylor when she first started out, Buddy Guy and Otis Rush down in Florida. When Freddie King came to Chicago I booked him, Harold Burrage, Magic Sam, Fred Below and his outfit and I booked every shake dancer in Illinois—Rosemary, Shake-A-Plenty, Tara Toxie, all of 'em.

A shake dancer is someone who gets up and does dances to attract the minds of people about sex. A lot of them will pull off some of their clothes and some pull off all their clothes and just make the movements and motions to attract the attention and get men upset.

They didn't care who'd book 'em so I'd send 'em a picture on somebody and book 'em. As long as I had the authority from the union that I could get advance money on these artists, I could send them to places. They'd get their money on that end and I'd give 'em their part of it. I was taking 10% from all of them.

Memphis Slim and I got together around 1957 because things had slowed down there in Chicago. We'd get a job on the weekend—if I got a job, I'd get him working with me and if he got a job, I'd work with him. We could always get a night or two together.

It got to the point where it was getting to be just one night a week in Chicago so Memphis Slim and I said we got to get out of here. We got to do something because when we took a record to someone, no one would play it. There was Big Bill Hill's station WOPA and the Chess station here playing blues and that was all.

Chess didn't own the station but Leonard and Al Benson were real tight and whatever Chess wanted, Al Benson was going to play on his station, WGES. I think Chess had made some agreement with Al Benson because Benson recorded Willie Mabon the first time. If Al Benson got something going good, he could always get Chess to handle it or distribute it one way or the other.

Slim and I worked around here and there in America and it was our intention to promote the blues. We played in California and Seattle and all the way up and down the West Coast, just trying to promote the blues, but there wasn't very much turnout for it in those days. We got a chance to go to the Newport Jazz Festival a couple of times.

On several occasions, we made tapes for VeeJay and some things with this Barbara Dane, a white girl who played guitar. We worked with her out in Los Angeles at Ed Pearl's place, the Ash Grove, and in New York and Chicago.

Me and Slim were working for Ed Pearl in 1958 or early 1959 when I made this song called "I Can't Hold Out ." I was talking to Marie on the telephone, that's the reason I made that song. I used to work with

Elmore James at Silvio's once in a while and the 708 Club on 47th
Street. When we got back, Elmore had a session and he wanted me to
work with him so I just jumped on that session and we made that "Talk
To Me Baby (I Can't Hold Out Too Long)."

When me and Slim was playing at the Ash Grove, Barbara Dane had
one of those Volkswagens. Hell, I had a bass fiddle in there, Barbara
was in there and I think Slim had a little portable piano. Everybody
would be laughing at us where we stopped at when we were getting in
there. We had the bass sticking up with the neck out the window.

You should have seen the time me and Buddy Guy went up to
Buffalo, New York. There were four or five of us in a little old two seat
car with the bass and drums and everything in there. You couldn't
hardly turn.

When me and Big Joe Williams and Slim came back from New York
one time, it was Joe Williams, his trunk and guitar, Slim and me and my
bass and guitar and clothes and this chick Big Joe had with him with
her clothes. There were the four of us coming back from New York
stacked up on top of each other like that.

One time Memphis Slim got pretty upset because we played this
place in Chicago. This VeeJay ad had a picture of this Barbara Dane on
the great big page and little bitty pictures of me and Slim and it said:
"White girl keeps blues alive." Slim was raising hell: "As long as I've
been playing blues—all my life—and this girl here that hasn't sung
but four songs, now she keeps the blues alive?" We discussed it pro
and con for a long time. I think that's the reason Slim got out of the
VeeJay company.

Slim said, "Maybe we ought to go to New York" because he was
telling me he could probably get some jobs around there. I had an old
Plymouth that I think I paid a hundred and a quarter for but we got it to
running pretty good. I had 10 or 12 bucks and he did, too, so we took
off for New York in this Plymouth. This was the first time Memphis
Slim and I played the Newport Folk Festival so it must have been
around 1958.

We almost got to Cleveland and I looked down and the charging
hand fell back and it's not moving. The battery was going dead, the
lights are dimming, dimming, down on low and we were running like
mad. We turned off the highway to go into Cleveland and we drove it
as far as we could—*chug, chug, chug*—and then it stopped.

We looked at each other and then we thought we'd find Robert Jr. Lockwood who had just moved to Cleveland. We were walking down the street when all of a sudden, Slim said, "Man, do you hear some music?" We started listening and sure enough, we could hear Sonny Boy Williamson just hollerin' like mad. We were about two blocks from where they was playing at this little club in Cleveland.

We went down there and there was Sonny Boy, Elmore James and Robert Junior. I was so glad to hear them I didn't know what to do. We walked in and after a while, Slim just walked onstage right up to the piano and moved somebody off it. He started playing and everybody started to hollering and going on.

When the intermission came, they said, "Hey, what you guys doing over here?"

"Man, the car's down there a couple blocks away. The battery's gone."

Robert Jr. called up some guy in the middle of the night and this fellow came over there with a battery and generator and fixed it. Elmore was a bragger who always pretended like he was in much better shape than he was and making more money than anybody. He said, "I got plenty of money. What do you guys need?" He gave us $20 apiece, we filled the gas tank up and went on from there to New York.

When we got to New York, we had to park the car in a garage. The woman let us stay at the Hotel Alvin on Broadway and 52nd for the weekend and Slim was up there calling around different places to try and find out where we could get a job because we didn't have any money. Slim would be calling like he was a manager—"Hi, I'm managing Memphis Slim and Willie Dixon and I got 'em in here for a couple of days. Better get them while you can because they're going to record."

PHILIPPE RAULT: I remember Memphis Slim telling a story about him and Dixon when they were going to New York to play at the Village Gate and they had to get a ride to the gig. There was Slim and Dixon and his double bass. Nobody would ever take them if they would ever see them together. They just couldn't fit in the taxi. Dixon would hide around the corner with his bass and Slim would stand on the street and hail the taxi. When he got in the taxi, Dixon would come down with the bass and haul it in.

WD: I would hide around the corner because a lot of times the guy wouldn't want to take that fiddle. The cabbie already turned on his meter the minute Slim would get in there and say, "Hold it, I got a buddy coming." Here I'd come with this fiddle.

"That thing can't get in here."

"The hell it can't."

The first one that recorded us there in New York was John Hammond because he had been coming around to hear Memphis Slim play at other places, you know. I think Hammond gave Slim about $300 or $400 to record an album so that gave us hotel money. I was so glad we could get something to eat.

Then we recorded for this other company in Newark, New Jersey, Prestige. This guy says, "Hey, you got any songs?" We said yeah but we were making up songs on the way to the studio. He had us in a rehearsal studio at first so we'd go in there and get to singing and didn't have nothing to write the song down with. He'd say, "Yeah, I like that one," and write it down. The next day guys would come back at us, "Play the song you played yesterday," and we didn't even know what the hell the song was.

We'd do a thing for Moe Asch's company Folkways, tell 'em it was this brand new song we'd never done before and we'd just done it for somebody else the day before. We stumbled into a thing where these companies found out they had the same identical song they wanted to release and this made both companies try to get the song out before the other one, you know. We would have the same song out on two or three labels at the same time and that gave us better publicity.

When Slim and I made those songs, we had to assign these songs with another company because Goodman and Arc Music had some of our songs. I don't know how in the heck Goodman found out but they was raisin' hell about me and Slim letting this other publishing company have our songs. They insisted on this—Goodman wasn't going to pay me on the songs of mine he already had unless I let him have these other ones. They went to this other publishing company in New York and got the songs. The next thing I knew, Goodman and Chess had 'em all.

We came back out West to California and other places until finally that old car broke down and we decided we'd go to Europe and try to promote the blues. We was working at the Gate of Horn club in Chicago and a lady came into the place.

She was from Israel and she was looking for some musicians. She didn't care what kind. Her name was Aviva and she had a little club out in Haifa called Hamoadan, which means "The Club." We went over there with her to promote the blues.

7

Tell Automatic Slim
To tell razor totin' Jim
To tell butcher knife totin' Annie
To tell fast talkin' Fannie
That we're gonna pitch a ball
Down to the union hall
We gonna rump and trump till midnight
And fuss and fight till daylight
We gonna pitcha a wang dang doodle all night long

Chorus: All night long
All night long
We gonna pitch a wang dang doodle
All night long

Tell Fats and Washboard Sam
That everybody's gonna jam
Tell Shakey and Boxcar Joe
They got sawdust on the floor
Tell Peg and Caroline Dine
We gonna have a heck of a time
And when the fish scent fill the air
There will be snuff juice everywhere

Tell Kuda Crawling Red
To tell Abyssinia Ned
To tell old pistol toting Pete

To tell everybody he meet
Tonight we need no rest
We're gonna really throw a mess
We're gonna break out all the windows
And kick down all the doors

The blues abroad was a crucial period both in Willie Dixon's career and in the history of the music itself.

Slim and Dixon weren't the first blues performers to head overseas. Big Bill Broonzy and Muddy Waters had already played to European audiences, usually presented on shows by the trad jazz clubs, i.e. appreciation societies made up of rabid fans and record collectors that sprang up throughout Europe during the mid to late 1950s.

Included in that network were a pair of German fans named Horst Lippmann and Fritz Rau. Rau was studying to be a lawyer and Lippmann was involved with his family's hotel business before their love of jazz prompted them, beginning with a 1957 European tour by the Modern Jazz Quartet, to start up a concert production company specializing in jazz artists.

The blues were viewed as an adjunct of the jazz world then and ultimately Lippmann and Rau decided to risk an all-blues package. Lippmann had become involved in producing and directing shows for a West German television station and, with that television tie-in to help cover the travel expenses, Lippmann & Rau brought the first American Folk Blues Festival to Europe in 1962. The line-up featured T-Bone Walker, John Lee Hooker, Memphis Slim, Willie Dixon, Sonny Terry and Brownie McGhee, Shakey Jake, Helen Humes and drummer Armand "Jump" Jackson.

The impact of that and the subsequent American Folk Blues Festivals was remarkable, for the American blues musicians arrived just in time for a generational shift that brought an entire new audience to the blues. They played in prestigious concert halls seating

1,800–2,500 people during three week tours of Europe with an extra week tacked on for dates in England.

Europe and England quickly became a more hospitable home for blues artists than America—the places where they could make decent money and receive the respect and adulation they never did at home. The festivals would run in Europe through 1971 and, in 1964 and 1966, took excursions behind the Iron Curtain. Lippmann built the momentum by recording an album of the revue-styled show each year—1968 excepted—and John Lee Hooker's "Shake It, Baby" became a substantial continental hit early in 1963. Memphis Slim would remain behind in Paris after the 1962 tour and became a star based in part on the exposure he received through the blues festivals.

Willie Dixon was a pivotal figure in the European breakthrough. He only went to Europe as the bassist/anchor of the performing band for the first three years—1962 through 1964. But Dixon's home on Calumet became Lippmann's base when the latter visited Chicago to arrange the festival line-ups and Dixon's contacts enabled him to function as associate producer for the folk blues and gospel festivals that went to Europe during the 1960s.

Nowhere was the impact of those shows felt more thoroughly than in England. The folk blues festivals triggered a whole new phase in Anglo/American music as the British rock 'n' roll bands who soaked up the licks and attitudes on the rare Chicago blues records that made the Atlantic crossing began making the return trip overseas. Among them were the Rolling Stones and Yardbirds, both managed by Giorgio Gomelsky, who also ran the Crawdaddy Club in London.

Gomelsky also happened to be the English representative for the Lippmann & Rau organization and that gave the English bluesheads who would come to define rock 'n' roll a direct conduit to the Chicago blues artists who performed on the festival bills. Willie Dixon, never a shy man when it came to pushing his own songs, took advantage of every opportunity to leave behind his material with those younger musicians. And within a few years, that proved to be the avenue by which Willie Dixon acquired his reputation as a great blues songwriter.

GIORGIO GOMELSKY: managed the Rolling Stones and Yardbirds early in their careers, ran the Crawdaddy Club and other London-area venues, and helped bring the American Folk Blues Festival to England.

HORST LIPPMANN: co-producer of the American Folk Blues Festivals.

PHILIPPE RAULT: see Chapter 6.

LEN KUNSTADT: accompanied Victoria Spivey on the 1963 American Folk Blues Festival and later founded Spivey Records.

LONG JOHN BALDRY: led several British blues/R&B groups, including the Hoochie Coochie Men and Steampacket. Among members of those groups were Rod Stewart and Elton John.

BUDDY GUY: a leader of the second generation of Chicago blues performers whose style influenced many prominent rock guitarists. He recorded for Cobra and Chess and played on many of the latter label's sessions during the 1960s.

CLIFTON JAMES: laid down the Bo Diddley drumbeat in the mid-1950s, was the drummer on the 1964 American Folk Blues Festival tour and later played frequently with Dixon in the Chicago Blues All-Stars.

Me and Memphis Slim went to Israel in 1960 to work for this lady named Aviva who had a place in Haifa called Hamoadan. We played everything in the club, blues and spirituals.

We went over there with the wrong impression that we would get 100 Israeli pounds and 100 dollars in American money. We thought the Israeli pound was the same thing as an English pound and, at that time, the English pound was worth $2.80.

We started running all over Israel after our first payday and got into a heated discussion about the money. We had a few bucks of our own going over and we were spending our money and keeping the Israeli pounds. People were glad to get the American dollar. When we found that the Israeli pound was only worth 33 cents, we hardly had enough to survive on.

We started trying to get other jobs at other places there to try to make enough money to get back home with. We went everywhere, down to Jerusalem, Haifa, the Red Sea and we got pretty popular over there.

One time, we were just going down by the Red Sea somewhere. I know it was hotter than hell and we were seeing people come along with camels and looking at this great big cat who was so tall he made Slim look like he was short. This guy had one of those great big sickles like you cut grass with but it was bigger. He had a rag around his head covering one of his eyes, looked like he might have been an old pirate or something.

We got to talking about him while we were walking around and we finally ran into a cat who had a camel. The camel was down and I decided to take a picture on there and, you know, when a camel gets up, it grunts. I was pretty fat so Slim thought that this camel was grunting because he couldn't get up with me on his back.

Slim was going to take my picture on the camel and when you're sitting on it and they raise up behind you first, you almost fall forward and when they raise up in front, you almost fall backward. Slim was all set with his camera to take my picture and he ain't got the picture yet. Some other guy took the picture of me on the camel because Slim was laying out, laughing.

We went a little further down there and here was a guy with some kind of van-like thing with a top pulled over there. I looked back in and he's got all these tiny women, young girls in there with those little veils across their face.

He said, "I sell you a wife. How much you pay? Three American dollars one wife as long as you're in Israel. Five American dollars, two wives, as long as you're in Israel."

"But they're babies."

"No, no, no full grown. They're women. You make love, they have babies."

"No, no, no." We were laughing at that guy.

We played the lottery all the time there, cashing them Israeli pounds because they weren't worth very much. People were trying to buy dollars and we couldn't get as many dollars when we left there as we brought in. We had all this Israeli money and they wouldn't change it for themselves.

While we were there, we started writing Horst Lippmann in Germany. We finally made it back to France with two pockets full of Israeli money but nobody would take it in France. We finally went to Switzerland and got the money changed but then we didn't have enough to get back home with.

We got a job at a place called the Trois Mailletz in the Latin Quarter on the Left Bank in Paris. Slim got the job and I would go work with him because this lady Madame Calvet wasn't able to pay us both. We were staying at the Touraine Hotel so I'd sit in at night and make a few tips, Slim would give me some of his money and we'd survive. It turned out the audience started coming down so good she started paying me, too.

Every weekend while we was working there, we had a fella named Bob Noss who used to come and book us Saturday and Sunday at some other place, just the two of us in a concert. He booked us in Strasbourg, Nice, all over Germany and we started getting a little popularity around there.

When we first went over there, all they had to do was advertise blues. They had these big places on the corner with a circle where everybody would be coming in saying they had blues from America, Memphis Slim and Willie Dixon at such and such a place, and the joint would always be loaded. They called everybody "blues"—you knew if they said blues, they were talking to you.

I must have been three months in Europe the first time with Memphis Slim. We went over to England. We were playing in Piccadilly Circus and youngsters used to come backstage telling us how they were going to have a group and liked this song and that song. They wouldn't let them come in the front door but they'd come around the back and me and Slim would talk with them.

We let a lot of 'em come in and stand there listening. They would peep around the curtain and see the people out in the audience but we would tell them to don't peep around there because they were going to put them out if they caught 'em in there.

GIORGIO GOMELSKY: We had a number of blues things at the Marquee and I had a little club for a while called the Piccadilly Blues Club. The Piccadilly Club was a bar that the guy would lend to us for one evening a week. You had to walk past the bar to go to the room and probably there were some restrictions there. There was a little courtyard in back where you could sneak in.

WD: Then I came back to France and toured around for a month or so. Most of the time, Memphis Slim and I were playing for a particular club. They'd put on one of those conga lines and everybody would be dancing around in a circle for a solid hour. After that, we'd take a half-hour break and go back and play another hour.

Finally Lippmann and Rau, who had been booking everything over the years, got in touch and we began to try and convince them how good it would be to have a blues show. They couldn't see it but after the public started coming to see me and Slim, we got together and made up the American Folk Blues Festival and started doing shows every year. I never actually met Lippmann before we came back to Europe with the first festival.

I told him we'd come back after we decided how we would get it together with the Lippmann & Rau Concert Bureau. I came back to Chicago and started getting that thing together. Horst Lippmann wanted to be sure the show was right and get a lot of blues artists that he knew nobody else knew. Big Bill Broonzy had been going over to Europe and telling people that he was the last of the blues artists in America.

HORST LIPPMANN: In 1959, a friend of mine, Joachim Berendt, was in America visiting in Chicago and Memphis Slim and Willie Dixon, I think, organized a blues jam for him. He returned and said, "Jesus Christ, blues is living." Then he had the idea of bringing these people to Germany for a television show called *Jazz Gesehn und Gehört*, which means Jazz Seen and Heard.

I was directing that show and it was about half a dozen times a year, on a steady schedule every second month or something like that. Naturally, to bring artists over, this is possible to finance only when you organize concerts and we came to the idea of organizing for the first time the American Folk Blues Festivals.

The problem was that I wasn't able to go to America and I needed a connection. I got in contact with Willie Dixon in Israel and he replied at once. When he was back in Chicago, we made the fixed plans for the first festival. I personally got in contact with T-Bone Walker, John Lee Hooker, Sonny Terry & Brownie McGhee—all old friends of mine so I had no problem—but the rest—Memphis Slim, Shakey Jake—was organized by Willie Dixon. Helen Humes was on the bill as well but Willie Dixon and I personally had not met. We only talked on the phone and exchanged letters.

I first met Willie Dixon at Frankfurt Airport—I think it was August 31, 1962 when they arrived from Chicago and the others came from Detroit and Los Angeles. We first went into the studio for four days to make a television show and Willie and myself got very friendly.

Willie was the right man to deal with but I didn't know that at first. I didn't know about Willie Dixon. I thought that's the bass player who did one album with Memphis Slim on Verve but I was not aware that in Willie Dixon, I really found the right man for the job.

I didn't know Willie was kind of a father figure in Chicago blues since he produced Muddy Waters, Howlin' Wolf and Sonny Boy Williamson. I was not so much familiar that he was a great songwriter and some of the songs Muddy Waters and Howlin' Wolf had been doing actually came from the pen of Willie Dixon. I found that out later so that was actually the biggest surprise I had with blues, to find a man like Willie Dixon who as a musician, singer, producer and songwriter was really the right person.

Willie was actually not the assistant producer on the American Folk Blues Festival; we worked together like brothers. It was very, very good cooperation—also by temperament because sometimes I do force things while Willie is always very cool and "yes, we're gonna make it." Once Willie goes into the studio or we sit together in the office, we really work on a thing. If he did not show up on the festival as an artist, Willie helped to organize it and all these people came out of Chicago with the help of Willie.

WD: When I went to try and get birth certificates for guys like Sunnyland Slim and Homesick James to go overseas, they went right back to where they were born and most of them didn't even know their names. When people are old, they figure if they can find any kind of record of anybody that knew them, that's how they make their birth certificate. They don't make them off of what was made at the birth. That's the reason they mix their ages up from one to the other.

They would write back and say his mother was named this and his father named that and they had a child on such and such a date named so and so. But it was always wrong. They would find out by the other sisters and brothers and the mother and father. My wife Marie's got a brother, they call him James and his name is Charlie. She just found that out since she got his birth certificate and her mama didn't even know anybody was named Charlie.

In Europe, each one of those countries would have different nationalities and we'd be talking with them all. It was a lot of fun—it was new to me, all these different people and I liked that. I like meeting people, especially trying to pick out a few words here and get an understanding about it.

English people had a certain portion of segregation—they treated black people more like Americans did at that particular time—but people like the Germans, French, Italians, and Polish always treated everybody alike. There wasn't very many black people over there so occasionally, a lot of people would point at you or something, which makes you wonder what the hell they were talking about. You couldn't understand their language but they always had a friendly attitude. They treated you nice and accepted you right into their homes.

People as a whole always treat a stranger better than they do their own people. They don't know who you are but you can never get the true identity of people as long as you're coming in with money in your pocket and as an artist. If you want to get their true identity, go somewhere without any money.

All the countries in Europe are so small and they're not together as a whole. The people are beautiful and they have their traditions and they couldn't live life as it's lived in America because America has had 400 years of slavery. Any country in the world that had 400 years of 15 million people working for free or practically nothing had to be one of the richest countries in the world so that's what America is.

The American Blues Festivals used to go from one country to the other with a big show. After they went to all the big cities all over Europe, they'd break it down into a small show where you'd put a couple of little bands in a couple of little vans and go to all the little cities with it.

That gave me a chance to get to just about all the countries over there. Frankly, you can't remember all the places when you go in and stay one night, you work damn near all night and chase sleep damn near all day so you can't get around and learn very much unless you have somebody as a guide.

HORST LIPPMANN: There was not much enthusiasm in Europe when we came up with the idea. Only Paris right away liked it. All the others said, "Oh, Jesus Christ, unknown blues people, nobody heard them, you want to make a tour out of this?" Everybody said we'll do it because we like you but we don't think the idea is good and there will be no people at the shows.

But we had the support of the television show, where at least part of the traveling expenses had been paid off, and we lined up three weeks. We had problems going to England but we did ten days in Germany, Austria, Switzerland, then Paris naturally and Scandinavian dates, too. Each concert was almost sold out and it was a completely different audience.

When we started the blues festivals, we did it from the aspect of a jazz lover. We like blues because we liked jazz and always thought that the blues was the foundation of the jazz. We thought a lot of jazz fans would come but they didn't show up at all. We found a new audience that was very enthusiastic, young people who started to learn a little about rock and really had sort of a feeling about folk music, rock music and jazz.

PHILIPPE RAULT: I was 17 and the 1964 American Folk Blues Festival was the first time I saw a blues show of that magnitude. I saw the show in Paris at the Salle Pleyel, a well-known classical music hall in Paris that was also involved in jazz.

Clifton James was the drummer and the main featured performers were Howlin' Wolf and Sonny Boy Williamson. Sonny Boy was wearing this suit and the coat and the pants were reversed. Half the jacket was in gray, the other half in white and the colors were reversed on the pants. Howlin' Wolf was amazing, just a monster. Hubert Sumlin and Sugar Pie DeSanto, it was amazing to see all those people at once.

The way they proceeded was basically the same rhythm section staying onstage through the whole show and then each artist would be featured for about 20–30 minutes during the performance. There was about eight or ten headliners on each show. It was like an old-time revue and really a great way to showcase all these people you had only heard of through the records and never had a chance to see on stage.

HORST LIPPMANN: With the exception of 1968, the festival was recorded each year and we released an album here. No record company wanted to record the blues festival over here at first. The very first one in 1962 we produced on our own and it was released on Brunswick, Deutsche Grammophon, Polydor. We paid for all this and actually got nothing for it.

We thought it was a good investment because it's part of history to document it on record. Two songs out of this recording got very popular in France—one was John Lee Hooker's "Shake It, Baby." Because of the impact of this record, Phonogram came in and for the next years up until 1967, all the festivals have been released by Phillips—Mercury in America.

PHILIPPE RAULT: *The American Folk Blues Festival* that had been issued on Phillips after the 1962 festival was one of my favorite records. John Lee Hooker's "Shake It, Baby" was a big hit all over Europe. I was still in high school and "Shake It, Baby" was *the* party record—John Lee Hooker recorded live with Dixon, Memphis Slim and all those people backing him up.

I was aware of all the Chess records Dixon had done. I knew of those records and the tunes he had written from every major English blues band playing them. "I Just Wanna Make Love To You" was a hit from the first Rolling Stones album and that was the big title I seem to remember.

Those shows had a really big impact. There was a bunch of English bands that put the fuse to the dynamite—like Alexis Korner and Cyril Davies—who really inspired all those groups like the Stones, but they were always the second-hand product. When those shows came over, there was a lot of attention, not only from the blues fans going to the shows but from all of the English pop stars of the time.

It was a major influence on spreading the blues in Europe at the time. Nobody had come to Europe in the blues field, except maybe for a couple of tours by Big Bill Broonzy. Through the American Folk Blues Festival, it was really the first time any serious presentation of blues was made and brought to European audiences. This was a really pivotal period, 1962–4—people were so starved for those shows because it was the real thing finally happening.

LEN KUNSTADT: Willie Dixon opened up the Lippmann & Rau blues festivals which opened the blues to Europe. Memphis Slim, owing to his European experience, was more of a front man for the Lippmann & Rau organization but Willie Dixon was in a supervisory role in terms of organizing and putting together the show and keeping it together.

All the blues festivals today owe their allegiance to the way Lippmann & Rau handled these things. We were handled in a prestigious way, the best hotels, the best food, an excellent bus. The blues was performed in the same halls that Mozart, Beethoven and Brahms were performed in.

A lot of the artists were bewildered by it. A lot of them were suspicious of what was going on. Horst understood most of them wanted cash so he would prepare cash payments. None of them actually believed him until the cash was on the table, and he paid real good.

HORST LIPPMANN: Usually when we signed someone, Willie and myself had a long talk with them explaining that everything would be looked after. There would be transportation, not only across the ocean but from town to town and from the hotel and all the hotels were booked and the currency—whether they can be paid in dollars or marks or the local currency. We explained any questions they asked.

There was a long preparation by word of mouth, and once they got here, they had been surprised because they had never been treated in their lives like we had been able to treat them here in Europe. It was something special because that was 25 years back, you know.

To be picked up at the airport—not only at the airport, but on the airfield because we got special permission to have a band, correspondents and television on the airfield treating them like kings and queens. They never had expected something like this. Can you imagine, you live on the South Side of Chicago, lucky to make it somehow and then you come by plane to Europe and there is something like a red carpet on the floor? That is something strange.

I think with each bluesman, once they came and toured Europe, there had been a sort of pride that they played Europe in front of a white audience and they had been elected to do this. They felt this was a special message they gave to the people so they acted a little different than in Chicago. I know that Little Walter in Chicago was a hard person, sometimes. This was one reason why I didn't take him the very first years. But over here, no problem.

GIORGIO GOMELSKY: They loved it because they had so much attention. I remember Sonny Boy talking about how he had this great deal playing at Silvio's on West Lake Avenue in Chicago. One day I got over there and it was 25 cents to get in and 50 cents a beer and the drum kit had a picture of palm trees on it with an electric bulb in it. When they played Europe, we put them in 1,500–3,000 seat concert halls and they were treated like artists. Some people would follow them around for days, from one gig to another.

LEN KUNSTADT: My memory of the 1963 tour is that we actually met at the airport—me and Victoria Spivey, who was on the show along with other greats like Muddy Waters, Otis Spann, and Big Joe Williams. I saw two cumbersome gentlemen come there all tired and worn out from their trips—the mighty Big Joe Williams and the mighty big Willie Dixon. Everybody was dog tired and there wasn't much conversation going on.

Willie Dixon saved the show from a major altercation over a window being open on the bus. Lonnie Johnson had such a pure voice he didn't want to get a cold and Big Joe Williams, who had high blood pressure, was always hot and wanted a window open. An altercation started and Sonny Boy Williamson, who was in the front of the bus doing a radio announcement, got into the middle of it and told Big Joe to shut the window.

Big Joe Williams reached into his pocket like there was something there and I remember Willie Dixon grabbing Big Joe Williams—these two ponderous men, maybe about 700 pounds between them— around the waist and getting him in the back of the bus.

Fritz Rau, the legal part of the Lippmann & Rau organization, inadvertently got in the way of Sonny Boy and Big Joe and the only one who would have gotten the damage was Fritz. He would have gotten cut up or hurt. If Willie hadn't grabbed Big Joe, we might have lost Fritz Rau.

We did somewhere between 21 and 30 days, in about nine countries and 20 cities. We gigged sometimes twice a day, in the afternoon and the night time. We traveled in class—in most of the cities we went to, we had police protection and were treated with great respect.

HORST LIPPMANN: When people realized after the 1962 tour that there was potential behind it, not only artistic but also financial, it was no problem to organize four week tours all through Europe. England was the last country to pick it up.

By accident, in 1963 I met a friend named Giorgio Gomelsky in Frankfurt at the Jazz Cellar and I told him we started the blues festival tour in a week without England. On this tour was Sonny Boy Williamson, Muddy Waters, Otis Spann, Willie Dixon, an all-star billing you can only dream about.

Giorgio said, "This is impossible. It has to go to England." He called a friend in England, Harold Pendleton, the manager of the London Jazz Club, and he said yes. Harold managed to get us two dates at the Fairfield Hall in Croydon near London, one in Manchester and I think one in Birmingham. We could have played a week only in Croydon— it was complete capacity and a big, big success with headlines in the *Melody Maker.*

WD: The first year, 1962, they called it the American Folk Blues Festival in England but Lippmann wasn't booking it over there. Another booking agent booked it in England that year and this agent went out of business. They still owe me money on that damn thing.

GIORGIO GOMELSKY: In 1963, Willie came over with Muddy Waters and Sonny Boy Williamson. At the time, I was running this little blues club where young bands were playing. There were only about four in the whole country—the Rolling Stones, Alexis Korner, a group later to be known as the Animals.

There were about 40 blues fans in London that had collected some records and had been looking towards the blues for regenerating the entire music scene, which was dying on its feet at the time. We didn't have access to records. If somebody found a Howlin' Wolf album, we would all sit around listening for hours. No one could afford cassette players so you had to get the records, listen to them and write down the words.

When Lippmann & Rau put together this package, they were

desperate to put it on in England because nobody in England knew much about the blues. We were able to do that and for all the young musicians, Willie Dixon and Muddy Waters were great, great heroes. The first time the American Folk Blues Festival came over, I got the Stones tickets. They were all broke so I got about 20 of these blues musicians tickets in the first rows and they were sitting there worshipping these wonderful people.

I started the Crawdaddy Club where the Stones were the resident band and then the Yardbirds, Julie Driscoll and Brian Auger, and the Moody Blues. I was concerned about material because the only way we could have known what was going on in terms of material was from records. A lot of the blues records were not released in England and it was a struggle to get them. The Beatles were the only ones that wrote music and the Beatles were not really a blues band.

We were chasing up B-sides and unknown and obscure songs from the 1950s. Muddy Waters' was a very important repertoire because it was exotic and this Delta style was very exciting to us. Willie had written most of those things so when he came, it was always a celebration. When Willie came, we sat him down and said, "Willie, you've got to give us some new material here because we've done all the versions of your songs."

WD: When we were working other places around there, kids would come and say they liked our music and wanted to sing our music. Sometimes I'd write it out for 'em. Sometimes I'd put it on tape, recording for 'em. When I got ready to leave there, I just load the tapes with everything and a few years later here they come in different groups and things. I wouldn't know one kid from another because years afterwards, when they came to the Chess recording studio, they were grown with a lot of hair on their face and I wouldn't know who was who.

I left lots of tapes when I was over there. I had different people, I'd make tapes for them and give them to them and tell them anybody who wanted to could go and make a blues song. That's how the Rolling Stones and the Yardbirds got their songs. I went back over there later with Sonny Boy Williamson, Muddy Waters, a whole bunch of us. I would always have a bunch of songs to take over.

GIORGIO GOMELSKY: My house was the place where all these guys came and exchanged records and listened to stuff. When the blues musicians came to London, they would come to my house. We became kind of a link between Chicago blues and British R&B, which is fundamentally blues-based music.

I'll never forget—it was an afternoon about four o'clock in March of 1964 or something. There was Howlin' Wolf, Sonny Boy and Willie Dixon, the three of them sitting on this sofa I had in my living room. Willie was huge, Wolf wasn't exactly small, and Sonny Boy was very towering and lean. These three grand viziers were sitting on this thing and there's like Jimmy Page, Eric Clapton and everybody sitting at their feet.

Willie was just singing and tapping on the back of the chair and Sonny Boy would play the harmonica and they would do new songs. To a degree, that's why people know of those songs and recorded them later. I remember "300 Pounds Of Joy," "Little Red Rooster," "You Shook Me" were all songs that Willie passed on at that time. Then there was a song that Koko Taylor did later on, "Wang Dang Doodle." We'd heard them really fresh, before anybody had made any records of them.

We were hanging out and having tea and coffee and a little Johnny Walker and listening to these guys telling stories and Willie sort of singing songs. Jimmy Page came often, the Yardbirds, Brian Jones, John Mayall came when Sonny Boy was there. It was only about 20 people—just about anybody that knew this was happening showed up. I remember my girlfriend getting upset about having to make tea every five minutes.

LONG JOHN BALDRY: Willie's leaving material actually caused a big row between Giorgio and me. I was very cross with Giorgio at one time because Willie had left a tape of some material for me in the Marquee offices and Giorgio saw it hanging and grabbed it for the Yardbirds to utilize.

Whether I'd asked Willie or whether he offered to leave me a tape, I can't quite remember, but I missed him leaving from England to go to the States so he had left this tape for me at the Marquee. That was 1962 or 1963, and I was furious with Giorgio over that. I didn't speak with him for a good year or so.

Willie was like a guru, I guess, for blues players. He really has been responsible for injecting the whole mystique of the blues into many of us. I think he was quite surprised and genuinely touched by the admiration when he first came to England.

The other Chicago blues musicians looked up to Willie because not only was Willie a musician, recording producer and songwriter—and most of them had recorded his songs—but Willie was the contact man in the States for blues people coming over to Europe. In a way, Willie was· responsible for getting them that break and coming over to Europe was a big break for blues players at that time. Willie was like the American representative.

BUDDY GUY: The first time I went to Europe in 1965, I think Willie Dixon knew somebody over there and set that up for me. The second time was in late 1965, when I went over for Horst Lippmann with Willie Dixon doing the booking. Willie booked the whole group of us over there and I had to give his booking agent percentage out of my $400 a week.

WD: It was '64 when we did Poland, Czechoslovakia and Russia [South Galicia, see below] and the reaction was beautiful. Over in Poland, they'd have these musical shows that would go weeks at a time. They'd play this kind of music one night, that kind the next and people would come out and bring their lunches. We played at this particular spot two nights. While we were living there in Warsaw, we went to a couple of places in Czechoslovakia and parts of Russia and we came back to Poland again. They had all of us buy these big Russian fur hats and somebody took mine.

HORST LIPPMANN: The first tour behind the Iron Curtain was in 1964 and that was only five or six people I took, namely Wolf, Hubert Sumlin, Willie Dixon, Sunnyland Slim and one or two more. We toured East Germany, Poland and Czechoslovakia. We recorded all of that session in East Berlin for Amiga, the East German company, and Hubert Sumlin played some guitar solos. Wolf wasn't on that session because of his contract with Chess but Willie, Sunnyland Slim, Hubert and Clifton James were on that session that was released by me on my L&R record label.

We did not get into Russia in 1964. That is one of the mistakes passed along, especially by Sunnyland Slim. We played South Galicia in the Polish countryside, which looks like Russia. The people came with the horses and the wagons behind it like you expect it in Russia, real countryside people that never saw any black people in their lives nor heard anything about blues or American music.

They had been very, very astonished, so there was not very much applause. Wolf said, "I'm going to get them," so he went on his knees and played a tango. It was a very, very strange thing. I think Willie might have thought it was Russia, too. There were big crowds of kids, you know, screaming and hollering because they never saw black people and Willie started to play with them.

I had a very funny problem with Wolf. When we played Poland and East Germany, he got the salary paid partly in dollars but we had to take 50% in local currency, which is not convertible, so we had to spend it in the country. Willie bought himself a mink hat which was stolen, Hubert Sumlin bought some jewels and stuff and Wolf didn't know what to buy so he said, "Give it to the YMCA." I said, "But, Wolf, there is no YMCA. This is a communist country." He said, "The YMCA is everywhere."

WD: We had a lot of fun over there, boy. People would come around to hustle money off the guys because American money was black market money but they didn't mind. We had so much of their money and we'd buy anything because we weren't going to be staying over there long and you couldn't get American money for it. They explained that to us going over there and had write-ups telling how they were going to give us so much American money and so much local money that was no good.

Well Wolf was getting quite a bit because he was paid more than anybody on that tour. He fooled around putting all that crap in his suitcase and kept it in his bag during that tour. I said, "No, you can't use that money—try to get clear of it before you get back here, buy equipment with it." Wolf packed his suitcase full of that Russian money and the law officers took his suitcase on the way back.

It took them several days to find the suitcase and what does it have but all this doggone money that ain't worth a damn. I was asking, "Wolf, what happened, man?"

"I had some money hidden where I was gonna keep it for a souvenir."

"Well, what happened to it?"

"Some of it I got, some of it they kept."

"Didn't they tell you . . .?"

"Yeah, but I thought they were lying."

The Russians were suspicious of everybody. They gave me a white button with a red star on it and every time we saw one of the Russians, he'd shake our hands and point to the button. That was the great thing—if you had that button on, they'd immediately come to make friends with you whether you were supposed to or not.

A lot of people used to follow us from place to place and here I wouldn't know what they're saying. It wasn't bad when we'd first go to a place, if we had a couple of days down there, you could learn a few greeting words and like that.

I had a bunch of books of all kinds. I learned the greeting words in most of the languages there and it was really fun. Sometimes you get two or three languages mixed up in your mind and start off speaking one and wind up speaking the other one. These guys wouldn't understand us. Boy, we used to laugh and then we started to do that on purpose and had a lot of fun.

In Poland they had these little hotels where everybody had their own room. They put me and Clifton James in a hotel where women worked at but no woman was supposed to live in the hotel. They had women all over the place so finally we get a couple of chicks up there. We know if they see them comin' out of there they won't let 'em in any more so we locked the room, told 'em to stay in there and lock the door from the other side.

When we came back from the show, each floor has a maid on it and this maid started saying to us, "Hey, you lock in girls."

"No, no savvy."

We spoke to this woman and she'd go get somebody else to try to make us understand. Whatever language they talked, we couldn't understand. Finally, they thought we were from Africa and they come in one time with a great big tall guy speaking Swahili. I got to be friends of his and he was teaching me some Swahili. We got on laughing about it and she's trying to tell this guy to tell us about no girls.

"No savvy, no verstehn, don't understand anything."

Boy, she was mad, walking up and down there saying, "You have girls in room."

"No, no, you come in." We'd grab her hand and make like we were trying to pull her in there.

"Oh, no, no, no, not me."

"Yeah, you say girl can come in room."

"No, no, you got girls in the room."

"No, you come in."

Boy, we had a ball. I never saw so many different people with so many different languages. They brought every nationality in the world in there, I believe, to try and make us understand. We couldn't understand anything. We were laughing and carrying on.

CLIFTON JAMES: We were on a show with Sugar Pie DeSanto, Sleepy John Estes and Hammie Nixon, Sonny Boy Williamson, Lightning Hopkins, Howlin' Wolf, John Henry Barbee. That was a heckuva show. The whole tour, everybody was just up there laughing. Even on the flight going over, we had all the stewardesses cracking up because we started to playing on the plane. Sonny Boy broke out his harp and we were walking up and down the aisle, people dancing—boy, did we have a party.

We were surprised by the reception. I didn't know that many people over there spoke English and they greeted us with open arms. We used to take long walks over there all the time, leave everybody and just cut out, go sightseeing and have fun. People would run up, stop and look at Willie like, "What the hell is this?"

Hey, Willie was big. Once when we were over there, Willie ordered a baked chicken, ate it up, ordered another one, ate it up, ordered another and ate it up, another one and he ate it up. I couldn't believe he did it. It might have been six whole chickens and he even had nerve enough to ask me for a piece of mine.

He was in perfectly good health but he would devour it, whatever it was. He was active and that cat could move almost like a track star or something. He used to herd people around a little because we had some that would go astray in a sense. Willie would put them under his arm, like a shepherd with his herd and they'd listen.

WD: I used to have to get Wolf off the stage and take him back in the alley and talk to him. I've threatened him and I even had him in the collar a couple of times but I don't remember actually coming to blows with Wolf. Sometimes, guys can be so illiterate by inexperience and all like that you have to take them off to the side and talk to them. If they won't act right, you threaten to send them home or something like that.

Another time we'd just got off from playing a concert in Baden Baden, Germany and everybody on the show was intending to eat. The restaurant downstairs in the hotel was closed and everybody roamed around a little while trying to find some place to eat.

Most of the entertainers were all on one floor of the hotel and just about the time everybody got into bed, all of a sudden we could smell something real good. It really aroused the appetite. Everybody would open their doors and all the way down this long hall, you'd see heads sticking out. Somebody said, "What's that cooking?" so we went down to the restaurant. We thought that maybe the restaurant had opened back up.

Finally, I heard a rumbling out in the hall and everybody broke to the door—some of the guys had their nightshirts and nightcaps on. Sonny Boy had a short German fella caught in the collar out there and his knife is open in the other hand. This little guy is trying to explain to Sonny Boy that he's the hotel dick but Sonny Boy can't understand this in German and says this guy is a peeping Tom. Sonny Boy says he was peeping through the keyhole but the fella was actually smelling around the door to find out where this aroma's coming from.

Just about the time it got good and quiet again, here's the same noise all over again. He's got him again in the collar and this guy's swinging back with all his might at Sonny Boy. I don't know what they were saying in German but whatever it was, it wasn't good. This guy was trying to back up and Sonny Boy's following him down the hall with this big knife in his hand. Sonny Boy hit this guy's red tie with his knife and cut it off right up to his neck and this guy tumbled backwards down the steps. Everybody was hollering and going on.

It was way early in the morning, about three or four o'clock, and finally it quieted down again. But this aroma is still smelling *goooood.* Every once in a while, I'd ease up and pull open the door real slow and look down the hall. Sonny Boy was living across in front of me and there he was standing up there bare-footed in a nightshirt that was just about to his knees.

He beckoned to me to come over there so I eased on over because I didn't want to wake anybody. He said, "Come on, man, get some of these pigtails." Sure enough, with the great big coffee pot he has, he's cooking pigtails and beans with onions and all the seasonings in it. So we ate pigtails and beans that morning.

I guess this little house detective figured everybody was asleep and I started out the door. He must have thought I was Sonny Boy coming out the door again and this cat took off down the hall and fell down the steps again. I laughed until I cried.

When they started the American Folk Blues Festivals, we were doing two shows a night at auditoriums with 2–3,000 people in all the big countries. Then they started writing about it over here in America. Naturally, people were getting jealous or something because here's a gold mine sitting in my backyard and I didn't know but over there people are making money. This is why America decided to get back into the blues because they found out that everybody in the European countries was going for the blues and it created all these different rock groups and things.

When we'd be in Chicago or America, we thought we was raisin' hell making $15–20 a night. We'd get over there in Europe and be making $100 and maybe more every night. We were making more than $1,000 a week a lot of times. That was a whole lot of money for a blues artist but after everybody started getting in on it, they're letting the prices back down again.

I haven't been over in Europe lately because I've been lucky enough to keep my salary up and get even better, even in America. That's the reason I haven't been over there, because I've been able to do pretty good here. I wouldn't have gone over there in the first place had I been doing all right here, you know.

8

It could be a spoonful of coffee
It could be a spoonful of tea
But one little spoon of your precious love
Is good enough for me

Chorus: Men lie about that spoonful
Some cry about that spoonful
Some die about that spoonful
Everybody fight about that spoonful
That spoon, that spoon, that spoonful

It could be a spoonful of diamonds
It could be a spoonful of gold
But one little spoon of your precious love
Could satisfy my soul

It could be a spoonful of water
To save you from the burning sand
But one spoon of lead from my forty-five
Will save you from another man

His overseas travel was only taking up a month of Dixon's year. The remainder of the time he was back in Chicago and, since early in 1959, back to full-time work at Chess.

Chess had done fairly well during Dixon's Cobra hiatus with its core four of Muddy, Wolf, Little Walter and Sonny Boy, but it was Chuck Berry and Bo Diddley that became the company's bread and butter during that period.

In May 1957, the label had moved its base of operations from the Cottage Grove locale up to its most famous set of offices at 2120 S. Michigan Avenue, a plain two-story building with a row of offices on the ground floor and a studio upstairs.

The demise of Cobra had left Chess and VeeJay as essentially the only major, old-guard record companies in town catering to blues artists and Dixon's influence helped artists like Rush and Buddy Guy slide on to the Chess roster. Dixon's increased leverage enabled him to implement more fully the sound and vision of his songs in the studio. The period from 1959–64 would see Dixon record the second batch of songs—most of them brought vividly to life by Howlin' Wolf—that would later bring him fame and notoriety courtesy of the blues-loving rock brigade: "Back Door Man," "Spoonful," "The Red Rooster," "I Ain't Superstitious," "Wang Dang Doodle," "You Shook Me," "You Need Love," and "You Can't Judge A Book By Its Cover."

But the same time frame also witnessed substantial changes in the way Dixon and Chess went about presenting the music. The advent of the electric bass meant that Dixon had largely abandoned playing on Chess records, except on select sessions with the label's bigger artists, by 1961. The arrangements had changed, too, by 1962–3 as organ and horn sections began cropping up in place of piano and harmonica more frequently on blues sessions.

Chess had expanded its artist roster as the rhythm & blues sound began to metamorphose into soul and its jazz division headed by Ahmad Jamal and Ramsey Lewis proved a lucrative complement to its gospel and blues base. Etta James recorded her first Chess session in 1960, several jazz albums (including one by Quincy Jones) dominated the releases in 1961 and comedians Moms Mabley and Pigmeat Markham had Chess albums mastered in 1962.

Additional producers and arrangers—Gene Barge and Ralph Bass prominent among them—came in to supervise other facets of the studio operation while Dixon remained the main man for blues and handled a good portion of the gospel division. Ahmad Jamal's But Not For Me: Live At The Pershing *album, recorded in 1958, had alerted the Chess operation to the potential profitability of the album market, but Chess was still treating the blues predominantly as a singles market. Despite Dixon's prompting, most of the company's blues releases still came out on 45s well into the 1960s.*

Typically, Dixon's activities weren't strictly confined to his work at Chess. Duke/Peacock, a heavyweight R&B and gospel label based in Houston, Texas, frequently hired him to produce sessions by their leading gospel artists when they hit Chicago in the early 1960s. A 1960 album session with the Five Blind Boys of Mississippi sparked a bitter court fight between Chess and Duke/Peacock over which label held a valid contract on the group. Chess won that battle, which dragged on for most of the decade, but Dixon's bass playing and arrangements with both Chess and Duke/Peacock artists left a major imprint on the classic gospel sound that became a bedrock foundation of the 1960s soul sound . . . in addition to his more widely known impact on the shape of blues and rock 'n' roll.

And reminders of his English and European travels kept showing up at his doorstep. The Stones came to Chicago and paid homage by recording their first American album at Chess in 1964; the Yardbirds made the city their American base when they toured in the mid-1960s and cut their groundbreaking "Shapes Of Things" single there late in 1965.

Horst Lippmann arrived each year to stay a few weeks and put together the American Folk Blues Festival line-up, and other European blues fans who made the pilgrimage in the early 1960s usually wound up being taken around town by Dixon. The house on Calumet Street became a clearing house for Chicago blues artists and fans and the site of an impromptu recording session with several lesser-known Chicago blues artists for Spivey Records.

BUDDY GUY: *See Chapter 7.*

JIMMY ROGERS: *See Chapter 4.*

RON MALO: *became the chief engineer at Chess in 1960, recorded the Stones and Yardbirds sessions, and stayed with Chess until its demise.*

MALCOLM CHISHOLM: See Chapter 5.

CLIFTON JAMES: See Chapter 7.

PHIL UPCHURCH: See Chapter 6.

CASH McCALL: Chess staff songwriter dating from the early 1960s who now lives in Los Angeles. A guitar player and singer, he began as a gospel and R&B performer but now concentrates on the blues.

HORST LIPPMANN: See Chapter 7.

BOB KOESTER: See Chapter 4.

DAVE CLARK: a legendary promotion man with over 50 years' experience in the record industry. He currently works for Malaco Records.

DICK LAPALM: a promotion consultant for Chess starting in 1958. He became the organization's executive vice-president of sales and promotion in 1963 and stayed in that post until the label folded in 1973.

GIORGIO GOMELSKY: See Chapter 7.

LEN KUNSTADT: See Chapter 7.

Chess wanted me back and they had been trying to get me back on several occasions but Leonard and Phil wouldn't come themselves. Eli Toscano kept his thing going with me by saying, "Oh, Chess doesn't want you back. They don't like you." He was telling me that it was me against them.

Finally, I met Phil one day downtown and he said, "Man, we're not mad at you or nothing. Why don't you come by and see our new place?" They had moved to 2120 Michigan when I got with Cobra so I went down there and we got together.

I was telling Phil, "If I did anything, I couldn't do it on the terms I was doing it before. I have to have some more salary." I had a contract but it was the kind of thing where he'd give me a definite amount—$75 a week—against my royalties. When I came back from Europe in 1960 with Memphis Slim, I told them I wasn't satisfied with that agreement so they raised me to $150 a week.

When I went back to Chess, Chess began to take in the artists that Cobra had. Just about all the Cobra artists got down on Cobra because Cobra wasn't giving them any money either. When they came looking for me over at Chess, if I could get them in there and thought they were good artists, I'd say yes.

BUDDY GUY: I don't think anybody would go into Chess doing any blues without Willie. When Eli died and there was no more Cobra, Leonard Chess got Otis Rush and sent Otis to get me. That was about as close as I got to Leonard Chess himself and then I signed up with them and got to know Willie Dixon real, real well.

Willie was around every blues session going on, especially with his songs. If it wasn't his song, I don't recall him messing around with it. A couple of sessions, I would go in and do Willie's songs like I had practiced and rehearsed with him and then say, "I've got my songs." He'd hear the song and we'd rehearse it and then he'd come back and tell me that line ain't strong enough.

That's the way things were working. I was a beginner and he had been there so I guess they would say if Willie says this line ain't strong enough, it ain't strong enough. I would say that my material got run through Willie for approval at Chess, yes.

WD: Sometimes songs would come out as co-written but most of the time because I would change verses or make new verses to it. I always made some kind of contract with them beforehand. People that haven't had very much experience in getting songs out there, sometimes you have to have it in a position where the company will accept it. I'd tell them up front but Chess never put my name as a co-writer without me telling the artists.

I didn't allow Chess to add my name because I didn't trust them. That's the reason for that song "I Don't Trust Myself." Nobody put my name on nothing that wasn't mine because then they'd turn around and put somebody else's name on something that was mine. If a dog will bring the bone, he'll carry the bone, too, so you can't give him any ground to do it on.

Most of the guys tried to cooperate in the recording studio because they wanted to record but Howlin' Wolf was pretty rough to deal with.

It required a lot of diplomacy working with him. He always felt everything was going the wrong direction and he'd try all kinds of angles. His band knew he was a rugged customer.

JIMMY ROGERS: Wolf was pretty hard to get along with, anyway, and in the studio he was *very* hard to get along with. He was slow to catch on. He'd take the stuff off, play around with it with the band or by himself and mold it into his head. He would never really get it right but he'd get it close enough to record with it.

He and Dixon had a few misunderstandings there in the studio because Wolf was set in his own ways. They were big guys, both of them. Dixon was pushing 300 and Wolf was well over 250, these two big freight car boxes, and we just laid back and tried to back them up. We wouldn't hardly get into the conversation.

RON MALO: Wolf was funny. He was one of the ones that couldn't read so Willie would have to yell in his ear the next lyric line on a new song. Wolf didn't know how to count so he didn't know where to come in.

Wolf was a natural singer and performer but he learned things one way and that was it. He had to learn and memorize it and if we changed the introduction from what Wolf had learned, he'd be completely lost and Willie would have to cue him in.

WD: Wolf didn't ever want to do none of the songs that I wrote for him but he finally would after a discussion with Leonard. A lot of times he would never learn the song. He couldn't read so he'd have to learn the words by heart but he really wouldn't be thinking about the song because I'd still have to whisper them into his ear after six months of training.

Sometimes we'd have a good cut all the way down and right at the end he'd turn around and say, "Oh, man, I didn't hear what you said," and mess up the whole damn thing. A lot of times you whispered so loud they'd pick it up on the tape machine.

"Wang Dang Doodle" meant a good time, especially if a guy came in from the South. A wang dang meant having a ball and a lot of dancing, they called it a rocking style so that's what it meant to wang dang doodle.

There used to be a place up north of Vicksburg called the Rock

House. It was built out of stone but it had a weak floor. On Saturday nights, people would crowd in there and when they would all get to dancin', the floor would rock up and down.

Everybody was saying, "Boy, the Rock House, I'm gonna pitch a wang dang up there." After I left Vicksburg, I heard the kids were there dancing one day and the floor fell in.

"Do The Do" was a dance they'd been doing ever since I can remember. They had so many dances when I was a kid—the black bottom, the fishtail, the cock crow, the dog, the mojo, the monkey. There was a mojo dance—I don't know how they did it but I used to hear guys going, "Do the mojo, man."

Boy, that fishtail was a dance. When I was a kid, my mother used to come in and make us stop any kind of damn dance. There was the monkey and the dog, the one where the guy rubs into the girl's back just like a dog when he's romancing her.

The idea of "Spoonful" was that it doesn't take a large quantity of anything to be good. If you have a little money when you need it, you're right there in the right spot, that'll buy you a whole lot. If a doctor give you less than a spoonful of some kind of medicine that can kill you, he can give you less than a spoonful of another one that will make you well.

But after you write these songs, people who have bad minds, their minds will tell them what they want to believe. If it's blues and they've been trying to degrade the blues all the time, I don't care what title you come up with, they'll say it's a bad title. I remember a time years ago that if I said sex, my mama would beat the hell out of me. People who think "Spoonful" was about heroin are mostly people with heroin ideas.

"Dead Presidents" was done during the time they had that payola thing going. There were two or three songs Billy Emerson and I did together and he was trying to claim all my songs after he got started. At first, I never got royalties on it but I know they put it out in Chicago.

"Three Hundred Pounds Of Heavenly Joy"—the average person that's heavy, especially while you're young, you don't feel like your weight is complicating your life or keeping you away from anything. You can have as much enjoyment in life as they can and the average person will like someone heavy or fat.

"Built For Comfort"—everyone naturally want to brag about the shape they're in whether they like it or not. People like you because you're happy, you're built for comfort. A dog don't like a bone—he just chews on it because he can't get the meat. The man feels like that extra weight makes him built for comfort and you don't have to make yourself uncomfortable by gnawing on the bone when you got plenty to eat.

Those weren't particularly made for Wolf. I think I made both of them for myself at that time but I didn't get a chance to record them. I did write "Wang Dang Doodle" when I first heard Wolf back in 1951 or 1952, but there's a time for these things. A lot of times you're too far in advance for the people or ideas you're dealing with so maybe a guy can see it at another time.

You see, a person has to put himself in the position of other people. I felt Bo Diddley was the type of guy that could sing a thing like "You Can't Judge The Book (By Looking At The Cover)" and when I told him about it, he liked it immediately. If you gave him a thing he felt fit his style, he knew it. He wanted to be acting happy, looking happy and being happy.

A story like "You can't judge the apple by looking at the tree/You can't judge the honey by looking at the bee/You can't judge a book by looking at the cover/So you can't judge me," that was his bag 100%. If you said the wrong words with the type of music he was doing, it took away from what he was doing.

For years, I tried to get in touch with guys, went from place to place, songs in my hand and pockets trying to sing to 'em and impress them with the same identical song. Once everybody else comes with it, everybody wants it: "You should have let me have that song."

That's just like Wolf and Muddy. Every song I'd give to Wolf, he'd say, "Man, you're giving Muddy the best songs." The songs I'd give to Muddy, he'd say, "Man, you're giving Wolf the best songs."

A lot of times you have to use backwards psychology on these guys. I'd say this is a song for Muddy if I wanted Wolf to do it. He would be glad to get in on it by him thinking it was somebody else's, especially Muddy's. They seemed to have had a little thing going on between them so I used that backwards psychology.

The average individual, when you hand him a thing that's a little different from what you hear out there in the public, he thinks, "It won't sell because it's not like what's selling." But people don't want to hear the same thing all the time. They want to hear something that's good but different and people will accept it.

The thing most people don't realize about recording artists is the music itself is the background that makes the artists sound good. There are certain little angles of things that can attract more attention to the artists and a lot of people playing the music don't know about it. When you're getting ready to go out of the musical part, you have to focus people's minds on the singer again and blues itself has to be properly emphasized. You have to get the point over of what you're trying to express.

You have to see the words are properly understood and administered so everybody can get the feeling and understand it. A lot of people think a singer is great but only a very few can walk out there flat-footed and sing a song where you can appreciate it without some kind of background.

As a whole, the public doesn't really understand music but they do understand the lyrics. If they understand the lyrics and there's a good song relating to any part of their life or understanding, you got the first half made. Now if you got reasonable music that sounds pretty good with a rhythm of some type that can hold their attention, that's it. All you need then is a little extra play and you're in business.

The first thing is to attract their attention with anything you can properly get that's within the boundary of reason. That's the reason the balancing of a record means so much. If it's not properly balanced, you'll hear all this stuff coming in between there that will distract your attention from the singer and message you're trying to get over. You can sell your song early or late but the later you sell it, the better the attention is.

When we get over there at the studio to go to a session, the first thing I generally told the guys was, "The reason I got you fellows is because I know you got the quality and you can do these things. We are here to sell this singer, first of all, and here to make good music behind it to sell 'em.

"I want every word this artist will sing to be heard and understood. When you come in there with hard things so that it distracts the artist and the attention of the public we are trying to get the message across to, we are messing up."

Family group, Vicksburg, 1916. Daisy Dixon is
holding the infant WD

Anderson (A.D.) Bell, WD's father

WD at 10, Vicksburg (*rear*), with (*L to R*) Lionel Turner and Arthur

WD with Mary Hunter, Vicksburg, 1933 (L.V Dixon)   WD at 18, Vicksburg, 1933

The Five Breezes at Martin's Corner, Chicago, 1941: (*L to R, front*) Freddie "Cool Breeze" Walker, Willie Hawthorne, (*rear*) WD, Jimmy "Eugene" Gilmore, Leonard "Baby Doo" Caston

WD in Chicago, early 1940s (L.V Dixon)

WD in Chicago, early 1940s (L.V Dixon)

The Four Jumps of Jive, radio broadcast, Chicago, 1945. (*L to R*) Bernardo Dennis, Jimmy "Eugene" Gilmore, WD, Ellis Hunter

The Big Three Trio: (*top to bottom*) WD, Leonard
"Baby Doo" Caston, Ollie Crawford

WD relaxing on the road near Denver, Colorado,
1949 (Leonard Caston, courtesy Josephine Caston)

The Big Three Trio, Amateur Night at Melby's Show Bar, St. Louis, Missouri, 1949
(courtesy Josephine Caston)

The Big Three Trio performing at the 607 Club, Chicago, 1947

The Big Three Trio with Dizzy Gillespie, Chicago, late 1940s· (*L to R*) WD, Gillespie, Ollie Crawford, Leonard "Baby Doo" Caston

The Big Three Trio with Louis Jordan, Chicago, late 1940s: (*L to R*) WD, Jordan, Ollie Crawford, Leonard "Baby Doo" Caston

WD with his first son, Willie James Franklin, Jr., Chicago, 1951

WD, Checker Records publicity shot, 1955

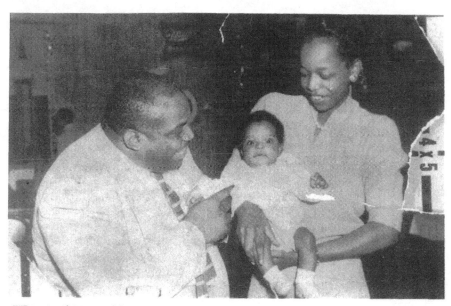

WD with wife Marie and daughter Pat, Apex Lounge, Robbins, Illinois, 1957

WD with Otis Rush, Chicago, 1957

WD (standing), Memphis Slim and club owner
Aviva, Hamoadan Club, Haifa, Israel, 1960

WD on a camel, Israel, 1960

WD and Memphis Slim in concert, Tel Aviv, Israel, 1960

T-Bone Walker, American
Folk Blues Festival, Manchester,
England, 1962 (Brian Smith)

WD with (*left*) Brownie McGhee and Sonny Terry,
Trois Mailletz Club, Paris, 1962 (Julien Quideau)

Matt "Guitar" Murphy,
Little Brother Montgomery and WD
performing in Chicago, 1963

Horst Lippmann working on
the American Folk Blues Festival
WD's basement, Calumet, 1963

American Folk Blues Festival arriving in
Frankfurt, 1963: (*bottom to top, L to R*) Big Joe
Williams, Len Kunstadt, Victoria Spivey, WD,
Sonny Boy Williamson, Matt "Guitar" Murphy,
Bill Stepney, Muddy Waters, Otis Spann,
Memphis Slim (Mickey Bohnacker, courtesy
Horst Lippmann)

Sonny Boy Williamson (*left*) and
WD prepare to board tour van,
Baden Baden, Germany,
1964

Chess studio, 2120 S. Michigan, early 1960s: (*L to R*) Leonard Chess, Howlin' Wolf, WD, Sonny Boy Williamson (courtesy Dick LePalm)

WD, Chess studio, mid-1960s (Mike Leadbitter)

Performing with J.B. Lenoir in Chicago, late 1950s: (*L to R*) unknown, WD, Lenoir, J.T. Brown

WD with Koko Taylor, Chicago, 1965

The Chicago Blues All Stars, 1969: (*L to R*) Walter "Shakey" Horton, WD, Clifton James (*seated*), Sunnyland Slim, Johnny Shines

The Chicago Blues All Stars, Blues Factory, Chicago, 1971. (*L to R*) Lafayette Leake, WD, Buster Benton, Frank Swann, Walter "Shakey" Horton

WD, Rising Sun Club, Montreal, Canada, mid-1970s with (*L to R*) Dou Dou Bouceil (club owner), Muddy Waters, John Lee Hooker

Quiet Knight pub, Chicago, 1978: (*L to R*) Muddy Waters, WD, Ron Wood, Keith Richards, Charlie Watts (D. Shigley)

WD performing with Muddy Waters (*left*) and Johnny Winter, Chicago, 1979 (Paul Natkin)

At recording session for soundtrack of *The Color of Money*, New York, 1986: (*L to R*) Robbie Robertson, Martin Scorsese, Gil Evans, WD (Richard Corman)

WD performing at the New Orleans Jazz and Heritage Festival, 1985 (Michael P Smith)

WD, 1980 (Donald Dietz)

Manager Scott Cameron, 1989 (Nancy Clendaniel)

WD with grandson Alex Dixon, 1988 (Carl Studna)

WD with Don Snowden, 1989 (Peter Sherman)

Willie and Marie Dixon, 1987 (Marc Norberg)

MALCOLM CHISHOLM: Will was absolute magic in dealing with other musicians. Will could handle us on any level and he prefers to handle things by being persuasive and doing his wonderful Buddha act. Will is interested in it coming out right and the people he works with. He's a genuinely nice man and he deals extremely well with musicians, even obstreperous musicians. I've never run across anybody who liked Little Walter but Will could deal with him well.

Will had pretty strict standards and would not put out a record without a mistake. If the master take is perfect, Will has been known to do another take. I suspect that it is superstition. I also suspect that it may be a trademark and I wouldn't be amazed if Will thought that a record should have, somewhere, a mistake in it to prove that it was played by human beings.

WD: It wasn't actually the policy of a mistake—it was the policy of a sound. The majority of the public today don't know right from wrong in recording. It's only the people that ain't gonna buy any music, the musicians and critics, that pay any attention to the little mistakes. You're making music for the public as a whole and this is why I would always try to get two or three things to pick from.

If it was what you considered a perfect record, it never sold. But if it had a good feeling and good time, even when some of the words couldn't be understood, it would be better to go with that than one that's so perfect the people don't enjoy it.

When you go to record, you want to be sure to start off with an introduction that's so attractive you want to hear the story. You go to tell the story and the story and the music is sounding good. Halfway through the song, *boom!*, you're out of the song into a musical thing, which gives you a little time to concentrate on what it said.

The last part of the song is mostly completing the story and if you have this music going so good until it stops at an odd disposition—on the upbeat, something that makes you feel like I didn't quite get it all—they want to hear it again. That second and third time around listening is the one that hooks people and most people don't realize that.

When people like it the first time, they'll say, "Oh, that's beautiful. Play the other one." When they say, "Oh, that's beautiful, but what happened that second sentence . . . play that again." Every time they play it, the hook is getting deeper.

MALCOLM CHISHOLM: He is an extraordinarily subtle man, not cagey. You can never be quite sure if you're dealing with Will or not—I suspect that I am but I'm not perfectly sure. Having been brought up in a milieu in which your whole childhood was spent learning how to deal with people who could basically shoot you in the nearest alley if they felt like it and get away with it, Will has very great social skills. And remember, there's a motive to get along on sessions because you ain't gonna work again if the session doesn't go smooth.

I should think he was viewed as Chess' man. He was a contractor for Chess and his publishing was always in Arc. He was intimately associated with the company as a Chess artist of very long standing and a Chess producer *per se*. On session, he would definitely be on the side of the session which would make the perception that he would be on Chess' side.

Outside that, it is more likely the paranoia among people who don't work regularly. The people who were professionals were the only people in the business who were steadily employed at that time. It was really unusual for somebody to be working steadily and someone who was associated with a record company was in an enviable position—you got to make a little money from time to time.

CLIFTON JAMES: A lot of people thought he was Chess' guy but I didn't see that and a lot of other musicians didn't. When you got a job, you got a job to do and you do the job. Willie didn't try to beat anybody out of anything. Willie would try to show you a way to go about this thing. A lot of them didn't understand this because a lot of them were illiterate so they misunderstood.

WD: You can't find a musician anywhere who will tell you that he gave me a penny, not one cent for being on a session. If a guy was a good musician, I'd call him. If he wasn't, I wouldn't and some guys always thought that I can play as good as this other guy but he don't ever call me and all this stuff.

A lot of the artists thought I had a lot more to do with the record company than I did. Because I had pretty good authority around there, the Chess brothers would tell me to do various things. They claimed they didn't have the time but a lot of times they didn't want to face the music.

They would tell me what to tell the artists sometimes and I would tell them that in good faith, thinking that the company was going to uphold these things. After it was done, I come to find out differently and the artists would say, "Man, I wouldn't have got involved if it hadn't been for you."

I told them that I didn't own the company. I was just working for a salary like they were. I found out that some people down South and other places thought I owned part of the company because I had so many songs out. I didn't own nothing.

RON MALO: The blues things with Willie were live. You did it three or four times and usually no more because the musicians and singers were ready to perform. When the red light went on, that was money time and they performed.

A lot of strange things would happen because it was live. Sonny Boy Williamson playing harmonica live and then dropping the microphone or banging it. We used dummy microphones—make him sing into one microphone but that's not the one we were using. It was the only way to keep him from banging up against the microphone.

WD: Sonny Boy Williamson was a beautiful guy, a straight guy. He wasn't a liar like a lot of guys. Most people, especially talking about themselves, exaggerate a little bit but if Sonny Boy told you it was, it was. I don't know about other people but if he told me anything, I could depend on that as far as I could anything.

One time Sonny Boy came in to the Chess offices and said, "Hey, I want to see Leonard Chess."

"Leonard's got company."

He stood around there in the reception for a little while and said, "Hey, I've got to see Leonard. You ain't gonna let me in there?"

"No."

He just walked over, laid that little glass window back, stepped right over on top of the little desk and down through it. Leonard started giving him the devil and he started cussing Chess out.

After a while, somebody said, "Sssh! Hush, man. The rabbi's back there."

"Damn the rabbi," Sonny Boy said. "I don't give a damn about the rabbi or nothing else. That rabbi wants the same thing I want, some money. This son of a so-and-so ain't given me my damn money." Leonard had to take him upstairs and give him his money to keep him quiet.

If Sonny Boy Williamson didn't have the right song on one of his sessions, he would make up something that would fit just as good and keep right on playing. One time he was recording and they had these isolation booths on wheels up there. He was playing harp and just as the drummer was making a big break in the song, *wham!*, the isolation booth came down, *bam!*, and Sonny Boy fell with the mike and kept right on singing and playing. Believe it or not, that was the take we took.

PHIL UPCHURCH: I hooked up with Willie probably in the early 1960s or mid-1960s. Any stuff I did that Willie was associated with, he was more in a supervisory capacity than playing, like conducting a session. He's totally easy to work with, knows what he wants and is just a simple, straightahead guy.

Willie would walk in, run the tune down a couple of times, roll the tape and that was it. It was basically that simple. Different guys would come up with ideas—"Hey, Willie, how about this?" "Oh, I don't think that would work. Why don't you try this?"—but nothing ever got heated. He was definitely open to suggestions and definitely a very democratic cat to work with.

You might be intimidated by Willie because of his credits and expertise before you meet him but Willie is the kind of cat that once you walk into the room with him, all that goes away immediately. He's got the same kind of persona as a Quincy Jones.

You say, "Aw, shit! I'm gonna work with Quincy?" but the minute you walk into the room, these people have a persona about themselves that relaxes you because they're such down-to-earth, for real people. They treat everybody the same and just cool you right out immediately.

Everybody was like brothers and sisters. One or the other of the Chess brothers would generally be at the sessions because they were fans of the music and wanted to be involved in every aspect. They would throw in suggestions but nine times out of ten they got run out of the studio if they got too much in the way. A lot of times Chess would be in there trying to run the session, telling the artist how to sing and we'd just throw him out of his own studio—"Get the fuck out of here, Leonard."

BUDDY GUY: They were doing this folk album on Muddy and I was playing acoustic guitar. Leonard Chess told Muddy and Willie to go find some guy that could really play that old acoustic blues. Muddy said, "Go get Buddy Guy." Leonard Chess laughed and said, "I told you to go get an old guy. What the fuck does he know about that?"

I went there in the studio and Leonard Chess was standing in that studio with his mouth wide open. Muddy and Willie knew I could play because that's what we all learned if you came up right behind those guys. I didn't start with an electric guitar.

CASH McCALL: I ended up on a Muddy Waters session in 1967 because I had written a song called "Bird Nest On The Ground" with Monk Higgins, and Willie Dixon walked in. I had been working at Chess for a while, writing songs at $25 or something like that—$22.50 after taxes.

When they brought that session on the floor, the strangest thing was being in the room with those guys, listening to them talk to each other. It was kind of a hard play with words there but you could see the camaraderie. They were calling each other jolly little names.

Phil and Leonard Chess would come up to the studio and create all kinds of havoc, to the point of guys like Muddy Waters and Howlin' Wolf inviting them, in no uncertain terms, "Why don't you get the blankety-blank out of here?"

They didn't call you by your name—your name was "m-----f-----" all day long and I was raised in a religious family. I wasn't used to being around that but after you get over the initial shock, it was fun to see how they put a session together. They'd come in talking all that stuff but then you'd count the song off and they get to it.

It was just a playful thing that everybody said and nobody took it to heart. Willie didn't use that kind of language. Out of 20 some years, I have never heard Willie ever use that kind of language.

Willie was definitely running the sessions I was on. He wrote the song and brought the musicians in. I remember a lot of situations where he'd be doing two jobs at once when he wanted to bring the musicians and singer together to get to a change. He'd be sitting there with the singer, touch him on the shoulder and point at the musician when he wanted a change.

You had to have ears at those Chess sessions. You couldn't just run all over the place. You had to pay attention and you had to feel what was going on. I never saw Willie lose his cool on a session. He explained to me what he expected me to do and explained to people what he wanted to do with the song.

RON MALO: Leonard felt that if he or Phil didn't show up at the session the artists would feel that he didn't care. These were his family. The blues and R&B stuff were where he started and they were still important to him. If he couldn't be there for the whole session he'd at least come in and shake hands.

Willie pretty well ran the show and even when Leonard was running the sessions, if Willie wasn't there on the blues things, there would have been no record. Nothing would have happened.

HORST LIPPMANN: When I went early in 1963 to America, I naturally went to Chicago and my first connection there was Willie Dixon. For the next few following years, I worked out of Willie's basement office at the Calumet Avenue house to organize all these blues festival tours and later, all of the spiritual and gospel festival tours. I came each year, sometimes twice a year, and stayed about two weeks. It became my home city in America.

We connected with a lot of other blues people because a lot of friends of Willie dropped by and said hello. That's how I first met J.B. Lenoir two years later and he played and sang some blues which were sensational so I decided right away to record him. That came to be the famous *Alabama Blues* album, which at the time no one was willing to release in America because of the political content.

Willie had guitars and the bass and the tape machine and a record player and hundreds of tapes and records and photos. When we looked for someone when he wanted to show me a picture or play me the tape, he'd say, "I know I have it somewhere," and then we'd look for two hours. There were hundreds of unmarked tapes and cases of photos. That was sometimes very good because we'd look together and I found a lot of things he forgot completely.

I did a couple of recordings in Chicago around 1964 or 1965 with the assistance of Willie which have been released on Scout—that was Magic Sam and J.B. Lenoir naturally and a little bit of Sonny Boy Williamson, artists who had not been signed under contract with an American company. Those sessions were cut at Ed Cody's studios, a white guy who had studios on South Michigan.

There was only one thing we didn't agree on. After two and a half minutes, Willie said, "Stop it, it's too long," and I wanted to run the three or four or five minute thing if one got in the mood. Willie was running the sessions and I made comments.

He had complete command on these things and he knew how to talk to blues people. He had a way of dealing with the people which got everybody feeling comfortable. Willie's a relaxed man because he knows his potential and he's confident because he knows what he's worth.

The second J.B. Lenoir album was Willie by himself. I said I wanted a follow-up album on J.B. Lenoir so we made this deal by telephone and Willie went to the studio that day and the man had enough material. I wasn't able to come to Chicago so Willie did the studio work and I mailed him the money.

Naturally, the songs were only one minute and 50 seconds. I almost fainted. There was really no reason to fade out because they could have played at least a minute longer. No, one minute and 50 seconds apiece, Christ! Willie was thinking of making singles to fit into the jukeboxes in America and I was thinking of making albums because nobody buys blues singles in Europe.

WD: In the early days, nobody wanted a record over three minutes because deejays had to have things timed out. It was a standard thing but I always liked the divided thing because it would give you a chance to get a contrast from the artist. I figured a good three or three and a half minutes with something and you get into another style, it will give you a better contrast and a way to figure out your artist and check the different ways they can do things. When you hear the same thing over and over, you get tired of it.

I recorded the J.B. Lenoir things in Chicago, a couple of albums and this one thing I made at J.B.'s house. This guy came by his house and was asking J.B. about things when he went to Europe the first time. I took it to Europe and was showing it around to different people. There wasn't really enough for an album but he'd be playing different songs and going through a lot of commotion and talk.

When J.B. went to Europe, Lippmann & Rau had copied that tape and added some of the stuff from his show in Europe to that homemade tape and made a record out of it. The record was selling pretty good in the States for a while, but at that particular time I didn't have control of the publishing. I didn't know all the loopholes and the publishing angles.

HORST LIPPMANN: Willie was my guide to all the clubs and most of the people. We looked after Washboard Sam almost for a week, parked the car in front of the house and waited until he came home late at night. Washboard Sam always had a gun in his pants because he lived in a rough neighborhood. I went to beautiful eating places in the South Side and West Side and it was maybe the first time a white person went into some of these places.

I'd go to all the main clubs where Muddy played and Wolf's place Silvio's and then little clubs on the corner you'd get in and suddenly there was Magic Sam playing—I didn't know anything about Magic Sam—and another West Side club where Otis Rush was playing. These were not very famous clubs but Willie knew them. At that time, Chicago was full of blues music, especially on the South Side.

We started gospel festivals in 1965, actually under the impact of the American Folk Blues Festival success, and Inez Andrews and the Andrewsettes and the Five Blind Boys of Mississippi I got through the help of Willie Dixon. In 1966, we had the Gospelaires of Dayton, Ohio and the Dorothy Norwood Singers.

There had been times when I came to Chicago where Willie and myself went through all the many black churches Chicago holds. Sunday especially was church day and we went to all these things like live broadcasts. Willie was not only a help on the blues but very strong on gospel.

BOB KOESTER: I usually saw Willie in the company of some visiting dignitary from England, France or Germany. They were ahead of most

Americans and people like Paul Oliver and Jacques Demetre and Horst Lippmann from Germany would come to town and Willie would show them around the clubs where the talent was.

Willie would come into my store (the Jazz Record Mart) more often than we would go anywhere. He would bring people in and hardly let me do the work of showing the guys around. If I hooked up with them, I could get shown around, too, and I was on quite a few occasions.

Once we went to the Masonic Temple over on Cottage Grove near 43rd and I heard a marvelous gospel piano player named Reverend Ballinger, Robert Ballinger, who died within a year. I regard Ballinger as the Fats Waller of gospel piano.

WD: There was a guy called Dave Clark. We had met years before because he was working for United and States Records in Chicago when I recorded Big Walter with them in 1955. Dave Clark was with Duke and Peacock by then and Don Robey would send me a letter to get the spiritual groups together and record 'em and I would.

Clifton James would be on drums, Lafayette Leake on piano, and I'd be on bass. We recorded some of the better spirituals with the Mighty Clouds of Joy, the Spirits of Memphis, Inez Andrews and the Andrewsettes, the Blind Boys, just about every group they had I recorded.

CASH McCALL: Don Robey loved Willie and would send his gospel and quartet acts, mainly, to him. I was playing with a group called the Pilgrim Jubilees from Chicago and Willie had produced the first gospel hit record they ever had, which was a song called "Stretch Out." It was their biggest hit record ever.

Willie not only produced it, he played bass on it and that bass line was a model for that particular tempo and kind of song. A cat named Roosevelt English was the cat who took the bass line that Willie instituted and after Roosevelt English, a whole bunch of bass players who were playing behind quartet singers started playing that line.

It's like a I-VI-V-VI-I-VI-V-VI . . . it just keeps going. It would fit through all the changes—like a I-IV-V—in any kind of quartet melody. He'd anchor on that I and use the VI and V. It was definitely unusual for quartets to be using a bass at that time but after that song became a hit record, most gospel bass players started using that line.

DAVE CLARK: Willie Dixon wrote a lot of gospel arrangements that have become standards now, like "Stretch Out" and "The Old Ship Of Zion" with the Pilgrim Jubilees. We worked on those things together and we recorded them at Universal Studios in Chicago.

I was right there in Chicago in 1954 and told him I was getting ready to do some gospel and wanted to do a new lead in gospel, use the upright bass. We recorded Reverend Ballinger on a thing called "This Train" that was the first thing with a driving, walking bass line in there. It was something new to gospel because before then most of the gospel sessions were cut with guitar alone. We added the bass and piano and that gave it a drive.

Willie was involved in most of the early 1960s sessions for Duke and Peacock playing bass and helping with arrangements. He wasn't involved in all the ones in Chicago because sometimes I used Maceo Woods. Quite a few of the gospel things Willie did became big sellers. A big gospel selling record—if you did 100,000 albums on a gospel group, you had a giant gospel record.

WD: Spirituals never sold—even the biggest ones never sold anything like the little blues. I actually wrote several spiritual songs but I never actually tried to get them over to very many people.

I don't actually believe in any religion. The whole set-up of activities was made to control the people by governments. The governments and classes that's handling the masses have to have certain things they work with that the masses can't know, otherwise they can't control them.

I don't think the average individual is born with fear. I think he's taught more fear after he's born and by the government keeping him in fear; this enables the government to control and handle the people to do various things they want them to do. Years back in slavery, they didn't allow them to pray or sing but then they found out a better way to control them—with religious activities.

Common sense will tell you there's a Supreme Being. Common sense will tell you there's a beginning to everything but there's also an end. I know a lot of people believe in Biblical things. I used to read the Bible all the time because my mother taught me ever since I was a kid by reading the Bible. To me, heaven is a condition and I've caught hell right here on earth.

According to the Scriptures, the only way you can get into heaven after you die is by doing the right things on earth. In one place, they'll tell you you'll die and go to heaven and then they turn around and tell you that when God was on earth and told us a prayer to pray, it's a place where the kingdom comes on earth as it is in heaven.

If the kingdom comes on earth as it is in heaven and you fly away from the kingdom, you'll probably miss the kingdom. If the prayer's right, you can have your heaven on earth, so why not have heaven here by treating each other right and having what we want and enjoying it here?

Ballinger and me recorded this song of mine "You Got To Move (When That Love Feeling Hits You)" two or three different times, I think, both for Chess and for Peacock, and we used to play it on the stage quite a bit. He always kicked on that. The last one we did at Chess and Gene Barge put horns behind it.

During the time it could have sold, I think the courts weren't allowing them to use that particular record because it was involved in a dispute. Chess and Peacock were suing each other for using their artists, the Five Blind Boys of Mississippi. I recorded both artists and all of them on both labels, because Chess was trying to hold me to their label and Peacock had me working for them, too. I couldn't afford to say no to either of them, because I needed the money anyway.

They was trying to get me to be a witness on somebody's side and I didn't have a damned thing to do with it. I just record for anybody. That was my job, recording. When the guys come with their songs, I'll record 'em and I'll try to get 'em right.

DAVE CLARK: I worked about six gospel sessions with Willie and after Dixon did this session with the Five Blind Boys of Mississippi, there was another session involved where the Blind Boys recorded for Chess and they didn't have a contract. That caused a big controversy between Peacock and Chess—a big league dispute between Chess and Robey—and out of that came a lawsuit.

Willie didn't have any exclusive contracts with Chess as far as recording is concerned, as a musician. I think he had something on contract with Chess as a writer.

WD: I had an agreement with Chess for songwriting, but the thing is they didn't want me to write for nobody else. I had a contract for that but it wasn't a properly drawn up contract. When Chess found out that I made recordings over in Europe with Memphis Slim, they started raising hell that I had a contract with them. But really I didn't have a recording contract with them—I had an agreement to work with other artists.

Most of the time, the Chess company was at 2120 Michigan Avenue when I was over at Cobra. They moved there in the late 1950s and stayed until the mid-1960s when they moved on to 320 E. 21st Street, right around next to Donnellys, this big place that printed a lot of books and magazines.

MALCOLM CHISHOLM: There was a change in attitude, an attitude of some contempt at Chess, because Will has not really changed a great deal. There was a period during which people were getting a little more sophisticated and thought of the blues as pretty grotzy stuff. He came back into fashion very rapidly when the Stones came in to record at Chess. Money does talk—loudly—and as soon as the Stones started selling records of this stuff, Arc had copyrights and suddenly Will's songs were making a lot of money.

DICK LAPALM: 2120 Michigan Avenue was a storefront. You walk into a little, tiny lobby with curtains and Chess Producing Corp. on the window. At the desk was Minnie Riperton, who might have been 16 or 17 and was taking the regular girl's place for a couple of hours. My office is the next one and the final one, of course, is Leonard.

We had this sliding glass thing and I hear, *tap, tap, tap*. I don't pay attention but I see this white guy who doesn't look familiar. Finally, Minnie comes in and said, "Do you know where Willie's at?"

"He's not upstairs. It's kind of early."

"This man is just driving me crazy. He keeps tapping. 'Is he here yet? Is he here yet?' He's got to see Willie."

From that lobby, you could see who was going into the studio. There were two doors and Willie came walking down the corridor about to go up to the studio and this kid almost went crazy. It was like he had seen God. It turned out to be Brian Jones and later one of the Stones came walking down into the same area and he was so proud to be able to say, "This is Willie Dixon."

WD: When the Rolling Stones came to Chess Studios, they had already met me and been doing my songs, especially "Little Red Rooster." I had heard it but I never got royalties from them for a long time afterwards. I met 'em, we all had a nice time. They were young and they seemed to be kind of bashful, you know.

GIORGIO GOMELSKY: When I went to visit Dixon in Chicago, he had an old Oldsmobile. He was really big then and I knew it was his car because he came to fetch me at the hotel and this Oldsmobile was leaning heavily to the driver's side because that was where he was sitting. We went down where he lived and it was cold outside but it was very hot in there. We were walking around in t-shirts in the middle of winter inside of this building/apartment.

Down in the basement he had this little publishing office. He played me hours of tape and I picked four or five tunes which the Yardbirds used to do onstage but they weren't meant for our situation. "300 Pounds Of Joy"—we didn't have anybody that weighed 300 pounds. We were all 17- or 18-year-old skinny English limeys.

We made Chicago our American headquarters city with the Yardbirds even though it was cold in the winter. Willie would always be there and he would take us around to clubs.

One time, we created quite a stir because I wanted to organize this jam and the local Musicians' Union found exception with this idea. I got all kinds of strange people involved in this at a club called the "Thumbs Up," I think. The guys that were running it were from the you-know-who and I spoke Italian really well and talked them into letting me do this. They called up the union and we were able to do this jam session.

I called Willie and said, "Let's bring some people up," because it was in the middle of town somewhere, not on the South Side. It was another one of those cold January or February days and it was the London blues guys meets the Chicago blues guys in Chicago with Buddy Guy and Jeff Beck. Willie played on that too.

LEN KUNSTADT: Willie Dixon was very instrumental in preparing the session in Chicago when Spivey 1003 came out. It was recorded in Willie's basement on Calumet. It was like any old basement loaded with musical paraphernalia. Victoria Spivey knew about Willie Dixon's great ability to get musicians and she told Willie to get some fellows together.

Willie Dixon is a peculiar combination of fine business sense and great artistic ability. He rarely loses his temper. Willie is a mediator of the first order and an amazing teacher of the artists who sing his songs.

Willie's cool disposition, his slow way of talking and those sharp eyes used to quiet a lot of folks down. Wear dark glasses around Willie Dixon because he would read you. He's a musical psychologist in a lot of respects.

He is also a taskmaster of the first order, especially when he's training artists. With Koko Taylor, maybe 20 times on one number, "Koko, stop, stop, let's do it again." Sometimes he would spend two hours on one part of a passage of a song until he was satisfied. By the time he finished with them, the artist knew the song better than he did.

That was the beginning of Willie Dixon's power in Spivey Records. Willie did this recording on a tiny $40-50 machine, a little monaural job and the sound was good in most respects. Everything was done impromptu, except for the furnace coming on every half hour. If the music got really vibrant, you didn't hear the furnace.

WD: The first basement, where I met Victoria Spivey, I was living over at Calumet and 52nd Street. It was a little old basement that we couldn't hardly get anybody in but down there is where we recorded Koko Taylor, Homesick James and a few others. I just had a little homemade set-up. It wasn't no big deal—two-track or four-track and I used to get all the different musicians.

Victoria Spivey had contacted me when I was in Chicago about a song Peter, Paul & Mary made called "Big Boat." I wrote this song when we had the Big Three Trio but we recorded it as "Somebody Tell That Woman."

A guy called Brother John Sellers came to my house one time looking for songs. This was around 1955 and he was considered a spiritual singer at that time. We got to talking and he said, "I like this song, 'Big Boat Up The River,' " and I gave him the words and forgot about it. He took it to New York and recorded it and every once in a while somebody would say Brother John recorded your song but I wasn't paying no attention to it.

Seven years later, Victoria Spivey called me and she wanted to have me talk with this Krasilovsky with Warner Brothers Music. Naturally, I was interested and I told this fella Krasilovsky I had made this song "Big Boat" and I think Brother John Sellers got hold of it. He told me Brother John was trying to claim it. I told him he couldn't have because we recorded it for Columbia years ago with my name on it and everything.

Victoria called me and said, "You come on in here to New York. If you ain't got money, I'll send you the money." I don't know whether she sent the money or Warner Bros. did but I went there. Brother John came up and I looked at him and started laughing, you know.

"Well, me and Big Bill wrote this song a long time ago," he said.

"You and Big Bill? You got to be kidding yourself. I recorded this."

"Well, the only time I heard it recorded was with me and Big Bill."

"You didn't record this song. That song is a different song altogether."

We discussed it and Brother John had some lawyers and they told him to forget the thing. When I found out I was coming to New York, I had picked up the dubs and records we had made on Columbia way back in the early 1940s.

We went into an office and they were telling me about how the song had sold a million copies. I had been working for Chess but I never saw money that was up in the thousands of dollars before in my life. They told me I could pick up roughly $10,000 if I wanted, right then and there, and they wanted to know could I assist Peter, Paul & Mary because they had made it big.

I made an arrangement that after I got the first money, I would cut them in on a second batch of records. I wound up with a third of the song and I'm still getting money from it today. They gave me $5,000 then in a check and cash money and that was the first time I ever had over $1,000 in my life.

Way later, when I got back to Chicago, the Goodmans and Chess found out and said, "Hey, man, why didn't you tell me you wrote this, that, and the other? I can get you $4–5,000 on that." Never mind, forget it. After then I started getting my notes together about publishing because I got a book through BMI that started coming regularly about publishing ideas and like that. That got me off to a much better start.

HORST LIPPMANN: We talked a lot because Willie was under contract to Chess as a composer. He had to deliver I don't know how many compositions a week and he was on the payroll to get about $150 a week but he got no royalties, no nothing out of these compositions. Once I got closer, I thought this was a very funny situation.

His payroll was just enough to feed the family, not enough to put away money on the side to register the publishing company. Willie actually thought it was a set thing, he lives not bad with his weekly check and he writes his compositions and that's okay. I made Willie aware that this is not okay; at least he should get part of the royalties.

WD: Horst helped get Ghana together over there for European publishing. I had him put all the stuff of mine over there into Ghana because Chess didn't want any of the artists to have publishing companies. I think that's what him and Chuck Berry got into it about.

Cash McCall was writing a lot of songs and letting Chess have 'em. I don't know whether he was sellin' 'em to him or what was going on, but I know he was writing a lot of songs. Cash was making songs and had his little crew doing his thing and I was doing mine but I would try to hip 'em occasionally about what was happening around there. Most of the time nobody paid attention to me because I think the Chess brothers had their thing in there.

CASH McCALL: He started educating me because when you're a writer and coming from the South, new in the business, you don't know anything about publishing, record vouchers, or anything like that. I had been a staff writer at Chess for about a year or year and a half.

I just went from the cotton fields into the army right into Chess. You're a country boy, you see your name on the record and you think you're gonna become rich, buy your mother the house and have her see some of the good things in life. Rude awakening.

For some reason, Dixon took a liking to me. One day down in the lobby, I met him and he said, "You're writing all these songs. Do you have any protection or anything? Are you collecting any money? Do you have your own publishing company?" I said no because at that point I really didn't know how the business was constructed.

He told me to meet him tomorrow and he went to BMI, picked up the papers for me and when I met him out there, he told me to sign these papers. He established, for me, my own publishing company. The man didn't know me that well but he took steps to help me.

He'd been telling everybody concerned up there what was going on. I think he got into trouble with Chess a little bit because he would tell a guy the truth. He'd worked for them a long time and he'd been shafted pretty much. Willie is the one that saved me from being shafted too much.

Chess and Arc really couldn't do anything about me having my own publishing company but if I wrote a song and put it in my company, they could do a lot of things to me without reservation. They would screw anybody, ain't no doubt about that.

After you've been in the business for a while, you don't remain ignorant of certain facts. Sometimes it's as plain as the nose on your face—"Hey, you're getting half?"—and that's just the way it was. I've been halved quite a bit myself.

WD: I gave advice about publishing companies to most of the guys when I found they didn't know what they were doing because the companies always took advantage of the artists. The companies, especially Chess, always underestimated the artists. They put all the artists in the same bag as somebody just trying to grab himself some money and didn't give a damn how they did it.

When I found out there were people that didn't know no more than I knew when I got there, I tried to assist them because I didn't want people to be going through all the hell and high water unnecessarily that I was going through. When you learn something about something that can make a better situation for someone else, you're supposed to do it.

9

You can't judge an apple
By looking at the tree
You can't judge honey
By looking at the bee
You can't judge a daughter
By looking at the mother
And you can't tell the book
By looking at the cover

Chorus: Now can't you see
You misjudge me
I look like a farmer
But I'm a lover
So you can't judge a book
By looking at the cover

You can't judge the sugar
By looking at the cane
You can't judge a woman
By looking at her man
You can't judge the sister
By looking at her brother
You can't judge a book
By looking at the cover

You can't judge the fish
By looking at the pond

You can't judge the right
By looking at the wrong
You can't judge one
By looking at another
You can't judge a book
By looking at the cover

Chess began to wind down as the mid-1960s stretched into the late 1960s. At the height of the civil rights era, the blues had largely fallen out of favor with a black record-buying populace. The last big blues hit the label had was in early 1966 with Koko Taylor's decidedly soul-tinged arrangement of "Wang Dang Doodle" on Checker.

Soul music was the dominant musical style of the period and Chess, ever the pragmatic, hit-oriented organization, naturally gravitated in that direction. There were fewer blues releases and fewer artists on the label beyond the twin towers, Muddy Waters and Howlin' Wolf. The deaths of Sonny Boy Williamson, Elmore James, Little Walter and J.B. Lenoir between 1963 and 1967 diluted the talent pool of proven blues performers. The change in emphasis translated into a reduced presence for Willie Dixon at the label as the decade wore on.

That shift in audience taste was complemented by a number of internal changes within Chess. Two decades of the constant hustle and physical grind of running an independent record label had worn Leonard Chess down. Leonard and Phil Chess had purchased radio station WTAO in Flint, Michigan in 1959 and four years later moved into the Chicago market by reportedly paying a cool $1 million in cash for station WHFC. Leonard began devoting more of his energy and attention to the station—re-named WVON—and the other facets of the Chess mini-empire.

Some time between mid-1966 and early 1967, Chess had moved to its final location—TerMar Studios at 320 E. 21st Street—in another cash-in-hand deal. At the six-story warehouse facility, Chess became a wholly self-contained operation with its own pressing plant, mastering facility and recording studios on the premises. The finished records were then released through its own distribution network.

But even as Leonard Chess' role on the musical end was being phased out, a new Chess family member was being phased in— Leonard's son Marshall was vice-president of the record company at 27 by 1969 and had already been given a large hand in shaping the company's creative musical policy. Chess attempted to swing with a tide that found the blues audience suddenly, surprisingly, turning into white college kids who bought albums rather than its core black audience that typically bought 45s.

There were attempts made to court the new blues audience, sometimes embarrassing ones like the late-1960s albums which presented the classic blues of Muddy Waters and Howlin' Wolf in tasteless psychedelic arrangements. Chess also tried to meet the psychedelic set on its own terms and enjoyed some success with groups like Rotary Connection (featuring Minnie Riperton) and the English band Status Quo, the latter hitting big with "Pictures Of Matchstick Men" early in 1968. But those forays into the rock world also led to Chess sessions for eminently forgettable artists with such cringe-inducing names as Attila & the Huns of Time or Salloom, Sinclair and the Mother Bear.

But with a jazz division buoyed by the mid-1960s pop success of Ramsey Lewis ("Wade In The Water" and "The In Crowd," the latter featuring Lewis' version of Dixon's "My Babe" on the flip side) and Ahmad Jamal, a slew of slow but steady-selling gospel artists and soul/blues performers like Etta James, Little Milton and Billy Stewart on hand to maintain an active Chess and Checker label presence on the R&B charts, Chess was still in fairly good shape even as its blues division slid into disrepair.

But Leonard Chess was increasingly fed up and in January, 1969, he sold Chess to the giant GRT corporation for a sum in the $10–11 million range. It was a shock to an organization that had always considered itself a family-style operation bound more by loyalty and out-of-the-pocket need than strict corporate principles of bottom-line accountability.

The Chess staff was still reeling from that body blow when it was struck by a deeper one that ultimately proved fatal. Leonard Chess had survived a number of heart attacks through the years . . . but not the

*one he suffered while driving from work on October 16, 1969. He was
52 and his death effectively sealed the company's fate. For all practical
purposes, Chess had been a one man operation—Leonard Chess'
baby—and the morale among artists and staff drained away.*

*The GRT regime made wholesale changes and the company quickly
slid down the tubes. Phil and Marshall Chess both left in 1971. Willie
Dixon had already recorded his last session for the label the year
before.*

*Dixon had been working on other projects throughout the final
stages of Chess—he had to, of course, since the flow of royalties from
Chess or Arc was never reliable and he was still supporting two
families. He maintained his managing and booking activities with
Koko Taylor and others, continued putting together European festival
line-ups for Horst Lippmann's organization, activated the Blues All-
Stars and began looking to a post-Chess career as a solo artist. And
there were the ever-continuing signs that all was not well within the
halls of Chess when it came to paying artists the money due them.*

RON MALO: See Chapter 7.

MALCOLM CHISHOLM: See Chapter 5.

*KOKO TAYLOR: hit big with "Wang Dang Doodle" in 1966 and actively
performs and records for Alligator Records today.*

DICK LAPALM: See Chapter 8.

*MARSHALL CHESS: ran Chess Records in the late 1960s before heading the
American division of Rolling Stones Records in the early 1970s.*

CASH McCALL: See Chapter 8.

PHIL UPCHURCH: See Chapter 6.

In the latter part of the 1960s, the Chess brothers were trying to back
away from blues, but they were always going to keep the few artists
they had in blues because they had become popular.

They wouldn't accept too many artists that were close to the artists
they had already in style and had good publicity on because they felt
that a new artist was detrimental to them. The company would take

these artists that had pretty good things in the style their artist had and put it on the shelf so it wouldn't be no competition for their artist. They wouldn't care if you lived or died as long as they took the best of the songs from other artists so it would give their artists more power.

During the 1960s Leonard was going all different directions and he wasn't too sure about what kind of stuff he was going to do. When he got WVON, he went right to work on it. He had a lot of deejays coming in there discussing working with him. Al Benson was the head man there, he got E. Rodney Jones from down in Texas and Don Cornelius of Soul Train was working with him in Chicago for awhile.

Leonard was still interested in the record company because I think he got the radio station to promote the records. He started promoting the records pretty heavy then and they couldn't squawk about how many of his records were being played. I don't know what the government was doing but I know a lot of Chess records were played there and a lot of his associated records.

I was associated with most of the blues and spiritual things. Cash McCall and Gene Barge were mostly associated with the jazz and sometimes they let them get involved with some of the spiritual things if I wasn't available.

When there wasn't but a few of us at the company, naturally I had more work to do in there. I could do just as much when the Chess company moved to 320 E. 21st Street if I wanted to but, naturally, when they develop into a different type of music, you've got to get people that are qualified to understand that type of music. I wasn't threatened at all because most of the guys didn't actually understand my style of things.

They were trying to ease themselves into some kind of modern jazz or bop but I was laying close to the bluesy things. I might have tried to change the style of 'em but I never did try to jazz 'em or put a lot of unnecessary things in there to attract the attention of the youngsters. I never was a real jazzy man.

We always had a basic background and a basic way of doing things to begin with. This is what we always practiced from the beginning with an artist so we had a definite way of doing it. If they went a different direction, we could still work it. A lot of times, they'd change the words or change the song completely around.

RON MALO: Willie wasn't really doing that much around Chess late in the 1960s and we weren't doing that much in the blues. The blues material was about a third of everything but it was really hard to say with Chess what was blues and what was R&B because it was constantly moving back and forth. You had Muddy Waters and those people—they had a market, they sold and it didn't cost a lot of money to put a record out so Chess would continue to do it.

When the cost of recording increased and the sales decreased in the mid-1960s, then we did less blues recording. The lack of blues coming out of Chess was more purely economics. The mid-1960s was a dead period for blues and it was costing more to record.

A big album at Chess Records was $3–5,000 for production costs. At five thousand dollars, you were really pushing the budget for an album and that's with an orchestra and everything. Studio time then was $20 an hour and that included just about everything. Tape was $10 a roll for quarter-inch tape.

Some of the artists had left. Koko Taylor may have been one of the last things done at 2120 Michigan Avenue because Willie was less and less involved when we went to the new studios at 320 E. 21st Street. I would still see Willie because we did things for him for other record companies.

WD: During the time of Martin Luther King, most of the artists, especially blues artists, didn't feel like they were going to have success with their thing. None of 'em felt like the company was actually going to push it or that they were going to have justice pertaining to what they was doing with the company.

They always felt like the company was out to beat 'em and cheat 'em out of what they did and most of the time the company did. In those days, they knew the artist didn't have enough money to carry it to court.

The common individual doesn't know anything about the law. If they carried it to court and consumed any time with it, the artist wouldn't be able to stay there because he didn't have any money. They could drag them out for so long the artist would give up. They always had a way, you see. Keep a lie rollin' and you just feel like there ain't no way out.

When these first rock artists came along, guys like Muddy and Wolf and Sonny Boy didn't get a whole lot of money. The company was telling Muddy Waters they was giving me the money and telling me Muddy Waters was getting the money. Muddy was rolling his eyes at me about, "You oughtta give me some of that money you're making off these songs I caused them boys to have."

"What boys?"

"You know, all them rock groups."

"I ain't gettin' no money."

"I know you're gettin' it because Chess told me you were gettin' the damn thing."

I was damned lucky to be getting anything. Me and Chess were fighting all the time because I'd be trying to get a reasonable amount to survive on.

If somebody didn't luck into a thing and have a good song the public would go for, nine times out of ten they wouldn't put pressure on anybody to play it and keep it going.

MALCOLM CHISHOLM: Chess exerted very little control over their artists and writers. They were accustomed to dealing with artists as stage musicians and simply got people they knew were doing well with the public and let them alone. They produced, from time to time, a thorough-going turkey.

However, they could afford to as they spent very little making records, very little producing records and almost nothing promoting. If a record didn't start to sell on its own, Leonard wouldn't spend a quarter promoting it. If it started to sell, he'd budget $20,000 to give it a little pat on the ass. Leonard was never strong for promoting records— "Let them live by themselves or let 'em die."

WD: I had recorded "Wang Dang Doodle" beforehand with Howlin' Wolf and they never turned it loose. When they put this thing out with Koko Taylor, they weren't expecting it to do very much and *bang*/that "Wang Dang Doodle" took off like a jet.

KOKO TAYLOR: "Wang Dang Doodle" was almost like a miracle record. They gave Dixon a sample copy and they had this deejay on WVON at night called Pervis Spann who could play almost anything. Dixon took "Wang Dang Doodle" over there and gave it to Spann. Spann started getting so many requests and phones that Dixon told him, "We gotta do something with this now. This tune is hot as July jam."

Leonard Chess was the owner of WVON at the time so it wasn't a problem getting played if he said play it. Sure enough, Leonard Chess told Spann to play it for three days and so many orders came for it he had to press it just like popping your fingers. Before I know anything they said, they had sold 100,000 copies right in Chicago.

WD: They make the contract with all artists that said that after the expense has been paid, then you split the royalty. They make the expense whatever they want it to be, let the artists have a few dollars at a time, and it takes a million records for 'em to see the expenses paid as far as they're concerned. When "Wang Dang Doodle" started selling, Koko and her old man were saying, "Dixon, why don't you give us some money? We know they're paying you."

They weren't paying me a damn thing. They were doing Koko like they were doing me, telling her I was getting the money and telling me she was getting the money. The song was really doing good but she wasn't making any money at all. You don't have a true way to check on it unless it's through some of their staff and people aren't going to jeopardize their job to give you the true facts.

DICK LAPALM: I knew what the sales were on "Wang Dang Doodle" because I had access to the books. I could walk in the office and say, "What did this distributor order today on 1135?" and Willie and I are on the back side of "Wang Dang Doodle" with "Blues Heaven."

When we had started to lose the people that passed away like Sonny Boy and Elmore James, I walked up to Willie one day and said, "There's got to be a blues heaven." Arc Music was the publisher and when I got my first check, I said to Willie, "I got a check for $16," and I knew what sales were.

I know Leonard and Phil were partners in Arc so I walked up to Phil and showed him this check.

"Phil, I just got a check from your music publishing company for my 50% share of 'Blues Heaven' and it's for $16."

He made some off-the-wall comment—"Well, you could buy a good breakfast."

"But the record sold, Phil, I'm right here with you, the record sold.

It's over 200,000 right now, the single."

"Don't be crazy. We're gonna get a lot of them back."

"No, we're not. They're all re-orders."

"Hey, just leave well enough alone."

But five months after I started working there officially in 1963, Leonard gave me such a Christmas bonus check that I went to the accountant and said, "Hey, man, you fucked up. Five hundred dollars, not $50?"

He said, "Leave well enough alone. He wants to give you $500."

That was a lot of money then.

WD: Koko Taylor has a beautiful thing now but when she first came to me, she told me, "I can sing but every time I go to somebody and sing, they tell me they don't like this growl, that heavy part of my voice."

"That growl you got to your voice will put you over."

"But I can't help it."

"I know you can't. That's what makes you good. You got a different thing and if you use it properly, it can be essential. It can really be great for you."

After I started working with Koko on different songs, I was telling her I wanted to do "Wang Dang Doodle." The first thing she said, "That ain't no song for a woman to sing."

"The hell it ain't. You're trying to get over and this is something different."

KOKO TAYLOR: I was introduced to Willie Dixon through a deejay, Big Bill Hill. Dixon was the one that first took me down to Chess and in fact wrote my first song, "I Got What It Takes." I thought maybe I had the wrong type of voice because I was about the only one that had this old rough, tough, strong voice. Dixon said to me. "You're the only woman I've heard that got that kind of voice and I think you got the right voice to sing the blues."

The reputation he had I knew and gathered from the beginning— when I first met him is when I first started meeting musicians. All the musicians would come to him and he always seemed to have had time and patience with musicians from all over town. It seemed like he was such a great figure in what he was doing until they all relied on him. They felt that if they could get with him, they could get their foot in the door and things would happen. They would be right there at his house and his phone would always be busy, someone wanting to know if they could do one of his tunes or audition for him or would he listen to something they had on tape. Most of his time went on other people that was trying to make it in music.

Willie wasn't a playful person. He was always business and had his mind on what he was doing—"Let's get this together. We're not here to fool around shootin' the bull." But you could say something funny to him or a joking word and he would laugh at it.

We didn't always agree to everything. Sometimes he would give me a song that I didn't want and here we'd go—"How come I gotta do this tune?" If he had a song or something he had confidence in for you and felt really strongly about it, you couldn't change his mind.

He'd tell anybody—"Well, you don't see nothin' in it because you're not looking further than the end of your nose. But I'm looking for tomorrow, next year, in the long run." The long shot is what he'd say he was looking at but we'd be looking at this tune right now and I ain't liking it so it made a big difference.

He was a very strong, firm person and a determined person with whatever he felt was right to do. It turned out later that the things he was saying were very true. Anything that you don't have faith in yourself, anybody else ain't going to have faith in it and over the years I've learned that to be true. This is what he taught me over the years, first to have faith in me and the rest will just follow all in place.

WD: The first two albums I made on Koko were beautiful sellers but at this particular time, the Chess company didn't want me to get involved with too much money. I noticed a couple of times the *Billboard* would come out and they'd either cut or tear the page out because they didn't want me to see it. They felt like if I got ahold of a decent sum of money, I probably would leave the company and they wanted to keep me around to assist.

The Chess brothers had quite a few things going on around there at the time. Chess had the radio station going and he'd send me over occasionally to hand checks to the different guys but I'd always have something of my own that I'd be working with on a record and wanted them to play it. Sometimes they would, sometimes wouldn't but if I brought it and it came from Chess, naturally they'd play it.

I also had things of my own and sometimes the Chess company wouldn't take a thing unless somebody else tried it out. If it seemed like it was going to be a hit or good seller, they'd jump in and take it, sometimes with a contract, sometimes without a contract.

My brother Arthur made this poem "Might Is Right" when he was in jail. I had this record of it out in Chicago but this was during the time of Martin Luther King. A lot of people wouldn't play it because they felt like it wasn't the type of song to be played at that particular time because of various incidents that were involved with Martin Luther King.

I had thousands of these records made but I couldn't get 'em played in a lot of places. They had the damned payola thing where they wanted you to pay for every damn thing. After that, I just put the records in my basement and water got to it and messed up a lot of them.

I started to march with Dr. King at one time. I had gotten in the game with them when they did the march right down South Park in Chicago. The guys over there were saying, "Now, remember, this is a peaceful demonstration. If we go out there and there's fighting going on, whatever they do, keep on marching."

I started thinking about that—ain't no way I'm going out there to look at somebody to jump on me and hit me and I don't knock the hell out of 'em back. I told 'em there's no use in me going out there and ruining your thing. I'll go back home because I can't tolerate that.

In order to try to keep the black man down, they have tried to psychologize them against their own culture and they do that even today. They show guys anything that is culture from way back, "Man, that's old timey and no good. This is the modern thing today that's happening."

They taught black people that being black was against themselves. Anything that would magnify you against black people, they found a way to say it. Black was dirty, white is clean. People in Africa were wild, they're savages and they'll chase you with spears, put you in a pot and cook you. They're still uncivilized . . . out in the civilized world, they drop the atom bomb and kill every damn body. They had black people starting to feel like everything that was black was wrong—the black customs was wrong, the black culture was wrong, the black religion was wrong, the black people was wrong.

A lot of people say it was because the majority of the black people didn't have knowledge enough to know they was being conned and the majority of the things they was making was being taken away from them. They were satisfied with everything like it was. They got more educated, black people, about things and naturally they became aware of some of the things that had been going down wrong.

All of a sudden certain guys said, "If they won't let you in their neighborhoods to do business, why should we let them in our neighborhood to do business?" That's the way it started. I know all over the South Side, everybody of every nationality under the sun had a place of business there.

They were all right up next to each other and doing good but they were taking the money and building their neighborhoods up to be sophisticated places and began to call these places where they had their business slums. Why should people take money out of our neighborhood to build up their neighborhood and call ours slums?

DICK LAPALM: When Fleetwood Mac came to Chicago in 1967, they, like the Stones, wanted to record at Chess Studios. Their guitar player was a wonderful player named Peter Green. They wanted to go to this club because of this blues artist that was one of our artists. It happened during that period when the marches and movement had started and it wasn't safe to go to the South Side of Chicago. I called E. Rodney Jones and he said, "Let me call Willie up."

We go to the club—was it Silvio's?—and Peter gets onstage and plays his ass off. People were standing and shouting, "Listen to that white boy, look!" As we're leaving the club, two guys try to take his guitar. The lifesaver was Willie, whose very presence said, "You sit in a club and applaud this man, carry on about him and then want to take his axe?" He convinced them of that.

MARSHALL CHESS: The record business was changing, spreading to white audiences, into albums and there were problems of change at the label. Some of the people in promotion couldn't do it. When FM radio was just beginning, I remember having horrible struggles.

DICK LAPALM: Marshall Chess, the heir apparent, started going over to London and said we better start moving in a particular direction. He brought that awareness into the company. There were varied opinions of the direction that the company should take as a result of this feedback we were getting from Marshall taking the trip overseas and from Willie Dixon telling us he's going over to London to play for thousands of people.

Leonard paid attention to the pressing plant. He loved radio and felt he could concentrate on this because he believed that he had surrounded himself with the right people who could see to it that Howlin' Wolf lives as well as Rotary Connection.

When you're Leonard Chess and you have a son named Marshall, who's grown up in the business and you go to turn the company over, you gonna turn it over to your cousin or your barber? You turn it over to your son.

We were not opposed to Marshall's movement with Cadet Concept. We encouraged it, but Leonard did not want to kill the goose that was laying the golden egg. He said, "Okay, do that, but let's continue what we're doing with the Soul Stirrers, the Meditation Singers, Koko and Wolf." We always felt that some day we were going to be able to sell Willie's material to these people in Seattle and Minneapolis.

WD: Those psychedelic albums that Wolf and Muddy did were mostly Marshall's idea. When you take away from the original, you create something different and those particular things never actually were creating anything different. It was doing the same thing using gimmicks on the instruments and gimmicks on the voice like putting extra echo on. If you were taking a new arrangement or making a different sound, that was saying something but a sound that ain't sayin' nothing didn't do anything for it.

DICK LAPALM: Marshall was always pushing for the 24-year-old who was listening to the Jefferson Airplane. They appreciated what Muddy, Wolf, Bo, Chuck and Willie did but because radio was going another way, they minimized it. They didn't fight for it and that projected into the company. It became the whole corporate thing—inter-office memos and that kind of bullshit.

CASH McCALL: I remember these new administrations coming through Chess and they wanted to throw away the blues altogether. There was a new breed of office cat personnel came around there that didn't care about Muddy Waters or Howlin' Wolf and didn't have any problems voicing their opinions about it. I was right there—I heard it. You know you're in a corporation then.

Of course, there was a change in attitude towards Willie. He took some adversity. There were times when he didn't get called to Chess to do sessions but he never let it stop him. There was more R&B going on than blues and jazz was happening. Nobody was that interested in the blues but the Chess brothers.

PHIL UPCHURCH: The only time the feeling it was over started setting in was after Leonard died because they were basically a one-man operation. When Leonard passed, everybody kind of felt, "Well, there goes the company," because he wasn't going to let his baby go down while he was on his feet. It started going downhill right after he passed.

DICK LAPALM: When Leonard was alive, he had us at the place. He came in and told me the deal he was making with GRT when he sold the company—"I told them that in order for the company to function and continue growing, you're one of the four people that must stay and this is how much money I got you." He really put it together. With the death of Leonard, it was like Chuck Barksdale of the Dells said, "It's over, man. It ain't Chess without Leonard."

I think Willie was saddened that Leonard died and before that it was a big blow to him when the company was sold to a corporation that was involved with tape. They were particularly concerned when the corporate people from GRT sent some of their accountants to take over. I thought they were going to kill one guy—they did manage to cut his tires. I told that guy people have been treated a certain way and if they wanted $100 to go to Detroit, Leonard gave them $100 cash.

Leonard was the big father. Phil . . . it wasn't that he couldn't make a decision but he could be overridden. But he could not override Leonard because Leonard was the big brother from a Polish Jewish family.

They cheated Willie. I know—I was there and I loved Leonard and Phil Chess for a lot of reasons. I know one of the reasons they had to do that is when you buy two full page ads in the trade magazines and you don't have the bread because this distributor hasn't paid you in time and you gotta find it somewhere, well—too bad.

WD: I don't know how much trouble they were in but the auditors were always auditing the records at Chess. The I.R.S. or somebody was in there, off and on, for close to a year because they had everything all over everywhere. But the company was still running. It didn't look like it was in any trouble.

MARSHALL CHESS: Chess went through a lot of heavy transitions when it was sold because our business was excellent. We had a much broader base—jazz, black comedy, the blues, quite a few R&B hits—so our dollar income was better than ever. This is one of the reasons they sold the company—the price was very good but the company itself was going through problems even though you could look at the sales figures and say this company is hot.

WD: After Leonard died, the company began slowing down quite a bit because he was the one who did most of the business pertaining to the company. When Chess stopped, financially, I was just like I was when I started with him—nothing, not a damn thing.

I wasn't making but $150 a week against my royalties when the Chess company stopped. After the end of royalty time, they'd take that amount out that they had given me and they'd give me a short royalty statement. I wasn't getting the right amount in the first place. Arc wouldn't send the royalty statement to my house. They'd send it to Chess and Chess would take out more.

I had a chance with my songs that other people had done but if I hadn't gotten my manager Scott Cameron I wouldn't have had a damn bit more than anybody else. You think of all that time Muddy spent with Chess, he got a few bucks but nothing like the amount of money you'd think he'd have.

Before Scott came on, I was getting a royalty statement of maybe $5,000 after six or eight months when I had all my best songs out there. We finally went to Arc Music in New York and they'd tell him they don't know about a thing but after that my royalty statement started moving up. We finally sued them and got some of the money.

10

Chorus: Give me some dead presidents
Give me some dead presidents
I ain't broke but I'm badly bent
Everybody wants them dead presidents

Now Lincoln, a penny, can't park your car
Washington on a nickel can't go too far
Jeff on two, good to play at the track
If you think you gonna bring some big ones back

Give me some dead presidents
Give me some dead presidents
I don't need Lincoln on the little old cent
I want great big Lincoln, to pay my rent

Hamilton on a ten, can get you straight
But Jackson on a twenty is really great
And if you talking about a poor man's friend
Grant will get you out of whatever you're in

Hundred dollar Franklin is really sweet
Five hundred McKinley is the one for me
And if I get Cleveland I'm really set
With thousand dollar Cleveland I forget the rest

Trying to tell the Willie Dixon story without dealing with Leonard Chess is as inconceivable as attempting a history of Chess Records and ignoring Willie Dixon. The Chess operation was patriarchal in nature, a one-man operation run out of Leonard Chess' pocket.

When anyone connected with Chess needed money, they asked Leonard for it. If they ran into some trouble, be it legal or financial, Leonard was usually the one who straightened things out. If Leonard preferred to operate on handshake deals and hand out money directly to his artists or employees rather than sign written contracts, that was just the way he chose to run his business.

It may seem a strangely informal set-up to anyone accustomed to the more structured approach of the modern record business, but the post-World War II music industry—particularly the small, independent blues/R&B labels hustling to stay alive—operated under different principles. It was a world where cash in hand today was infinitely more valuable than a check in the mail six months in the future, where a song's life was measured in terms of the sales it generated when it first hit the market and what might happen ten years down the line was rarely considered.

And it was a world where payola was largely viewed as an accepted, inevitable cost of doing business. During the early 1960 investigations of payola by the Federal Trade Commission, Chess apparently refused to sign a unilateral cease and desist order until uniform restrictions were passed by Congress. And Chess claimed that it operated above board by itemizing payments to deejays as a legitimate business expense and declaring them to the government on 1099 forms come tax time.

The role of a record producer was markedly different as well and didn't carry the creative importance then that it does now. Usually, the producer was the person who bankrolled the session rather than the contemporary model who commands a substantial advance payment plus a percentage of royalties and plays a substantial role in selecting material and shaping the performance in the studio.

Leonard Chess has been touted as a great blues producer who truly understood the music—an opinion shaped largely on the sound of early Chess records and the one, well-remembered occasion when he went into the studio to play the bass drum when Muddy Waters' regular drummer couldn't pick up the rhythm to "She Moves Me." But the nuts-and-bolts, day-to-day arranging and fashioning of the music—the kind of work identified with producers today—was largely the province of Willie Dixon during his tenure at Chess.

But the chief bone of contention among Chess artists concerned the company's symbiotic relationship with Arc Music, the label's in-house publishing company formed in 1953. The Chess brothers were partners in Arc Music with Gene and Harry Goodman, who ran the publishing company from New York. Ironically, given the number of court claims that have been filed against Arc Music by black blues artists, the Goodmans were the brothers of Benny Goodman, who had effectively broken the color barrier in jazz in 1936 by including pianist Teddy Wilson and later vibes player Lionel Hampton in his group.

It was common practice for the early independent record companies to start up their own publishing wings—and sometimes placing the rights to their songs with the in-house publishing company was a condition of an artist getting recorded. Label owners could, with a stroke of the pen, split songwriting credits by adding names or pseudonyms to the copyright. The most famous example at Chess was "Maybellene," credited to Chuck Berry, rock 'n' roll deejay Alan Freed and Russ Fratto, the man who was printing up the record labels for Chess at the time.

It was a situation ripe for exploitation since an artist was completely dependent on the publisher and record company to supply accurate information that would let the performer know what was going on. Blues artists were particularly vulnerable since many were marginally literate and trapped in a situation where any deal was no better than no deal—getting a record out on the market meant the chance to pick up some cash through live performances.

The intricacies of the music publishing world were often enough to stymie those who did have some inkling of what was going on. Willie Dixon formed his own Ghana Publishing company and registered it with BMI in 1957 but he didn't join the organization as an individual writer until the following year. He wound up transferring the administration rights to Goodman at Arc in the mid-1960s because of the time involved and contacts required to keep tabs on his songs around the world.

Any earlier material was registered in Dixon's name but the copyright itself was owned by Arc. The one recourse was the courts, and a suit initiated against Arc Music resulted in an out-of-court settlement in 1977 which provided for the return of his copyrights as they came up for renewal, the return of the Ghana catalogue and other benefits.

But Leonard Chess was a far from one-dimensional man. When Chess purchased their Chicago radio station, the call letters were changed to WVON—the Voice of the Negro—and Leonard was once quoted as saying, "I made my money from the Negro and I want to spend it on him." He was a life member of the NAACP, a contributor to Martin Luther King, Jr.'s Southern Christian Leadership Conference, a director of the Chicago Urban League and voted that organization's Man of the Year in 1966.

The Chess clan was always quick to characterize the label as a family operation that took care of its own. Phil and Leonard Chess have both been quoted as saying that if they stole from their artists, it was taking sales numbers from good-selling jazz artists like Ahmad Jamal or Ramsey Lewis and shifting them to the empty accounts of their blues artists so the bluesmen could get some money. But if Chess was a family affair, the distribution of income certainly favored the fathers–the Chess family and the Goodmans—who wound up wealthy over the sons—the artists—who ended up with next to nothing in the bank for the music they created.

SCOTT CAMERON: a former booking agent and vice-president with Willard Alexander, Inc., he became the manager of both Muddy Waters and Willie Dixon early in 1973.

RALPH BASS: a noted blues/R&B producer for Savoy, King and Chess Records.

MALCOLM CHISHOLM: See Chapter 5.

AL DUNCAN: a well known Chicago drummer and sessionman in the 1950s and 1960s working for Chess and VeeJay Records.

DICK LAPALM: See Chapter 8.

RON MALO: See Chapter 8.

DAVID MEYERS: played guitar with Little Walter on many of Walter's early Chess recordings.

LUTHER TUCKER: played guitar with Little Walter and Sonny Boy Williamson on many of their late-1950s Chess recordings.

JIMMY ROGERS: See Chapter 4.

MARSHALL CHESS: See Chapter 8.

HORST LIPPMANN: See Chapter 7.

CASH McCALL: See Chapter 8.

SCOTT CAMERON: When I hooked up with Muddy and Willie early in 1973, Chess itself was under the wing of the GRT corporation and Willie had no recording contract. The only agreement he had with GRT and Chess was a very simple production agreement he had signed with Phil Chess in the mid-1960s and a production agreement to produce Koko Taylor for the Chess label through GRT.

RALPH BASS: Muddy came to me in Europe and said, "I'm broke." All he had was his ticket—his manager had stolen all his money. I said I'll get you somebody and made some phone calls to some of the big booking agencies and see if the money was straight. I called up the Willard Alexander Agency and talked to Scott Cameron. Muddy signed with him, Muddy brought Willie in and Willie got with Scott.

WD: Ralph Bass told me, "I got Muddy with a good guy called Scott." I got talking to Muddy about it and Muddy said, "He's doing pretty good, man, because he made old Goodman and them come up with more of my money." Naturally, I got interested.

SCOTT CAMERON: Willie called me up at Willard Alexander and came down to the office. He brought his wife and a couple of kids along and they were out in the waiting room. I got off the telephone and I went around to meet him.

As he came around the corner to meet me, I came around to meet him. He's looking for a big, tall guy and I'm looking for a guy of average size. We just looked at each other and cracked up. I ended up staring at his navel, probably. It was an instant camaraderie.

I saw two people in Muddy and Willie who were living in a day of education necessity who did not have that. I had seen and heard some of the things they had gone through in their careers and they deserved to get their own piece of a pie that everyone else had eaten.

One of the most unfair things with all this is that they never got the benefit of enjoying the money they should have had. I heard all the things: "Muddy was bought Cadillacs and Muddy was bought this and that." Hell, if they'd given him his money, he could have bought his own damn car.

A lot of the songs Willie had written were personal favorites of mine. As far as music publishing, I personally thought when I met Willie Dixon that he should have been quite a wealthy man. When he first gave me his old statements, I would look down and say, "God, he has to be making more money than this."

After I started managing them and making inquiries, their royalties increased dramatically. The Chess family and the Goodmans looked at me defensively. I remember being told that persons there didn't have time to teach me the publishing business and I should stick to my booking.

My knowledge about copyrights and writers' royalties was really not that wide. I had to teach myself. I think it was late 1973 or early 1974 when I first made a trip to the Library of Congress. I spent a lot of time at the Library of Congress—at that time, everything they had was on 3x5 recipe cards. I came on a couple of agreements.

There's a little-known portion of the copyright law called employee for hire which generally is used in film and on the stage if you're scoring something for a play. A music publisher will hire a writer to write a specific score. The writer is paid a salary and the publishing company owns the rights to that song, not the writer.

I found that both Muddy and Willie, without having the wildest idea of comprehending what they were signing, signed those agreements. They were both a little shocked to find out what employee for hire meant. Muddy signed his for $2,000 under the understanding, as it was presented to him, that he was signing a straight-out songwriting agreement.

In Muddy's case, it was in fact a retroactive employee for hire signed in the early 1970s but dating all the way back to the 1950s. As I interpreted it, that meant that when one of them dies, their families don't have a right to any income derived from the copyrights. Because of that and what I felt was incorrect accounting, we filed a lawsuit against the Arc Music Corporation and its principals, which included some of the Chess family and Gene and Harry Goodman, which was subsequently settled prior to reaching court.

WD: We could have gotten a bigger and better cash deal out of it but we both were green about what was happening. By never being able to accomplish any real money out of these things, you never know where to start. The main thing is I got all my songs back and those that I didn't get back right away, they'll come back to me gradually as the years roll around.

SCOTT CAMERON: The legal basis of the action for Willie was mostly dealing with the employee for hire. I felt I had to get him and Muddy back the rights to their own copyrights so not only could they appreciate something regularly for as long as they would live but their families could benefit from what they created and not have a cold door slammed in their face.

One of the points that worked in our favor is that he was not given a weekly salary. It was an advance against royalties and that's where they had the employee for hire worked in. He was paying himself to work for them and he was paid at a figure that was ridiculously low compared with the amount of money that his copyrights were regularly providing.

He never had to go to work and he'd have made just as much money. The one thing about going to the studio was continuing to get his music recorded and out there, which kept the snowball going of royalties coming in.

MALCOLM CHISHOLM: As far as count, Will was screwed over by Chess and Goodman. I know for a fact that 10% of Chess records were sold by Chess but it wasn't by Leonard. It was the people on the shipping dock. Leonard was a firm believer in letting everybody steal as long as they didn't steal too much and he never could quite understand that engineers won't. If you stole too much, Leonard would get rid of you but everybody in the company was stealing a little bit—it gave them an interest.

AL DUNCAN: The first Chess studio was a garage on Cottage Grove. I used to leave every day from the studio and Sonny Woods would tell me, "Hey, Al, you getting ready to go? Would you drop this package off down at the record store for me?" I didn't know what was happening so I said, "Yeah, I'll be glad to. Give me a big old bag there."

I'd take 'em down to the record store. Sonny was cleaning up. Finally Chess caught him and fired him and called him right back. He couldn't get rid of Sonny because Sonny knew the number of every album that Chess had and Chess didn't know himself.

DICK LAPALM: When they released things, there were four people at the company that the brothers, specifically Leonard, would play a record for. One was a girl named Cary Sanders in the accounting department, another was Sonny Woods in the stock room.

Sonny was the best because he was very blatant—he'd listen to something and go, "This ain't shit," or "Put that motherfucker out." When he heard "High-Heeled Sneakers," he said, "Let's get that one on the street right away." The others were Dotty Lange, a Southern white also in the accounting department, and Willie.

There were a number of people who would just hang out and write and fight for studio time but Willie always had preference. He had priority as far as the brothers Chess for almost everything.

SCOTT CAMERON: Willie was always kind of looked down on, from what I've read and heard, as Chess' guy, unless it came to a point where he would point out that something was wrong to an artist and all of a sudden he was against the Chesses. Willie always seemed to be on a tightrope.

They kind of kept him in a corner, in the studio producing, writing, a sideman. They didn't promote him as an artist because his value to them was to keep him in the studio working with people like Muddy and Wolf.

WD: Pretty good artists would come from other places and Chess would make songs and a contract with 'em and he wouldn't give them money. He would have the artist thinking he was going to release the tune in a certain amount of time and he never would.

A lot of times they would do that to keep the artist from recording with somebody else. People would call and Chess would say, "Yeah, he recorded for me and don't record him." I remember Leonard Allen, the one who had United and States Records, told me about asking Chess if certain artists belonged to him and he said, "Yeah, you don't make a record on this guy. I just recorded him and I'm gonna release him." Then he never would

A lot of times it would make a guy disappointed because he recorded his best material and couldn't go somewhere else. A lot of record companies did this at that particular time, you know. Any recording company that's got out four records has got 15 they didn't put out. Me and Memphis Slim found out the best way to do that is record all you can with everybody you could and that's what we did.

RON MALO: An independent record company was a bust your ass and make your record thing. Leonard literally went on the road to promote his records. He went to the disc jockeys and slipped them their $5-10. That was big payola for these little R&B disc jockeys but it wasn't payola. It was thank you for playing my record and in some cases the disc jockeys were happy to get the records because there wasn't that much R&B recorded material to play.

Nobody would record the blues people but the little guys and only the black radio station would play the R&B stuff so there wasn't much. When I was working at WJLV in Detroit in the early 1950s, one of the disc jockeys got fired because somebody at the station opened a record and it had $15 in it. It was that down low at the R&B stations.

It got bigger. I can remember delivering envelopes. I'd go to Detroit to visit my folks and I would be told that Joe would pick up this envelope at my folks' house at eight o'clock on Saturday night. At eight o'clock, *knock, knock.* "I'm Joe. You have something for me? Thank you. Good night."

I don't know who was picking up the money or what it was for, but it was a plain white envelope for somebody. I remember people that worked for us who would be going to Philadelphia or wherever and they'd be carrying envelopes. It wasn't dealing in dope or anything like that.

Malcolm [Chisholm] told me that one thing Chess wasn't involved with is the syndicate. Leonard managed to sidestep syndicate take-over when the other companies in Chicago couldn't. He had good relations with the syndicate people.

The blues and gospel people would usually rather sign with Chess Records than some of the other companies that had screwed them. If they were going to get screwed, they would rather get screwed by Leonard because Leonard at least was honest about it. I never heard any griping about Leonard and I certainly heard a lot about other record companies.

SCOTT CAMERON: I think the black artists from the late 1940s through the mid-1960s really had very little choice as to whom they recorded for. In the long run, it was maybe better to have a bad deal and something out there than no deal. The great white hope labels were not signing those particular artists—the choices were independent labels.

The word I'd heard from everybody for years was that they got ripped off. They heard it, they talked about it and they knew. They just didn't know what to do or how to go about it. They found it very hard to put their trust in anyone.

The artists were always looking for their little royalty check. That's the way they always put it to me—"Yeah, I'm waiting for my little royalty check"—because it was never big and in their mind it was never going to be big. It's just something they get twice a year and whether it's $800, $8,000 or $80,000, that's what they get. They had no idea that they could challenge this and had absolutely no knowledge of how they could.

They never had a lawyer look at their contracts. It was like a family affair. Somebody would put something in front of them with a pen, say sign it, and *zip*, they'd sign it, take the money and run.

"I'm not gonna turn down anybody that's going to give me money" was the mentality of the blues people. They lived from hand to mouth. If they could go sell a song of theirs for $50 to a publisher, they'd sign every right in the world away for 50 bucks. They needed that 50 bucks to get from New York to Philadelphia or Chicago to Detroit, or to pay the rent or because the kids were hungry.

WD: I can't remember anybody in the whole Chess organization that would admit, among the others, that they had justice. Sometimes you just get in a position where you can't say anything. It's better just doing like I was doing, take what I could get and be satisfied because there wasn't anything better out there.

I can definitely say, of all the things I produced for the Chess company, I never got one cent for any arrangements or part of anything but the writing. They would list themselves as producers and they never produced nothing but arguments. If you don't think so, listen to Sonny Boy Williamson's "Little Village."

MALCOLM CHISHOLM: Leonard would occasionally function as a session producer not so much in the sense of "That's good enough" but in the sense of "I don't think I'm going to be able to sell any of these." Leonard had a very strong feeling about records and I heard him quote the line any number of times: "Fuck hits. Give me 30,000 on everything I put out." Considering his half of the estate was settled for 28 million dollars and he was in business for 20 years, it wasn't a bad business philosophy.

Mostly his production work consisted of: "We're going to do these tunes with this artist and why don't we get these guys." He was also a firm knothead, to his credit—when he thought something was right he'd go for it. He functioned very well as the theatrical kind of producer (the one who puts up the money and hires the musicians) and was then, by and large, perfectly content to let the people on the floor do the job. Will would run 'em off in a corner somewhere and rehearse them a bit and we'd do the session.

DAVID MEYERS: Chess was a funny guy. He did things when it popped up, on the spur of the moment. If he got something set up to cut you, when the day comes you're supposed to record, you don't see or hear from him. After that he would call you right in and say we're gonna cut it and it throws everybody off. On "My Babe," I was in a pool hall that day shooting pool so how the hell is he going to find me?

When we cut with Little Walter, the only thing I thought Dixon was into was the song. He would just play his bass and elaborated some to the guys about how the song should be expressed. Otis Rush, I think he was up on these sessions because you can hear nothing but Dixon in Otis' music but, with Little Walter, we already had what we wanted together.

LUTHER TUCKER: Willie Dixon was almost like a second boss man. Everybody would go to him and say, "How you think this should go?" He'd just sit there on the stool right by where his bass was and say, "This is how it's going to go and this is what you do."

The only complaint I had was me and Leonard Chess didn't get along too good. He'd say, "Why don't you get somebody that knows what they're doing?" I'm so proud that Little Walter, Muddy Waters, Willie Dixon and Howlin' Wolf were all in my corner. It was a nice feeling but when I recorded Little Walter they would take my bass and since Willie Dixon had just about put it all together, he would go over my bass part with his bass and that set me in the background a little farther.

JIMMY ROGERS: After we would get through with a session, Dixon would be one of the men who had a little say so—like "This should be this way or take this out," overdubbing, things like that. Dixon had a big hand there because he was working around the studio just about all the time. He didn't do any performing at all when he got his foot in the door.

WD: Any time they thought it wasn't quite right in certain places, they'd always try to see which way I could straighten it out to make it sound better. I overdubbed so many different things for different people that it's hard for me to tell. You couldn't get a lot of guys to say the complete word at the ending of a song and sometimes I even used to dub my voice at the end.

They didn't have but two tracks. Sometimes you'd overdub one track and if you've done a good one here and you're gonna repeat the same thing and the next one wasn't good, you'd have to take out that whole piece of tape and put in another one. A lot of people never knew they were dubbed.

AL DUNCAN: There was a close relationship between the abilities of Willie and Leonard Chess. Willie knew all about music and Chess knew all about business. Neither one interfered and Chess, smart as he was, kept a lot of things from Willie, assuming that he didn't know. Willie knew but Willie didn't say anything.

Chess was in a position to form a monopoly because he had an empire. He had Willie Dixon to find, develop and record the artist. He would take the artists' master and send it to his own pressing plant and press it. He would put it in his own distribution company and then play the record on his own radio station. That's all there is to the business. That's the position he was in when he died.

Chess was a phenomenal person. He was a brain and what made it so bad was that the cat had a magnetic personality. He'd be sitting up patting you on the back, grinning and telling you how great you was and be laughin' all the way to the bank. You wound up without anything and he got all your money in his pocket.

RON MALO: Leonard Chess was a one-man operation just as Berry Gordy was at Motown. To paraphrase Leonard's favorite line, "I don't want to know about that bullshit. I don't care if it's technically great as long as it sells." One of his more famous quotes was, "If shit is gold, we'll sell shit." Leonard was a very practical person.

One of our little jokes about Chess Records was that normally you have a command structure in the corporation with a president and it breaks down into different departments. The chart at Chess was like a bicycle wheel. It had a hub and that was Leonard Chess and everything else was a circle around it. Leonard would even fix the toilets himself rather than have a plumber fix a $6.95 valve.

MALCOLM CHISHOLM: There's an odd relationship there, and to understand that, you have to realize that Will Dixon, who is a more than ordinarily bright man, tricked Leonard Chess, who died thinking Will was stupid. Will had the best stupid act going that I may have ever seen in my life. I didn't find out that Will was an intelligent man until I had been working with him for two years and that was because he let me. Leonard never did, I think, find out but there's an excuse for that.

We had artists like Muddy Waters, who was a little above average intelligence, I think, and never made any attempt to conceal it. Howlin' Wolf, who was one of the greatest musical talents I've ever come across, was bone-stupid, unless *his* act *was* the best thing I have ever seen. He had the paranoia of the very stupid man. He was paranoid from the day we knew him and Little Walter was the same way. So there was something for Leonard to hang his hat on in the idea that Will was a great musical talent but not very bright.

WD: What Malcolm is probably talking about is when they would try to get me to sign a lot of different papers about signing my rights away. I had knowledge enough to read a paper and know the meaning of power of attorney and a few things like this. Naturally, I wouldn't let on that I knew like that around Chess. I wouldn't get involved with them and they'd have to take it to an attorney and they didn't want to fool with it then.

A lot of the other guys would say, "Yeah, give me some money. I don't give a damn what you do with the songs, man." I never would tell the guy the song is yours. I'd say I'd sell the song but I always put such a price on it they wasn't going to give it to me.

They'd say, "We can't give it to you, but if you sign this, we'll do this."

"No, I don't want to sign."

"Well, what are we going to do? We can't put this song out."

That's the reason, I guess, they always had a lot of songs of mine available there that they had recorded but they couldn't release. It wasn't no smart act—it was just the idea of somebody underestimating your ability.

SCOTT CAMERON: I believe Gene Goodman still feels like Willie is dumb and unworldly. I find it distasteful when I have to put Willie in the same room with Gene Goodman because he talks to him in plantation talk and m.f. this and m.f. that. I think that's talking down to Willie rather than accepting Willie as an equal who may not have had as complete and proper an education.

WD: You couldn't get nothing from Goodman unless Chess agreed and 10 to 1 you couldn't get nothing from Chess unless Goodman agreed. I tried to discuss things with Goodman but how the hell are you going to talk to Goodman? He'd never have time. I've even called in from Chicago: "Man I'm coming in here because I want to discuss that."

He'd tell me to be here at two o'clock and I'd be there before two and he had something else to do. If you stayed there for three days, he still wouldn't have time. They'd use anything or nothing for an excuse. They'd just wear you out and keep you sitting around there.

MARSHALL CHESS: I felt my father and uncle had a really high esteem for Willie. He was one of the extended family, definitely a Chess guy. I'm really speaking of this heyday period because in the later 1960s, when my father got into radio, Willie did less work at Chess because the blues weren't selling and the resurgence hadn't begun.

At one point, the blues was a major part of the business. By the late 1950s, when we started selling Chuck Berry and Bo Diddley to whites, the volume was an immense difference. A blues would do 20–30,000 copies, nothing in comparison, and that would be a hit.

Our first album hit was Argo 628, *But Not For Me: Live At The Pershing* by Ahmad Jamal. That was recorded in 1958 and we were shocked at how much money we were making. The album business was a new thing—in those days, we'd get album covers from one place, records from another and inner sleeves from a third and have to assemble everything.

We put out *The Blues, Volumes 1–4* in the early 1960s so we were not that far behind with the albums. It's when we got the first inkling that we could make money with it. It wasn't like CBS where they say, "We're gonna put out $2 million and hope it clicks." This was a family-type business; get as many sides as you can in three hours and make as big a profit as you can.

Many times my father would put out a record, always on a Friday, and he'd have the radio covered so it would be blasted. You could buy a blues record in Chicago Friday and Saturday night until two in the morning and we put 'em out just to make money on the weekends.

We were distributing our own records and a Muddy record, when you knew you'd do 6–7,000, that was $6,000. That was a lot of money. It might not have been a giant hit but it was quick in your pocket.

Arc was the publishing company and they definitely tried to get every song into Arc. Look at the publishers with any label—that's what all independent, first generation record guys did then. It was part of the thing to try and get all of an artist's songs.

They made the rules and they didn't follow any models. They had no idea at all what publishing would be worth. A song was finished aside from what your single made.

SCOTT CAMERON: I think the real relationship was between Gene Goodman and Leonard Chess. I think the Goodmans and the Chesses worked out a 50–50 deal on who owned Arc Music and the Goodmans took care of all the publishing and the Chesses took care of the recording.

There are a lot of ways in creative accounting to melt down a dollar because a lot of the blues income is foreign. The way that some publishers have done it is they'll set up wholly owned companies in several different countries.

If you earn a dollar in France, the company they own in France will retain 50% of it and send it to another wholly owned company in Switzerland who will retain 50% again, another quarter. They'll send the quarter to another wholly owned company in England, who will send 12½% to the wholly owned company in America, who will give 6¼% out of the dollar to the writer, if that.

I'm not a lawyer but it's my understanding that these sub-publishing agreements from one company to another like that are not illegal. It's a question of ethics rather than legality. You hear about these motion pictures that make millions of dollars and the star never gets a penny of his percentage because of creative accounting.

After I got the 100% copyright renewals, I found it was more than I thought it was. I didn't understand the entire scope of getting them. I understand it now as we've recovered them and collecting ourselves world-wide what a tremendous difference it is. It's like getting a dollar on a dollar instead of a quarter on a dollar.

The statements back in the 1950s and 1960s were all handwritten. Some publishers have forgotten to account particular songs on statements. I would be certain, too, that on some royalty statements from some publishers, you get 33 ⅓% instead of 50% when there's a lot of money in it.

I'm certain that major publishers make mistakes and not necessarily contrived mistakes. It's being human and I'm certain that somewhere down the line any songwriter of prominence has missed a few dollars here and there.

But I think there are instances where those misses are perpetrated from the beginning to be missed. Especially on the older blues labels, I think the record company and publishing company wing, if it was house-owned, would get together and decide on the numbers they would provide.

WD: Goodman was interested in Ghana because I began to tell him about different things. After I found out I wasn't getting my proper royalty statements, I tried to figure a way that I could get other people to claim one of my things and put them in my publishing company. Some of them I had split like that with me and another guy like J.B. or Leake.

The Goodmans and Chess couldn't bother me, because they made an agreement with Ghana and they didn't know Ghana was mine for a long time but they started catching on to it. When they found out I owned Ghana, naturally they would want to get it, too.

Goodman wasn't paying me all all my money but at the same time I wasn't getting very much accounting from other places. I had quite a few songs going overseas that I couldn't actually keep proper communications with the sub-publishing, you know, and I was trying to book all that stuff at the same time.

Something is better than nothing, especially when I had been running overseas and putting these songs down in other places and didn't have correct business arrangements to contact them backwards and forwards and Goodman was doing it all the time, anyway. We reached a decision that he would pay me a percentage in collecting on it and that's what we did. He offered me a reasonable sum of money to accept it so what else could I do?

The early sessions for Chess, they were only making 45s and these 45s were selling pretty good but we didn't have an idea of the impact it was making around the world. When we'd go to ask people about our record sales and like that, you wouldn't believe some of my early royalty statements after the songs had been out there as long as they was.

A lot of times, Goodman forgot to pay certain songs and I'd have to warn him. Arc would send it to Chess and Chess would take me to the bank when I'd get it and say, "You got to shell me out this much," depending on what I made.

If I got as much as $5,000, I'd say I'd have to give him at least $1500 although he was getting his money off the recording and everything else. The God's honest truth, if I didn't give him that money, he threatened me all the time: "You know, I've already got the money and I don't have to give you a straight count. If you don't treat me right, I'm going to do what I'm supposed to do in the first place." I would always write on my statement when I gave Chess some money back.

I just let him have the money to keep from going into all the argument. Leonard himself told me, "If I happen to hear you're going to tell somebody about what they're getting, you gotta get your own, you know." I know I never got a true accounting from him but I felt like you have to pay something to get something.

Phil had a different attitude—I'd say Phil even had a little heart, you know. He always had a pretty good thought but a lot of people aren't going against their own brothers or sisters or kinfolks whether it's right or wrong.

After Leonard died and I'd get the record company royalty statement, Phil would say, "Hey, I ain't gonna do like Leonard did, make you pay me so much money, so get me a couple of silk shirts." He wouldn't care if I didn't get him anything but I always tried to remember.

Leonard always told everybody when you'd come in there with a song that if your song didn't have a copyright don't worry about it because the publishing company has the copyrights in your name. But I found out the publishing company did copyright some in your name and those they didn't want they didn't copyright.

Luckily enough, most of mine the company didn't publish and sell, I got a chance to see my name on the label. Naturally, they wouldn't put it on the label unless I wrote the song. A lot of times they'd take my songs, and put other people's names on the labels.

Chess would write in other people's names on anybody's songs if he thought he could get away with it. They wanted to do that—write my name in on songs that I hadn't done—on a couple of occasions but I wouldn't accept it.

After Sonny Boy Williamson died, people at Chess came up and wanted to put my name on some of his things. Max Cooperstein one time said, "I don't see why you won't go on and put your name on there. He's dead."

I don't want nobody to give me nothing. I wanted my own thing and here you want to give me somebody else's and then you'll be taking mine. I just wouldn't accept it. I want my stuff, only mine. I know one thing—if a guy takes from him to me, he'll take from me to give to somebody else. That's the old philosophy of my mother's—do unto others like you want them to do unto you.

I'm practically certain there was no change when the rock bands started covering my songs because I don't feel like I was getting justice then. They would always try to sweet talk me with a lot of things and they expected me to believe 'em. But when your head's in the lion's mouth, you can't snatch it out or be too rough. You just have to be cool until you get in a better position.

RON MALO: Chess did not belong to the RIAA so we never got official RIAA gold records. Leonard would not open his books for RIAA certification so he made up his own gold records and gave them to his artists. He didn't want anybody to know, officially, how many records we'd sold. That was the way he worked, not that he was dishonest. He just didn't feel it was anybody's business.

Leonard was a shrewd businessman but Leonard lived up to his contractual agreements. You didn't have to have a contract in writing. If you negotiated, you generally came out on the short end because he was a good negotiator.

MALCOLM CHISHOLM: How many records Chuck Berry sold or Muddy Waters sold, who knows? Whether this was intentional cheating of the artists, I kind of doubt. Leonard, in his own way, was a fairly ethical man. Leonard took care of his people, a typical small businessman. You may not make a lot of money but if anything goes wrong, he did really take care of his people any number of times.

JIMMY ROGERS: Chess was like the Quiz Kid. He knew the answers and if you would come up and approach him from an angle of the situation, he'd always have his way of answering the question in his favor. We couldn't prove it otherwise.

WD: Leonard definitely wouldn't let you know about hidden things. He always felt that certain things was just his business and not yours. When I'm doing business with you, it's yours and what he's doing with somebody else is over there and like that. He was just like the average businessman and he felt like the majority of people felt like at that particular time. There wasn't any law that was forcing him to do all the things legitimate with black people.

There wasn't any law the black man had that the white man had to respect because nobody paid attention to the 14th and 15th amendments. After the Martin Luther King era, people found out that if you didn't treat the black folks like they treat the white ones, they could be sued and the government agreed. That's the reason things started getting better on behalf of black people because they had laws that other people had to respect. They didn't have to respect the law before then and Leonard knew that.

I felt like Leonard was just doing the things like the majority of the people were doing at that time. Leonard had the full say of everything because he was the one that had established the company.

Leonard would take it away from the little fellow and make his business bigger and better by dealing with the big fellow. Leonard was a businessman and what they called business in America, especially before the 1960s, was if anything wasn't against the law, it was good business.

HORST LIPPMANN: It really came to a fight between the Chess brothers and myself in 1964 or 1965, because I recorded Sonny Boy Williamson with the Yardbirds in England. The Chess brothers naturally said I'm not allowed to do this because he's under contract with Chess, which is true. But I knew they didn't live up to the contract because they didn't record Sonny Boy for a long, long time. They put him on the side and forgot him.

Only because of my recording in England with the Yardbirds did they start recording him again so they didn't live up to the contracts for years. Plus I had the feeling that this contract was pre-dated because they didn't even think to sign it in time.

They had a black lawyer, Willie Dixon was present at the office and also Chuck Berry, who at that time was just getting out of prison because of some thing with a girl in the South. I had this thing with the Chess brothers and blamed them that this was sort of a new slavery, what they were doing to their black artists. That turned even their black lawyer on my side and Willie Dixon really got pale because nobody thought to have the nerve to talk to the Chess brothers like this so the situation changed after this fight.

WD: That's why Chess didn't want us to record over there because

Horst had been givin' 'em hell about what they were doing to the musicians. The people in America were trying to force the people over there to give us great big money and they weren't giving us any money in the States. Lippmann was coming up and giving us more money on accident than we was getting on purpose over here.

If it had been left to Chess, there wouldn't have been no blues festivals over there. Chess didn't mind Horst taking 'em back over if Horst made a deal through them but they didn't want him to make a deal with artists by themselves. I might have told Horst to be careful because the Chesses didn't want him to record their artists and take them back over there without some kind of deal with them.

HORST LIPPMANN: The Chess brothers said they will sue me and I said, "Yeah, go ahead and sue me." But they didn't do it because they knew if it came to a boil, they might have lost the case. They tried to work with me like they got used to with the black artists because they thought this guy comes from Europe and he doesn't know anything. But I'm not that type of person.

My experience with the Gestapo, I had to face that, you know, so that's harder than the Chess brothers. I must say the Chess brothers did a lot for the blues but they did even more for their own money. That's okay in a way—only when they do tricky things, then it becomes problematic.

MARSHALL CHESS: Every independent little record company of that era was treating their artists the same way. So many guys sold songs or did things to get that $1,000 or $2,000. My father was a businessman—a guy comes to you, he wants to sell you this, he needs the money, you know? It seemed like they were just doing normal kinds of business. The company very much ran out of Leonard's pocket. It was a family business but he was definitely the king.

CASH McCALL: You got your money right out of the pocket. There was a beautiful lady there named Dot Lange who had worked for Chess for 20 years. She had a loyalty to Chess that cannot be questioned and she didn't betray her trust in the company, but she would tell you to get your business straight. As you know, most didn't listen.

There was a saying going around at the time, "If you find a fool, you whup his head." Unfortunately, there were a lot of fools. I won't count myself as being one of the privileged ones—it went in one ear and out the other. Another saying was going around at the time—"Fool me once, shame on you. Fool me twice, shame on me."

I don't have any bitter feelings and I haven't felt from Willie that he does. He always had a phrase that made all the sense in the world to me: "Don't get mad. Get smart."

I don't care for Arc Music and I don't have any qualms about you quoting me on it. Leonard and Phil had a hand in it in some way. My differences did mostly center around Arc Music even though I knew the Chess brothers weren't unapprised of the situation.

I can say this—if Leonard told you he was going to do something, he was a man of his word. If he gave you his word on something, put it in the bank. With Phil, the same thing.

When Willie started opening up my eyes and explaining the music business to me and I started understanding, I started speaking up. When I played hardball with Leonard and Phil, I'd get some satisfaction. You have to speak up for your rights.

Fear is the thing which kills most of it. You figure you're doing what you like and if you raise a stink, you create a lot of problems and a lot of people just didn't want to be bothered. I can't say they were just some dirty bastards and leave it hanging because they also returned something.

I found a lot of areas to disagree with company policy but I dare say this—in the sum total of it, his music was black music. For whatever differences the people who worked there might have had, when you walked up on that sixth floor, you had a lot of black people employed up there.

11

Now all you girls that think that your days are done
You don't have to worry, you can have your fun
Take me, baby, for your little boy
You get three hundred pounds of heavenly joy

This is it, this is it
Look what you get

You've been sneakin' and hiding behind his back
Because you got a man that you don't like
Now throw that man, baby, out of your mind
And follow me, baby, and have a real good time

Hoy, hoy, I'm the boy
You get three hundred pounds of heavenly joy
I'm so glad you understand
You get three hundred pounds of muscle and man

The demise of Chess Records hit Willie Dixon hard, stripping him of his chief source of regular income and the main outlet for his music for most of the previous 20 years. But the new, wide-ranging awareness of the importance of Chicago blues left another avenue open for him: a return to performing.

Through the continuing stream of cover versions of his songs performed by leading rock bands in the late 1960s, Willie Dixon had become a certified blues legend and he put together a new version of the Chicago Blues All-Stars in 1969 to reactivate his career as a solo artist. The first edition included Johnny Shines (guitar/vocals), Sunnyland Slim (piano), Walter "Shakey" Horton (harmonica) and Clifton James (drums). Dixon had sufficient name recognition to land a deal with Columbia, which released I Am The Blues, *a nine-song collection featuring his versions of some of the most popular songs that rock artists had re-worked.*

But he was continuing to record other artists and write fresh material. Dixon released the Peace *album on his own Yambo label in the early 1970s, recorded a 1973 collection for Spivey Records in New York.* Catalyst *and* What Happened To My Blues *came out on Ovation in 1973 and 1977, respectively; both records received Grammy nominations.*

His Yambo label put out singles by Koko Taylor, Margie Evans, Lucky Peterson and McKinley Mitchell. Dixon even showed up outside Cincinnati's Riverfront Stadium on the night in 1974 when baseball slugger Hank Aaron broke Babe Ruth's home run record. He was there to sell copies of "That Last Home Run," the song Dixon wrote and Mitchell sang on a Spoonful single to commemorate that feat.

In 1967, the Dixon family had moved from its long-time Calumet address to a new home at 7636 Throop Street, far from the heart of the old South Side blues scene. Not that the musical activity tapered off—when the constant rehearsals got too noisy for the neighbors, Dixon purchased a storefront around the corner at 7711 Racine and turned it into the Blues Factory studio. And those home front activities were balanced against the demands of a performing schedule which kept him on the road for six months of the year annually until 1977.

PHIL UPCHURCH: See Chapter 6.

SHIRLEY DIXON: Willie Dixon's daughter.

CLIFTON JAMES: See Chapter 7.

I was still working with Chess when this fellow Abner Spector came along. He was the go-between between me and the Columbia record company on this particular deal. I've been trying to get in touch with the guy ever since then because the royalty statements from the company say we're still in the hole today.

He recorded some of the best of my tunes that I had out there at the time, like "I Just Wanna Make Love To You," "Little Red Rooster," and all like that. Columbia said they were going to release three albums and they only released one, *I Am The Blues.*

They had a truck strike for six weeks that started the same day they released the Columbia album. They had a bunch of 'em pressed up and I couldn't get the doggone things myself for nearly a year. I was right there in Chicago where they were supposed to have plenty of them.

It could have got pretty good exposure but you'd call for it and couldn't get it. Some guy up north had a distributorship for Columbia and I'm the one who went up there and sold just about all the ones he had. I was sellin' 'em right and left, because I didn't want it to die out before the publicity stopped.

People were calling for the record for the four or five weeks they had it advertised after it was released but by the time the strike was over, hell, folks had got into something else. A record is a funny thing. If people can't get a record while they're in the mood and while people are playing it, they get tired of trying to get that record and they go for another one.

I had a chance to do some producing with several different labels but you ask some of the other artists and they say, "Man, they're talking a lot of baloney." It's just like B.B. King once asked me about coming to Chess in the early 1960s when him and Chess were just about to get together.

I told B.B., "Look, you'd be doing the wrong thing if you worked for Chess," and he didn't get with him. I don't know whether I was the cause of it but I knew damn well what Chess was doing to everybody else. Why the hell should you get on the same boat?

I had been getting my record companies, Yambo and Spoonful, together off and on for some time but I never had produced anything on them. Every time I would get somebody for my label that sounded pretty good, I'd wind up letting Chess have them.

I really didn't put nothing out until the latter days of Chess.

I found out that if you produce an artist and don't have sufficient things to give him the proper publicity and advertise him like you should, it's just a waste of time. You just got a lot of good material sittin' there doing nothing so I'd get me somebody who'd probably do something with it rather than keep it on the shelf.

A lot of people wouldn't really take the number unless they had a good recording on it because if you bring the song to the average man in the rough, he can't see it or hear it. After you get it halfway shaped up, then they'd get interested.

There was a woman named Miss Jones who brought the Jackson 5 over to my studio at 7711 S. Racine when they were young but I wasn't there. She was trying to get me to record 'em. I didn't have nothing to record 'em with because I had sunk my little bit of money into Lucky Peterson, the little five-year-old boy who was playing organ.

I had done a few recordings on him and started getting him on television and radio around there. By the time I got him to a place where he could make some money, his old man run amok and decided he wasn't going to let him come out to this school. I had a school yard full of 4,000 people, rented the organ and had everything set up in the middle of the field and this boy didn't show up. I called up and Lucky answered the phone and said, "My daddy won't let me come."

This boy and I could have been heavy in the chips. Everybody remembered him even more than the Jackson 5 at that time because he was five years old, playing and singing. I recorded him and he was doing a song called "1-2-3-4" and "Good Old Candy." All this would relate to kids, you know, and every kid in Chicago damned near was singing those songs. Then I had to fall out with his old man and Lucky ain't done nothing since.

I know a lot of guys right now who could make it good but they're not gonna make it because they ain't got nobody to nurse them. I lost about $25–30,000 trying to get this Lucky Peterson over in practicing the guys to get ready for the recording session and the actual session. I had to take it to the radio station and pay through the nose to get the record I made played.

I even had Columbia Records, the central A&R man up there, check him out. When the guy came back, he told me the boy is beautiful and can get over big but you're going to have trouble with his old man. I had him playing guitar along with his son in the band and was paying him extra money.

"For what? I got him under contract, too."

"Yeah, but the contract don't mean a damn thing. The guy doesn't have what it takes to understand progress in any form and you'll never make it with him."

I had my Blues Factory studio with Ed Winfield and Ed said, "Well, Dixon, we're gonna have to string along with him." Every time Lucky's father would call up he would have something to say that was wrong. Frankly, I think the old man was a little jealous of Lucky. Finally I was cussing out everybody.

I had to run backwards and forwards up to Buffalo, New York, where the old man had a little tavern, just trying to keep communicating and get this thing together for him. They had a lawyer up there in Buffalo named Rabo and Lucky's father was telling me about Rabo was going to do this.

I had a contract on Lucky and we finally wound up filing suit against Rabo and made a deal that they were going to give me all the money I spent on Lucky Peterson. They sent part of the money for a little while but the last couple of thousand I never got.

But I made an arrangement that Lucky couldn't play nowhere without my consent. He played a couple of places and we snatched the money at the last minute so they had to start him playing with other groups.

I used to train these guys and get them in good shape. The average big company knows the deal so well they aren't gonna fool with someone until they are in good shape. That's why the average individual has to pay their dues because the company knows all the little hassles they're going to be bothered with—like if you don't have some management, you ain't going nowhere.

The average person doesn't give you respect if you don't have somebody considered as your agent. If you ask for money or anything yourself, they can't see it but if you have somebody representing you, they can. I was a representative for Lucky and a lot of people knew me from the Chess organization. They figured if Dixon's got him, he must be good.

I was doing all these things for everybody else and couldn't do it for myself so I had to get a manager. I tried to get Ed Winfield to manage me and put Ed Winfield right in my own quarters. It was working pretty good for a while but Winfield had matrimonial troubles, too, and naturally I had to drop him. He really wasn't my partner.

An artist wants to find out what you can do for him and he hasn't done a damn thing for himself. He hasn't got money or somebody to help support some of these things you need, he doesn't know how to sing or how to express things. Somebody has to start from that low end with him and work him up.

By the time you work him up to where he's pretty good, here come the leechers—the guys with the money sayin', "I can do this for you" but they couldn't do it until somebody else got him in shape. They don't want to give you credit for anything. You won't get a quarter back for all that long time you did.

Frankly, I had said I was going to slow down on my performing. I booked Leake and Matt Murphy, just about anybody that needed booking. Some I'd get commissions for pay and some I wouldn't.

I booked this fella Big Moose and a drummer down in Texas. I sent 'em down there for three weeks and gave 'em enough money to go down on their own. They were going to send me back 10% but them guys went down there and stayed five years and I didn't get a quarter. Every once in a while one of 'em would write a card: "I'm doing this and we're gonna take care of you."

I had a little, two-story house at 7636 Throop. I got a nice big garden spot on the side where I used to raise everything. I miss it because I'd get all my fresh vegetables there all summer. I raised everything around there to eat—beans and vegetables, watermelon, cantaloupe, you name it.

In the garage back there, that's where Muhammad Ali's first Cadillac is nailed up. I used to book Steppin' Fetchit different places and he was down in Kentucky during the time Ali was getting ready for the fight with Sonny Liston. Somehow or other, he said Muhammad Ali gave him the Cadillac. He kept it awhile—somebody kept it awhile because the engine was in bad shape but I had it remodelled by a fella down on Wabash and 22nd.

Step kinda got in rough shape there and needed a few hundred dollars so I let him have it and he kept trying to give me the damned car. He said he was going to junk it anyway so I took it and kept it back there in my garage. Some guy offered to give me a new Cadillac for it and I wouldn't take it. Ali won the championship a second time and I found out, hell, I got me a collectors' item. After it got to be 20 years old, automatically that makes it an antique.

The Blues Factory was at 7711 Racine, about two blocks from my house when I was living at 7636 Throop. This was a place I got together just to write blues songs, where I'd be away from everybody. I had a couple of cassette machines in there and started writing a lot of songs, contacting other people and giving them songs.

PHIL UPCHURCH: Willie called me for help—like what equipment to buy—in setting his demo studio up and I came over and helped and did a few rehearsals over there. I was one of the few black guys in town with a serious recording set-up going at that time and probably the only one that was non-commercial. Willie would say, "Call Upchurch. He's into it."

He had rented out a storefront place on Racine in the 1970s and he used it for rehearsals, making demos, pre-production. They didn't call it pre-production in those days—they just called it rehearsing for the sessions. The kids were helping him operate the stuff, too. He talked about perhaps eventually having a full-blown studio, which is generally what's in the back of most people's heads when they're putting a demo studio together.

WD: I was using the studio as a place to try to educate my kids, keep 'em out of the streets, messin' with dope and stuff, you know. I'd have 'em all come in the studio and they'd be playing, singing, typing, recording instruments and all like that.

SHIRLEY DIXON: We always had a little studio under our home before he bought the Blues Factory and was able to have real music sessions. Phil Upchurch was the teacher—he was teaching us how to run all the equipment and chose all the equipment that Daddy would have here. He taught us how to run the studio and make recordings. I always did his typing for him so I got a chance to see a lot of his songs.

When he'd come in from the road, it would be the same routine. He'd always work there and there would always be artists waiting to see him or someone calling for him or someone that would be recording and want him to sit in or help with their arrangements. When he was at home during this period, he was either working with artists or helping to teach students. He did a lot of seminars during that time, on the blues and where it came from and where it was made.

WD: At first, I would be at Chess until four or five o'clock, and then go home and I'd meet half the gang that was at Chess right at the house and start a new thing. I used to let everybody practice there until the neighbors up on the second floor—we were living on the first floor— and my wife got tired of the noise.

I think I paid about $15,000 to buy the store on Racine around the corner and that's when I put the Blues Factory together. I had a mind to make a big thing of the Blues Factory but I didn't have enough money to get involved into the place in a big way so I was just doing dubbing for different people.

I made the *Peace* album there and I got some good albums of stuff that was made with McKinley Mitchell that has never been released, Willie Williams, Wild Child Butler and all of Koko Taylor's first stuff was made there. I was managing Koko when she first started but I couldn't keep up with it. When you're trying to do too damn many things without assistance, you just can't do it.

Most people, even today, automatically condemn it when you say blues because they're brainwashed against the blues. Whenever you get with somebody that might take a chance, they want to take advantage of every damn thing and don't want you to have nothing out of it. That's the reason I didn't get involved deeper.

I recorded a couple of professional things there—they were supposed to be making them for dubs and they wind up puttin' 'em on professional records. Willie Williams had a thing that got pretty popular because E. Rodney Jones, the deejay, was supposed to have been his manager. I never got my money out of it but it turned out to be a pretty popular record. From then on, I just started pushing my own songs as best I could, trying to get back in touch with some of my songs.

The Jubilee Showcase was a spiritual program on Sunday mornings on one of the big television stations in Chicago. All the different spiritual groups would show up there and I'd sit with all of them—a group, a choir, everybody.

A lot of times the guy didn't want to rehearse with me because they knew I knew all the songs. They may rearrange them but I can follow the pattern of anything. Once you're a first class musician, all you have to do is get someone to tell you what key you're in. I did that show just about every Sunday morning off-and-on for years, as long as I was there in Chicago.

When I first moved to 7636 Throop, I used to go into my basement late at night and early in the morning to write songs. Later, I had to move to 7711 Racine in order to have some peace and quiet. I always did have some kind of place where I could get away in order to think good.

You can write songs anywhere you can get the imagination and peace and quiet to think about it. Sometimes this imagination will get so strong you can be right in the middle of everything and still write it but other times you get your mind focused off into something else and the little things you need to see, you don't see. A lot of times we'd be on the road somewhere, driving along and you get ideas and the guys are asleep so you can get them together in your mind.

I used to go out in Washington Park early in the morning. They had a great big place out there where the people could drive out and park, walk out to the park and play ball and cards. I'd go out early in the morning just a little bit before the sunrise and get out of the van and walk way out in the middle of the park. You could hear the cars way off, everybody was running down here or somebody was tooting the horn over there.

Out in the middle of the park, you couldn't hear nothing. At that particular time in the morning, there wouldn't even be birds singing. The noise is way away and you go out there with something in your mind and you kind of thought about it a little bit and you can get deeply into this.

After you walk out way in the middle of this park, you can see anything coming within half a mile of you. Sometimes, I'd be out there by the little diamonds where the kids could play ball, concentrating deeply, and feel like nobody's around me. I used to be in such a deep thought that one time some guy walked all the way across that wide open space and got close enough to me to scare me. I jumped.

Sometimes I'd take my car and go way out on the edge of town somewhere in some wooded area or levelled land spot, cock my legs up on the wheel and sit out there and think. Sometimes you have the ideas together and go out there to finish it and sometimes you get your ideas together out there.

When I decide I'm going to write about something, I get the idea of what the interest of other people would be into it and how other people would feel about such a subject. Is it really worth writing about? Then you start thinking on all the related things to that subject and then the various things that sound poetically towards whatever I'm writing about.

When I go into writing something, I've got to have all that it means, all the know-how and all the understanding of it because people are definitely going to ask you what does this mean and why did you make it like that? There's an answer to all that if you wrote the song from the facts of life.

If you're writing about cars, you have to think about what the car does, why it does it and all the related things from the making of it to the end results of it. If you're going to think deeply enough about it, you gotta think where it comes from and all the various parts.

You have to think all the way back to maybe the rubber was made somewhere in Africa on some plantation, guys chopping trees to make the rubber run out. Some guy in some mine somewhere else is mining copper, another guy's cutting sheep's wool somewhere to make the interior parts of the car and another guy is in a steel mill. The things that make it run come from all different parts of the world.

A piano—you might think about somebody cutting trees to make the piano, some poor elephant that dies in Asia for the ivory that's on there, the brass and copper and paint, the nails of the carpenter—it took everybody. There's nothing one man can do that can keep us as comfortable as we are today.

The whole world, in general, helps the other part to be comfortable so it's necessary for the whole word to understand these things and remember them. A guy who ain't directly associated with you is associated with you unconsciously, one way or another.

I started using the name the All-Stars in the early 1960s. I would get various musicians I felt would be pretty good and use them as studio artists. When I'd have to go somewhere, I'd just take 'em on the road with me. Most of 'em had been a star in their own rights, anyway.

CLIFTON JAMES: I don't think I ever saw Willie getting angry. Sometimes he'd get a little angry at the guys in the Chicago Blues All-Stars. He'd lay into Buster Benton and Carey Bell but that was because maybe Carey had been drinking too much and forgot what he was doing instead of concentrating on his music the way Willie wanted it played. He would wait until the next morning and go in there and talk to him after he'd sobered up. I never saw him rake somebody over the coals publicly.

WD: Once you get a good outfit with you, it makes it so easy, you know. But when you get a bunch of those amateur youngsters, you go to tell them something and he thinks he knows every damn thing and he don't really know east from west.

These guys can be hazardous because they feel like they're young musicians and supposed to be getting high and drinking. When I discourage those kind of things, sometimes the guys get mad and that attitude shows in their music and on the stage. So I started to get to dumping them fast as I get 'em and that's the reason I've changed so often.

Guys like Shakey Horton and Sonny Boy had been drinking so long, 10-1 the only way you could tell Shakey was drunk was when he'd stand up and half-stagger around. Sonny Boy Williamson could be completely loaded but would never stagger. He was always raising hell one way or another so you wouldn't know whether he was drunk or sober.

That cat drank up a two gallon jug of something, some kind of alcohol, one time. Somebody gave him a great big jug in Germany and that sonuvagun stayed in that jug until he drank it all. Nobody else could stand to smell it.

After I got involved in playing music again, I was playing all over the world and didn't cater to too many of the places in Chicago. All of the old places was going, anyway. We always played at Biddy Mulligan's up on the North Side every time we went back there because that was kind of home for us.

Whenever we'd get back in town and wasn't playing at Biddy Mulligan's, we'd be practicing and getting ready to go on the road. The last ten years or so in Chicago, I didn't actually go to very many of the other clubs. When you're in this kind of business, you don't have time enough to stay involved in other people's things because you're trying to keep your own thing happening.

The only reason we kept the job at Biddy Mulligan's is that we'd tell people that when they came to Chicago, they could connect with us there. You'd be surprised how many people from all over the world ask you, "When I come to Chicago, where can I see you and where shall I ask for you at?" Naturally, you don't want to tell 'em your house because, boy, people can overcrowd your house in a hurry. A lot of people will drop in unannounced.

12

Blues heaven, where can this place be?
Blues heaven must be mighty sweet
Did you ever think of a blues heaven
And the many sights you can see
Where the people who always sang the blues
Could sing till e-ter-ni-ty

Like old King Cole, he sang with soul
And Bessie Smith sang so sweet
And poor old Sonny Boy sang the blues
And played his harp for me

Where the Big Bopper could blow his top
And Big Bill sang the blues
And Dinah, she sang like an evil gal
And Billie Holiday just croons

Elmore James sang dust my broom
And Sam twisting time a-way
And Blind Lemon Jefferson played the blues
Until the break of day

Did you ever think of a blues heaven
And the many sights you could see
Where the people who always sang the blues
Could sing till e-ter-ni-ty

"Blues Heaven" by Willie Dixon and Dick Lapalm
Copyright © 1965, Hoochie Coochie Music/Arc Music

One thing that could slow down Dixon did—illness. The diabetes that he had suffered from for years brought him off the road and into a Chicago hospital in 1977. Gangrene set in and his right leg was amputated above the knee.

But his financial situation was changing for the better when the revenues from his songs, the result of his 1977 settlement with Arc Music, gradually began coming to him directly. By 1980, he was again averaging about four months annually on the road, working shorter stints with revamped editions of the Chicago Blues All-Stars. There were more recordings—the Live! Backstage Access *recorded at the 1983 Montreux Jazz Festival and* Mighty Earthquake And Hurricane, *both on Pausa, were released in the first half of the decade. There were Grammy nominations for* Backstage Access *and Dixon's one live track on the* Blues Deluxe *album recorded at the 1980 Chicagofest.*

Dixon maintained that touring pace until 1983 when the Dixon family moved to southern California to escape the Chicago winter and for the greater songwriting opportunities. Dixon picked up work acting in commercials and also got involved with the movie sound-track world, producing a new version of "Who Do You Love" for Bo Diddley on the La Bamba *soundtrack and performing his own "Don't You Tell Me Nothin'" on* The Color Of Money *soundtrack. He continued writing, working with artists and recording new songs which reflected an increased concern with social issues.*

The majority of his time has been devoted to establishing the Blues Heaven Foundation, a non-profit corporation designed to increase awareness of the blues through scholarship awards and donations of musical instruments to schools. A long-range goal is providing assistance for blues artists and/or their heirs who suffered from the lack of financial safeguards in writing and recording their music.

And Willie Dixon himself was not yet through with matters of proper crediting and adequate compensation. The year of 1987 saw an out-of-court settlement of a suit filed in 1985 regarding the similarity of Led Zeppelin's heavy metal monster mash "Whole Lotta Love" to Dixon's "You Need Love." The original version of the latter was recorded by Muddy Waters in 1962 and released on an obscure Chess single but never on an album in America. But in England, the song had been a favorite rave-up tune for aspiring groups to cut their teeth on during the British blues boom of the mid and late 1960s.

Nor was Dixon through with recording. In 1988, the Hidden Charms *album (for Bug/Capitol) brought him back to the studio for the first time in the CD age. It won the 1989 Grammy for Best Traditional Blues Recording and, the same year, MCA released* The Chess Box, *a three album retrospective of Dixon songs recorded during the Chess years by the original artists as well as some of Dixon's unissued performances for the label.*

Later in 1989, Dixon returned to the studio to record his Grammy Award-nominated soundtrack for the film "Ginger Ale Afternoon." The Austrian label RST/Blues Documents also released "Gene Gilmore and the Five Breezes" that year, a collection including all eight tracks cut by the Five Breezes—the first time Dixon's earliest recordings have been available on record. And both Sweden's Dr. Horse label and Columbia have tentative plans to release collections by the Big Three Trio in 1990. The Columbia compilation marks the first time any of the group's recordings for the label have been re-issued in the U.S.

SCOTT CAMERON: See Chapter 10.

I had sugar diabetes but I was just taking a pill for it. The doctor was telling me to keep on my diet and I would never have to do more than take that pill. But how you gonna keep on a decent diet when one night you're here, one night there, one night you sleep, the next night you don't, running all over the country and trying to take pills and your medicine in time when the time is two hours different and you got to eat all that garbage out there on the road?

I had had diabetes ever since I was about 30 years old. I was overweight all the time and my pancreas was making insulin but it wasn't making enough to support the size body I was carrying around because I was around 380 pounds at one time. Little by little, I finally got down but before I got my weight down they had to amputate my leg.

I figured that as long as I took the medicine for the diabetes, it wasn't a serious thing, but a sore came on my foot when I was on a tour. I never paid attention to little things, you know, and I figured it would get well. Scott and my wife didn't want me to go on this tour of the South because it was hot but I decided I would anyway because I needed the money. Marie and Scott pulled me in off the road when my foot got sorer, but when I got back, I had to have my leg amputated.

They tried to save it first because they just cut off part of my foot but later on I had to have the whole leg amputated. Boy, I caught hell then because the diet they had me on was nothing. I had been used to eating and I was losing weight and I had a whole lot of trouble. Even after I got halfway straight, I'd start back eating again and wound up in the hospital.

When a man loses his thoughts and mind, a thing that can be made for a bad thing can also be a good thing. It all depends on the way you look at it and the way you feel about it. I feel like the early part of my life had a lot to do with my having diabetes and because of not being able to eat properly and drink various things and have the proper education and all like this. I could feel like, "Why me?" when I was just starting to get some money and recognition.

But at the pace I was going and had to go in order to survive, I feel like the diabetes actually done me a favor. Believe me, I couldn't have kept this pace up going into my 60s and survived. I'd been carrying too much weight from overeating the wrong things all my life to a certain extent.

Poor people don't have a lot of good things to eat and they had a lot of things that were definitely against them, things that gave you sugar like a lot of starches because you were trying to fill up with a little bit off of less money. This operation has slowed me down to a pace that it's hard for me to get exhausted. This really is doing me a favor and is gonna cause me to live many years longer than I would have lived under the circumstances that I was going.

It feels like a reprieve or something—it leaves me more to work with because I'll have a chance today to use some of the money I'm getting. Yesterday, at the pace I was going and not being directed into the proper foods and all these things, I might have flipped my own lid and knocked myself out.

A song I wrote like "If I Could See," nobody knows what it's like to be blind. You got an idea, but . . . like I didn't know what it was like before my leg got amputated. I figured that a man with one leg, hell, when I was a kid I used to hop all over the place with one leg but I could always drop the other leg when I got tired. It wouldn't hinder me from nothing but then when you go to put on your clothes and underclothes, I didn't think about all the complications that's involved.

Ain't no way in the world I can tell you how I felt when they took my leg off. The first time I was ever really afraid in my life was when they amputated my leg. See, I never was afraid of nothing but I got afraid when they said they were going to have to take it. I was a nervous wreck—I was lucky I didn't die from fear. After they took it, I made up my mind that other folks have done it and survived.

My mother always used to say, don't care what shape you're in, there's always somebody in worse shape. I looked over in the hospital and saw another guy—he was in much better shape than me overall but he had had both his legs taken off. He was staying right across the hall from me and this guy was telling me about how the week before, "Man, last week, I swore I would have been dead. Man, you're in good shape. At least you got one leg to walk on and you can get yourself an artificial limb."

He built me up quite a bit of hopes, you know. This guy started going on the floor and he said, "Man I ain't never had to travel like this before but I'm still traveling." That knocked me out. I said, "Hell, if this cat can lose both his then you know damn well I'm going to make it."

I had a helluva time getting accustomed to that extra leg. That stump is so tender and I began to think of it like a baby. He's gotta learn to get his feet tough. When you first go to putting on an artificial leg, you put it on five minutes and then take it off three or four times a day, then ten minutes. You don't try to walk in it, just put it on, then you learn how to stand up in it and keep trying to toughen up that place. When you get to the place where you can just walk across the room in it, you feel like you're really raising hell. Then they take you up to therapy and show you how to walk.

It'll take a good four years for you to get to where you feel like you can halfway walk with it. I fell before my leg got well and it kind of set me back a while because you fall on that open stump. I went to the damned doctor's and he wasn't in. I was sitting around there and the thing was hurting, boy, and they gave me all kinds of painkillers.

A guy was going to help me. He saw that I had this amputation and I was on two crutches. I aimed to come in the door and just as I pushed the door, he opened it, thinking he was helping me and *bam!* I hit the damned floor. By being accustomed to 60 years with a leg, the first thing you're going to do is stick out your foot and there ain't no foot there, so you fall right on that. Boy, that hurt. It started that thing to bleeding all over again.

I could always find something to do. I was even writing songs up in the hospital when I had the operation. That was about the only thing that gave me consolation. I could get my mind off it by writing songs, just think about the different places I'd been, where I'm going and what I'm going to do. It was the same year my mother died, 1977. I was on crutches when I went to see my mother's funeral.

Around 1980 I had a program I was introducing at the radio station every Sunday night. This program was just to promote the blues—a guy named Larry Streeter was handling it—and I paid for an hour show right out of my own pocket for about three or four months.

I would play my songs and everybody else's, songs of different artists from a long time ago just to keep the blues in the minds of the people. The blues was going out of the minds of people so fast right after the Chess station, WVON, considered itself closed that I really feel like the blues would have gone out. The guys at WVON started playing everything but blues and that was about the main station that had played blues.

Most of the songs you hear now I wrote years and years ago. The songs that I'm writing now you'll begin hearing 'em in a couple of months. Most blues artists haven't been able to get their rightful dues. They do the songs and lose 'em and get lost in the copyrights and publishing.

This is why so many youngsters today don't really know about the blues until they hear about 'em from some other source. They hear 'em after they've been doctored and rearranged by somebody else. A lot of times, these other people get the biggest of the royalties and everything.

My daughter first brought "Whole Lotta Love" to my attention. She was all raging about it and that's what really turned me on to it. I wasn't sure I was going to have any justice pertaining to it. We made a deal where I was satisfied and that was a very great thing as far as I was concerned because I really wasn't expecting very much.

SCOTT CAMERON: Prior to my working with Willie in a management capacity, there were two Willie Dixon songs on *Led Zeppelin I* that were properly credited, "You Shook Me" and "I Can't Quit You, Baby." When *Led Zeppelin II* came out, Arc Music brought a claim against them claiming that "Bring It On Home" was Willie's song and that "The Lemon Song" was Wolf's "Killing Floor." They had a settlement, all of this without Willie's knowledge.

I discovered it going through his royalty statements that he kept and all at once here was this huge amount of money for "Bring It On Home" out of the middle of nowhere. I contacted Arc Music and they sent me that portion of the settlement agreement which dealt with Willie.

When I was on the road with Willie or Muddy, people would say, "You know, Led Zeppelin ripped off a Willie Dixon song." We thought it was "Bring It On Home" and it had all been taken care of.

In 1962, Muddy recorded a song Willie wrote called "You Need Love" which was kind of an obscure single on Chess in America. It was never a big seller and never appeared on an album. Long John Baldry told me it was on an EP in England.

We felt that "Whole Lotta Love" was directly imitative of Willie's song. I never heard Muddy's version of "You Need Love" until Willie called me up. We had to search for it and finally found someone who would give us a tape.

I never heard a lot of Muddy's songs and I don't know all of Willie Dixon's songs today. People say the publisher should have known that and I don't think that's necessarily true. I believe with all my heart that if the publisher we're talking about thought there was money there, he'd have been knocking on the door.

The Zeppelin suit took a couple of years. The hardest point we had was what they called "latches"—the time when purportedly the thing took place versus the time when the suit was filed. As big a mega-hit as that was, should it have been known within a reasonable period after its release versus discovering it some 12 years later?

I think what got us over that hump was their not wanting to go all the way through the courtroom battle. There are areas with the settlement I'm very happy in and there were things I felt Willie should have had that we just couldn't get.

WD: When you're a writer, you don't have time to listen to everybody else's thing. You get their things mixed up with your ideas and the next thing you know, you're doing something that sounds like somebody else. Once you write a song, you can always remember certain portions of it. A lot of times I'll run into titles of songs that are the same as my song, but it's not my song. When I hear the words, I know immediately whether it's my song, words and tune.

When a person knows what his background is, it gives him a chance to be proud. The majority of things that America has damn near came from black people themselves but, regardless of what a man makes or what a man does, there was no way for him to expose his project. The one who controls him is the one who's the owner.

Naturally, the white man has control of everything that the black man had made in America, so that makes him the owner. Naturally, they didn't write the history of the guy who made it—they wrote the history of the guy who got it.

We weren't taught to read and write and understand. Nine times out of ten, you have to have a high school education before you learn the knowledge of copyrights. They got it so complicated today where you have to go through a long series of different questions to copyright a song and the people without the proper knowledge don't know.

I remember great blues artists that never had a future, that have made many great songs that blues artists from all over the world have recorded. These people were popular as blues artists and no one knows their names. No one knows their picture. They have no history of it.

With any other music, they have their rightful dues and get money on it and blues artists have been writing songs through generations. There are many millions of people that became rich from the blues and various parts of the blues and none of the blues artists today can receive one quarter because it wasn't qualified in the copyright.

All these people who never recorded need to have their blues thing properly told to the world. We don't know their names—like Little Brother Montgomery would say, hundreds of people died who never had a chance to record before there was a real recording. These people have been forgotten about.

Ma Rainey, Bessie Smith, Clara Carter—nobody knows who the heck they are unless you have been in research with records. Blind

Tom, Victoria Spivey, Jimmy Yancey, Mama Yancey, all of them. Nobody knows them, very little's been written on them, damn few people heard 'em and no one seems to care but still they use their ideas in their music up until today.

This is the reason for the Blues Heaven Foundation because we've got to correct some of the past mistakes. We aren't trying to fight. We're just trying to catch up to some of the stuff we left behind and some of the things we didn't get a chance to do.

If we can just get to some of the people that know they inherited millions through the blues, we can help some of the blues people's children or grandchildren to reap some of the benefits and have an opportunity to do something in their music and build up from their own heritage—not just of the blues, but many things.

You're gonna fly away to heaven—that's somebody else's idea and you accepted it, but the things of the blues are facts, the possible. I don't see myself flying in the air—I see heaven as a condition and hell, too. That's why I'm planning on making Blues Heaven while the majority of people that want to enjoy heaven can know and enjoy this one now and won't have to worry about the next world.

Why I'm the one to do Blues Heaven is very easy. Naturally, nobody wants to be at the bottom of the totem pole. He's there by force, not want. Somebody's got to be at the bottom of the pile, so why me? Naturally, everybody wants a better condition and if everybody else is standing on him, you want to get out from under the pile.

When you get to be a certain age, there ain't very much you can do with the pile but you can start preparing somebody else to help work on the pile. Frankly, no man is bigger than the least one of his race or no bigger than the biggest one of his people.

The reason for doing Blues Heaven is when something is rightfully owed to somebody, they deserve to have it. I want it to be in a position where it can help the underprivileged people, especially under-privileged musicians that don't have any way of assistance. The average musician doesn't have any income and no social security so when he becomes old, he's got nothing and nobody to be leaning on. These people need protection and if you can start an organization or foundation, everything starts from a little.

On top of that, Blues Heaven is a historical thing. The blues are a part of the history and heritage of our people and these things are supposed to be known through the rest of history.

Most people emphasize the bad things of life and don't think about the good ones. Pretty soon, you'll find generations that will judge you on the past. Your past helps you on your present and your present helps on your future. If you don't have a past to look back to, what are you living on in the present and why should you live in the future if you haven't been any good?

The past will be registered with the future generations. If a youngster can't see today where he'll be tomorrow, why should he work for something tomorrow? If black people knew what their own heritage is, they would never let it down. Nobody lets something that is history die because of ignorance, especially something that means something about holding their people together.

I've got as high hopes as anybody in the record business for future stuff. One of the main reasons I got out to Los Angeles is because this is the best market in the world for songs. In Hollywood, they need songs for all occasions and I happen to have them.

You get to the place in the recording business where people wonder which way to go and what to do. Somehow, I've been lucky enough that, in advance, I could always have the idea for which way to go to make it move. Even if they didn't accept mine, they went that way. I think I got the kind of future ideas for the next ten years.

Today, you've got all kinds of angles on the blues, just like you've got the facts of life. All blues must say it in poetic form but as you change the time, it changes the blues. Every time you change the news, you got to change the blues because the news ain't always the same. The blues changes just like everything else changes.

Years ago, they were singin' about cotton and corn because they were raising cotton and corn. Today you got political ideas, ideas of other things like peace, because the world has gotten so outrageous today with fighting going on. Everybody's fighting each other and nobody knows what the hell they're fighting about. Every time somebody fights to win something, the next thing you know they want something else. You can't make peace like that.

The world has advanced in everything. The pattern of everything changes so the pattern of the blues has changed to be better just like changes from a wagon to having an automobile. If you come in singing one of them old-time blues today that are singing about something of yesterday, it ain't gonna work.

I can't go back to talking about slavery days, picking cotton and pulling corn. They got these electrical instruments and things to do all that. I can't even go back and talk about my job because they don't give a damn about jobs. They got computers and everything doing all kinds of jobs now.

All that's yesterday's news. The only thing you can go through is what's popular as of now, that people are interested in. The popular thing is to be smart enough to out-smart somebody else, forget the old and bring in the new ideas of what's happening today.

Singing about them old-time things wouldn't move anybody but you say something about being smart, being over-hip and relate more things to politics . . . politics carry the whole world today. Everything today is political, one way or the other, so when you go to dealing with political and world affairs, you've got to interest more people than anything else in the world.

If you make blues and don't make 'em about world affairs or something pertaining to political things, yours are too far gone. I made blues yesterday about the things of yesterday and what would be the hopeful future of today. Today I make blues about today and what the hopeful future of tomorrow is.

POSTSCRIPT

You have made great planes to scan the skies
You gave sight to the blind with other men's eyes
You even made submarines stay submerged for weeks
But it don't make sense you can't make peace

You take one man's heart and make another man live
You even go to the moon and come back thrilled
Why, you can crush any country in a matter of weeks
But it don't make sense you can't make peace

You can make a transfusion that can save a life
Why, you can change the darkness into broad daylight
You make the deaf man hear and the dumb man speak
But it don't make sense you can't make peace.

「It Don't Make Sense (You Can't Make Peace)」 by Willie Dixon

"It Don't Make Sense (You Can't Make Peace)" by Willie Dixon
Copyright © 1984, Hoochie Coochie Music

People always come up and ask me what is my favorite song out of all
the hundreds of songs that I've written. Most everybody figures I'll call
some song that made a lot of money or that one of the rock bands did
that got my name out there to the public. Frankly, it's a song I wrote
some years ago that I had on this Pausa recording: "It Don't Make
Sense (You Can't Make Peace)."

I did "It Don't Make Sense" many times on the stage and the
audience always was spellbound when we did it. The place would

228

come to a complete standstill, big or small, but somehow we never did get much radio play on that.

The blues are supposed to put thoughts in the minds of people but any time you get involved with something that's really good for the people, you can't get much publicity on it because everybody is banking more on trying to get financial rewards on a thing than they are on the wisdom of it. The blues was made for wisdom but they'd rather play the record they know that some kid is going to dance to and buy whether the song has wisdom or not.

This wisdom of the blues can be used all through life and that's why most blues songs are written as a statement of wisdom. I'd say that from 95% up to 99% of the world believes that it don't make sense you can't make peace.

It couldn't make sense you can't make peace if you want to make peace. You can make anything else you want on earth—the best plane, the biggest ships, everything to fight with—but suppose we spend just half the time and amount of money making peace that we have spent making war? There wouldn't be a mouth on earth that wouldn't be fed and nobody would have to suffer.

Out of all the things we did and made on earth, regardless of how we use them, it don't make sense unless we have peace enough that we can enjoy the world. God made man the greatest of all the animals but you ain't satisfied with that. You think you're smarter and you have to get to killing each other. For what? It's all vanity, anyway.

If you learned anything from this book, you learned the facts of life and the wisdom and knowledge of the blues are these facts of life. I feel that if the proper songs get to the various people of the world, it helps their mind to concentrate on what's going on in the world and this will give you a better communication. That's the real meaning and the real good of the blues, a better education and understanding among all people.

The blues being the true facts of life, we know it has been a fact of life that the people in the world have always made whatever they wanted. In making the many things of the world, we've made everything but peace. If you accept the wisdom of the blues, we can definitely have peace.

APPENDIX 1

Discographical information was drawn from the following sources:

Ruppli, Michel, *The Chess Labels: A Discography, Vols. 1&2.* Greenwood Press, 1983.

Leadbitter, Mike and Neil Slaven, *Blues Records, 1943–1966.* Oak, 1968.

Dixon, Robert M.W. & John Godrich, *Blues and Gospel Records, 1902–1943.* Storyville, 1982, third edition.

Whitburn, Joel, *Top R&B Singles, 1942–88.* Record Research, Inc., 1988.

Rowe, Mike, *Chicago Breakdown.* Drake Publishing, 1975.

Willie Dixon's Individual Recordings

1940
Chicago
15 November

THE FIVE BREEZES
Gene Gilmore (v/p-1); Leonard Caston (v/g); Willie Dixon (bass v); Joseph Bell (v); Willie Hawthorne (v).

049462-1	Sweet Louise – 1	Bluebird B8590
049463-1	Minute And Hour Blues – 1	BB B8590
049464-1	Laundry Man	BB B8710
049465-1	Return, Gal O'Mine – 1	BB B8614
049466-1	What's The Matter With Love? – 1	BB B8679
049467-1	My Buddy Blues – 1	BB B8614
049468-1	Just A Jitterbug	BB B8710
049469-1	Swingin' The Blues – 1	BB B8679

1945
Chicago

THE FOUR JUMPS OF JIVE
Gene Gilmore (v/p); Bernardo Dennis (g); Ellis Hunter (g); Willie Dixon (b).·

101	Satchelmouth Baby	Mercury 2001
102	It's Just The Blues	
103	Boo Boo Fine Jelly	Merc 2015
104	Streamline	

1946
Chicago

THE BIG THREE TRIO
Leonard Caston (v/p); Bernardo Dennis (v/g); Willie Dixon (v/b); unk (d); unk female (v-1).

UB-2898B	Lonely Roamin'	Bullet 274
UB-2899B	You Sure Look Good To Me – 1	Bullet 275, Dot 1104
UB-2900B	Signifying Monkey – 1	—
UB-2901B	Get Up Those Stairs Mademoiselle	Bullet 274

1947
Chicago
11 March

THE BIG THREE TRIO
Leonard Caston (v/p, lead v-1); Ollie Crawford (v/g, lead v-2); Willie Dixon (v/b, lead v-3); Charles Saunders (d).

CCO-4750	Signifying Monkey – 3	Columbia 37358, 30019
CCO-4751	If The Sea Was Whiskey	
CCO-4752	Money Tree Blues	Co 37584, 30055
CCO-4753	Lonely Roamin'	

Chicago
10 June

ROSETTA HOWARD WITH THE BIG THREE TRIO
Rosetta Howard (v); Leonard Caston (p); Bernardo Dennis (g); Willie Dixon (b); Charles Saunders (d). Big Three Trio (bkg v-1).

CCO-4788	Ebony Rhapsody – 1	Columbia 37573, 30053, 40494
CCO-4789	I Keep On Worrying	Co 30127
CCO-4790	When I Been Drinking	Co 37573, 30053
CCO-4791	Help Me Baby	Co 38029, 30105

Chicago
3 September

Alphonse Walker, d, replaces Saunders.

CCO-4837	It's Hard To Go Thru Life Alone	Columbia 38145, 30113
CCO-4838	Where Shall I Go	— —
CCO-4839	Too Many Drivers	Co 38029, 30105
CCO-4840	Why Be So Blue	Co 30127

THE BIG THREE TRIO
Howard out.

CCO-4841	After Awhile (We Gonna Drink A Little Whisky)-1	Columbia 37893, 30103
CCO-4842	It Can't Be Done	Co 38064, 30108
CCO-4843	No More Sweet Potatoes – 3	—
CCO-4844	Baby, I Can't Go On Without You	Co 37893, 30103

Chicago
30 December

THE BIG THREE TRIO
Dennis replaced by Crawford. Unison v-4.

CCO-4982	Reno Blues – 1	Columbia 30142
CCO-4983	Just Can't Let Her Be – 1	Co 30144

CCO-4984	Big Three Boogie – 4	Co 38125, 30125
CCO-4985	Since My Baby Been Gone	Co 30144
CCO-4986	Evening – 2	Co 38125, 30125
CCO-4987-1	88 Boogie	Co 38093, 30110
CCO-4988-1	You Sure Look Good To Me – 4	— —
CCO-4989	I'll Be Right Some Day – 1	Co 30142

1949
Chicago
18 February

	THE BIG THREE TRIO	
CCO-5029	Get Her Off My Mind	Columbia 30174
CCO-5030-1	I Ain't Gonna Be Your Monkey Man No More	Co 30166
CCO-5031-1	I Feel Like Steppin' Out – 1	Co 30156
CCO-5032-1	Big Three Stomp	Co 30166
CCO-5033	Hard Notch Boogie Beat	Co 30156
CCO-5034	No One To Love Me	Co 30174

Chicago
4 May

BU-6508	Don't Let That Music Die	Delta 202, Columbia 30190
BU-6509	Till The Day I Die	— , Co 30222
BU-6516	Appetite Blues – 2	Delta 208, Co 30329
BU-6517	Dry Bones	unissued
BU-6518	Why Do You Do Me Like You Do	Delta 205, Co 30328
BU-6519	Goodbye Mr. Blues	— , Co 30222
BU-6531	Cigarettes, Whiskey And Wild Women	Delta 208

Chicago
16 December

CCO-5094	There's Something On My Mind	Columbia 30228
CCO-5095	Don't Let That Music Die	Delta 202, Co 30190
CCO-5096	Blip Blip	Co 30329
CCO-5097	Practicing The Art of Love	Co 30190

1951
Chicago
29 May

	Add Baby Duke (v-5; probably "Baby Doo" Caston).	
CCO-5265	Blue Because Of You –3	OKeh 6863
CCO-5266	It's All Over Now – 5	OKeh 6842
CCO-5267	Tell That Woman – 3	—
CCO-5268	Lonesome –3	OKeh 6807
CCO-5269	Violent Love – 3	—

1952
Chicago
3 January

CCO-5296	Got You On My Mind	OKeh 6863
CCO-5297	Etiquette (inst.)	unissued
CCO-5298-1	You Don't Love Me No More – 5	OKeh 6901

Chicago
16 June

CCO-5356	Come Here Baby	OKeh 6944
CCO-5357	O.C. Bounce	unissued
CCO-5358	Cool Kind Woman	—
CCO-5359	Juice Head Bartender	—
CCO-5360-1	My Love Will Never Die – 3	OKeh 6901

Chicago
16 December

CCO-5393	Torture My Soul – 3	unissued
CCO-5394	What Am I To Do	—
CCO-5395	Be A Sweetheart – 3	OKeh 6944
CCO-5396	Too Late – 3	unissued

1951-54
Chicago   WILLIE DIXON AND THE BIG THREE TRIO
Willie Dixon (v/b); Ollie Crawford (g/v); Leonard "Baby Doo" Caston (v); Lafayette Leake (p); Harold Ashby (ts); Al Duncan (d).

	Violent Love	Chess LP CH 3-16500
	Alone	Teldec (W. Germany) LP 6.24802

1955
Chicago   WILLIE DIXON AND THE CHICAGO BLUES ALL STARS
Willie Dixon (v/b); Harold Ashby (ts); Lafayette Leake (p); Fred Below (d).

U-7842	If You're Mine	Checker 822
U-7843	Walkin' The Blues (no ts)	Teldec (W. Germany) —, LP 6.24802, LP 2173, Argo LP 4034, Chess LP CH 3-16500
U-7942	Crazy For My Baby	Checker 828, Chess LP CH 3-16500
U-7943	I Am The Lover Man	—
U-7944	Pain In My Heart	Checker 851, Chess LP CH 3-16500

1956
Chicago   Substitute Al Duncan (d).

8190	29 Ways	Checker 851, Chess LP CH 16500

1962
Chicago   Willie Dixon (b/v); Lafayette Leake (p); Clifton James (d).

U-11694	Home In Indiana	Teldec (W. Germany) LP 6.24802
U-11695	Wrinkles	—
	Firey Love	—

1963
Chicago
26 July   FOLK BLUES FESTIVAL LIVE/LIVE AT BIG BILL'S COPA
Willie Dixon, Muddy Waters, Buddy Guy (v); Guy (g); Otis Spann (p); Jack Meyers (bs-gtr); Fred Below (d); Jarret Gibson (ts); Donald Hankins (bs).

	Wee Wee Baby	Argo LP 4031

233

Bremen, W.
Germany
13 October   THE CHICAGO BLUES ALL STARS
Willie Dixon (b/v); Memphis Slim (p); Matt "Guitar" Murphy (g); Bill
Stepney (d).
Sittin' And Cryin' The Blues   L+R (W. Germany) LP 42.023
Crazy For My Baby

1964 (probably)
New York City

Willie Dixon (v/g).
Weak Brain! Narrow Mind!   Chess LP CH 3-1600

1964
Chicago
26 March   Willie Dixon (v/tambourine); Homesick James, Evans Spencer, John
Henry Barbee (g); Washboard Sam (washboard).
So Long!   Spivey LP 1003

Chicago 4 April   Willie Dixon (v/g).
Weak Brain! Narrow Mind!   Spivey LP 1003

Berlin, Germany
1 November   Willie Dixon (v/b); Sunnyland Slim (p); Hubert Sumlin (g); Clifton
James (d).
Blues Anytime   Amiga (E. Germany) 8 50 043
My Baby

Willie Dixon (v/g).
Big Legged Woman

1969
Chicago May   Sunnyland Slim (v-1/p); Johnny Shines (v-2/g); Cryin' Marie Dixon (v-3);
Willie Dixon (b); Clifton James (d); Shirley Dixon (tambourine).
Down In The Basement   Spivey LP 1011
Blues Drove Me Out Of My Mind –1   —
Three O'Clock In The Morning – 3   —
Lonesome Bedroom Blues – 2   —

Cologne, W.
Germany
1 July   THE CHICAGO BLUES ALL STARS: LOADED WITH THE BLUES
Walter Horton (v-1/hca); Sunnyland Slim (v-2/p); Johnny Shines (v-3/g);
Willie Dixon (v-4/b); Clifton James (v-5/d).
German Babies-5   MPS (W. Germany) LP 15.244,
                                 MPS 15003; BASF (U.S.) LP 20707
Baby I Need Your Love – 1   —   —
29 Ways – 4   —   —
Put It All In There – 2   —   —
She Got A Thing Going On –2   —   —
Every Time I Get To Drink – 2   —   —
Fat Mama – 3   —   —

Little Boy Blue –1   —   —
See See Rider –3   —   —
I Love The World – 3   —   —
Chicago Is Loaded With The Blues – 5   —   —

**1970
Frankfurt,
W. Germany**

Walter Horton (hca); Lafayette Leake (p); Lee Jackson (g); Willie Dixon (b); Clifton James (d).
Introduction   L+R (W. Germany) LP 42.021

1981 Chicago

Willie Dixon (v); Billy Branch, Snooky Pryor (hca); John Watkins (g); Butch Dixon (p); Freddie Dixon (bs-gtr); Jimmy Tillman (d).
Wang Dang Doodle   XRT LP 9301
(From the Grammy Award nominated *Blues Deluxe* album)

**1986
New York City
August**

Willie Dixon (v, hca); Robbie Robertson, Hiram Bullock (g); Delmar Brown (keyboards); Mark Egan (b); Kenwood Dennard or Ricky Sebastien (d); Gil Evans (arranger).
Don't You Tell Me Nothin'   MCA 6189

Willie Dixon's Albums

**1959
Englewood
Cliffs, NJ**

WILLIE'S BLUES
Willie Dixon (b/v); Memphis Slim (p); Wally Richardson (g-2); Al (probably Harold) Ashby (ts-1); Gus Johnson (d).
Nervous – 2   Prestige/Bluesville
                                    BV-1003 (re-issued as
                                    OBC-501), Prestige France 68414

Good Understanding –1   —
That's My Baby –2   —
Slim's Thing   —
That's All I Want Baby – 1   —
Don't You Tell Nobody   —
Youth To You –2   —
Sittin' And Cryin' The Blues –1,2   —
Built For Comfort –1,2   —
I Got A Razor   —
Go Easy   —
Move Me – 1   —

New York City

MEMPHIS SLIM AND WILLIE DIXON
Memphis Slim (v/p); Willie Dixon (b/v).
Joogie Boogie   Folkways FA 2385. Le Chant
                                   Du Monde (France) FWX52385
Stewball   —
John Henry   —
Kansas City 1   —
Kansas City 2   —

Kansas City 3	—
Have You Ever Been To	
Nashville Pen	—
Roll And Tumble	—
Beer Drinking Woman	—
Chicago House Rent Party	—
44 Blues	—
Unlucky	—

1960
New York City
January

MEMPHIS SLIM AND WILLIE DIXON: THE BLUES EVERY WHICH WAY
Memphis Slim (v-1/p); Willie Dixon (v-2/b).

Choo Choo – 1	Verve MSV 3007, Verve (France) 2304 505
4 O'Clock Boogie	—
Rub My Root – 2	—
C Rocker	—
Home To Mama – 2	—
Shaky – 2	—
After Hours	—
One More Time – 2	—
John Henry – 1,2	—
Now Howdy – 1,2	—

New York City
April

MEMPHIS SLIM AND WILLIE DIXON: AT THE VILLAGE GATE Memphis
Slim (v/p); Willie Dixon (v/b); Pete Seeger (v-1).

Somebody Tell That Woman	Folkways FA 2386
My Baby Don't Stand No Cheating	—
Stewball – 1	—
Slop Boogie	—
Misery Falls Like Rain	—
Wish Me Well	—
T For Texas – 1	—
I Just Want To Make Love To You	—
Try To Find My Baby	—
One More Time	—
Nobody Loves Me	—
We Are Going To Rock	—

(Memphis Slim and Willie Dixon are featured on Folkways FA 2450, PETE
SEEGER AT THE VILLAGE GATE.)

1962
Paris, France

MEMPHIS SLIM AND WILLIE DIXON: LIVE AT THE TROIS MAILLETZ
Memphis Slim (v-1/p); Willie Dixon (v-2/b); Philippe Combelle (d).

Rock And Rolling The House –1,2	Polydor (France) 46.131, Polydor 658.148
Baby Please Come Home	—
How Come You Do Me Like You Do – 1	—
The Way She Loves A Man – 2	—

New Way To Love – 2   —
African Hunch With A Boogie
   Beat – 2   —
Shame Pretty Girls – 2   —
Baby-Baby-Baby – 2   —
Do De Do – 2   —
Cold Blooded – 2   —
Just You and I – 1,2   —
Pigalle Love – 1   —
All By Myself –1,2   —

1969
Chicago
Summer

WILLIE DIXON—I AM THE BLUES
Willie Dixon (v/b); Walter "Shakey" Horton (hca); Sunnyland Slim or
Lafayette Leake (p); Johnny Shines (g); Clifton James (d).

Back Door Man	Columbia PC 9987
I Can't Quit You, Baby	—
The Seventh Son	—
Spoonful	—
I Ain't Superstitious	—
You Shook Me	—
I'm Your Hoochie Coochie Man	—
The Little Red Rooster	—
The Same Thing	—
Big Boat	unissued
Bring It On Home	—
Country Style	—
Crazy For My Baby	—
Hidden Charms	—
Hoodoo Woman	—
I Am The Blues	—
I Don't Care Who Knows	—
I Just Want To Make Love To You	—
Little Baby	—
My Baby	—
My John The Conqueroot	—
My Love Will Never Die	—
Tail Dragger	—
29 Ways	—
Wang Dang Doodle	—
When The Lights Go Out	—
You Can't Judge A Book By Its Cover	—

1971 (probably)
Chicago

PEACE
Willie Dixon (v); Walter Horton (hca); Lafayette Leake (p); Dennis
Miller, Buster Benton, Joe Young (g); Louis Satterfield, Phil Upchurch
(b); Clifton James, Frank Swan (d).

I'm Wanted	Yambo 777-15
Peace	—
It's In The News	—

I'd Give My Life For You	—
You Got To Move	—
Suffering Sun Of A Gun	—
Jelly Jam	—
You Don't Make Sense Or Peace	—
Blues You Can't Lose	—
If I Could See	—

1973 Chicago CATALYST (Grammy Award nomination)
Willie Dixon (v); Carrie Bell Harrington (hca); Lafayette Leake (p); Buster Benton, "Mighty" Joe Young, Phil Upchurch (g); Louis Satterfield (b); Morris Jennings (d).

Bring It On Home	Ovation OVD/1433
I Don't Trust Nobody	—
God's Gift To Man	—
Hoo Doo Doctor	—
My Babe	—
Wang Dang Doodle	—
When I Make Love	—
I Think I Got The Blues	—
But It Sure Is Fun	—
I Just Want To Make Love To You	—

Brooklyn, N.Y. MAESTRO WILLIE DIXON AND HIS CHICAGO BLUES BAND
Willie Dixon (b); Carrie Bell Harrington (v/hca); Buster Benton (v/g); Lafayette Leake (v/p); Larry Johnson (v); Professor King (d); Victoria Spivey (v).

WILLIE DIXON: Intro	Spivey LP 1016
BUSTER BENTON: Must Have A Hole In My Head	—
LAFAYETTE LEAKE: Leake's Trouble Trouble	—
LARRY JOHNSON: My Hoodoo Doctor	—
VICTORIA SPIVEY: I'm Taking Over	—
CARRIE BELL HARRINGTON: When The Evening Sun Goes Down	—
BUSTER BENTON: Every Day I Have The Blues	—
LAFAYETTE LEAKE: Fine Little Girl	—
LARRY JOHNSON: Put It All In There	—
CARRIE BELL HARRINGTON: One Day You're Going To Get Lucky	—
VICTORIA SPIVEY: It's A Mighty Poor Rat That Ain't Got But One Hole	—
BUSTER BENTON: The Thrill Is Gone	—

1976
Libertyville Illinois WHAT'S HAPPENED TO MY BLUES? (Grammy Award nomination)
Willie Dixon (v/b); Carrie Bell Harrington (hca); Dennis Miller, Buster Benton (g); Freddie Dixon (bs-gtr); Clifton James (d).

Moon Cat	Ovation OV-1705, Intercord Germany. 164.211

What Happened To My Blues	—
Pretty Baby	—
Got To Love You Baby	—
Shakin' The Shack	—
Hold Me Baby	—
It's So Easy To Love You	—
Oh Hugh Baby	—
Put It All In There	—
Hey Hey Pretty Mama	—

1982
Chicago
1949–1965

(Re-issued material)
WILLIE DIXON—BLUES ROOTS VOLUME 12
Various personnel.

WILLIE DIXON: Walking The Blues	Teldec (W. Germany) 6.24802
WILLIE DIXON: Home In Indiana	—
WILLIE DIXON: Wrinkles	—
ROBERT NIGHTHAWK: Black Angel Blues	—
LITTLE WALTER: My Babe	—
WILLIE DIXON: Alone	—
KOKO TAYLOR: 29 Ways	—
KOKO TAYLOR: Wang Dang Doodle	—
MUDDY WATERS: 40 Days And 40 Nights	—
WALTER HORTON: Gonna Bring It On Home	—
WALTER HORTON: Good Moanin' Blues	—
WILLIE DIXON: Firey Love	—
SONNY BOY WILLIAMSON: The Hunt	—
HOWLIN' WOLF: The Red Rooster	—

1984
Chicago

WILLIE DIXON—MIGHTY EARTHQUAKE AND HURRICANE
Willie Dixon (v); Billy Branch (hca); Lafayette Leake (p); John Watkins, Johnny B. Moore (g); Freddie Dixon (bs-gtr); Jimmy Tillman (d); Mae Cohen, Ayo Kason, Ellen Samuels, Zora Young (bkg v).

Earthquake And Hurricane	Pausa PR 7157
It Don't Make Sense (You Can't Make Peace)	—
After Five Long Years	—
Everything's Got A Time	—
Wigglin' Worm	—
Flamin' Mamie	—
Grave Digger Blues	—
Pie In The Sky	—

1985
Montreux,
Switzerland

15 July, 1983 LIVE! BACKSTAGE ACCESS (Grammy Award nomination)
Willie Dixon (v/b); Sugar Blue (hca); Arthur "Butch" Dixon (p/v); John Watkins (g/v); Freddie Dixon (bs-gtr/v); Clifton James (d).

	Closing Blues	Pausa PR 7183
	I Don't Trust Nobody	—
	It Don't Make Sense (You Can't Make	
	Peace)	—
	Shakin' The Shack	—
	Wang Dang Doodle	—
	Built For Comfort	—
	Spoonful	—
	I've Got My Mojo Workin'	—

Chicago
1946–1952

(Re-issued material)
THE BIG THREE TRIO: I FEEL LIKE STEPPIN' OUT
Willie Dixon (b/v); Leonard "Baby Doo" Caston (p/v); Bernardo Dennis or Ollie Crawford (g/v).

Signifying Monkey	Dr. Horse Sweden, H-804
Reno Blues	—
After Awhile (We Gonna Drink A Little Whiskey)	—
You Sure Look Good To Me	—
Big Three Boogie	—
No More Sweet Potatoes	—
My Love Will Never Die	—
Ebony Rhapsody	—
I Feel Like Steppin' Out	—
Just Can't Let Her Be Lonesome	—
Appetite Blues	—
Evening	—
I'll Be Right Some Day	—
Blue Because Of You	—
Violent Love	—

1988
Los Angeles

WILLIE DIXON—HIDDEN CHARMS (Grammy Award winner)
Willie Dixon (v); Sugar Blue (hca); Lafayette Leake (p); Cash McCall (g/v); T-Bone Burnett (dobro); Red Callender (b); Earl Palmer (d).

Blues You Can't Lose	Bug/Capitol Cl-90595
I Don't Trust Myself	—
Jungle Swing	—
Don't Mess With The Messer	—
Study War No More	—
I Love The Life I Live (I Live The Life I Love)	—
I Cry For You	—
Good Advice	—
I Do The Job	—

Chicago
1951–1969

(Re-issued material)
WILLIE DIXON—THE CHESS BOX

LITTLE WALTER: My Babe	MCA/Chess CH3-16500
WILLIE DIXON: Violent Love	—
EDDIE BOYD: Third Degree	—

240

WILLIE MABON: Seventh Son —
WILLIE DIXON: Crazy For My Baby —
WILLIE DIXON: Pain In My Heart —
MUDDY WATERS: Hoochie Coochie
Man —
HOWLIN' Wolf: Evil —
LITTLE WALTER: Mellow Down Easy —
JIMMY WITHERSPOON: When The
Lights Go Out —
MUDDY WATERS: Young Fashioned
Ways —
BO DIDDLEY: Pretty Thing —
MUDDY WATERS: I'm Ready —
LOWELL FULSON: Do Me Right —
MUDDY WATERS: I Just Want To Make
Love To You —
LOWELL FULSON: Tollin' Bells —
WILLIE DIXON: 29 Ways —
WILLIE DIXON: Walkin' The Blues —
HOWLIN' WOLF: Spoonful —
OTIS RUSH: You Know My Love —
BO DIDDLEY: You Can't Judge A Book
By Its Cover —
HOWLIN' WOLF: I Ain't Superstitious —
MUDDY WATERS: You Need Love —
HOWLIN' WOLF: Little Red Rooster —
HOWLIN' WOLF: Back Door Man —
LITTLE WALTER: Dead Presidents —
HOWLIN' WOLF: Hidden Charms —
MUDDY WATERS: You Shook Me —
SONNY BOY WILLIAMSON: Bring It
On Home —
WILLIE DIXON: Weak Brain, Narrow
Mind —
KOKO TAYLOR: Wang Dang Doodle —
MUDDY WATERS: The Same Thing —
HOWLIN' WOLF: Built For Comfort —
HOWLIN' WOLF: 300 Pounds Of Joy —
LITTLE MILTON: I Can't Quit You, Baby —
KOKO TAYLOR: Insane Asylum —

1989
Los Angeles

WILLIE DIXON—GINGER ALE AFTERNOON (Grammy Award
nomination/Film soundtrack)
Willie Dixon (v); Cash McCall (g, bs-gtr); Stanley Behrens (hca, ts);
Arthur "Butch" Dixon (p); Chucki Burke (d); Charlotte Crossly (bkg v-1)
Miseries of Memories   Varese Sarabende
                                                        VDS-5234
Wigglin' Worm   —
I Don't Trust Nobody   —
Earthquake and Hurricane   —

241

The Real Thing	—
Move Me Baby	—
Save My Child	—
I Just Want to Make Love To You	—
Sittin' & Cryin' The Blues	—
Save My Child II	—
Shakin' The Shack	—
That's My Baby	—
Ginger Ale Blues	—
Save My Child III	—
Good Understanding-1	—

Chicago
1939-1940

(Re-issued material)
GENE GILMORE AND THE FIVE BREEZES—COMPLETE RECORDINGS
(1939-1940)

GENE GILMORE: Brown Skin Woman	RST/Blues Documents Austria BD-2065
GENE GILMORE: Charity Blues	—
GENE GILMORE: She Got Something There	—
GENE GILMORE: The Natchez Fire	—
BABY DOO: I'm Gonna Walk Your Log	—
BABY DOO: The Death of Walter Barnes	—
FIVE BREEZES: Sweet Louise	—
FIVE BREEZES: Minute and Hour Blues	—
FIVE BREEZES: Laundry Man	—
FIVE BREEZES: Return, Gal O'Mine	—
FIVE BREEZES: What's The Matter With Love?	—
FIVE BREEZES: My Buddy Blues	—
FIVE BREEZES: Just A Jitterbug	—
FIVE BREEZES: Swingin' The Blues	—

1990
Chicago
1940-1952

(Re-issued material) BIG THREE TRIO, VOL. 2 Bernardo Dennis, (v-1) BABY DOO: I'm Gonna Walk Your Log	Dr. Horse Sweden H-808

BIG THREE: Since My Baby
Been Gone   —
FIVE BREEZES: Return, Gal
O'Mine   —
ROSETTA HOWARD: I Keep On
Worrying   —
BIG THREE: Don't Let That
Music Die   —
BIG THREE: If the Sea Was
Whisky   —
BIG THREE: Big Three Stomp   —
BIG THREE: It Can't Be
Done-1   —
GENE GILMORE: She Got
Something There   —
BIG THREE: Signifying
Monkey   —
ROSETTA HOWARD: Where
Shall I Go?   —
BIG THREE: You Don't Love
Me No More   —
BIG THREE: Till The Day I
Die   —
ROSETTA HOWARD: It's Hard
To Go Through Life
Alone   —
BIG THREE: Got You On My
Mind   —
BIG THREE: Cigareets,
Whisky and Wild Women   —
ROSETTA HOWARD: Why Be So
Blue?   —
BIG THREE: Hard Notch
Boogie Beat   —

(Note—Track listing and release date are tentative as of publication date)

Chicago	(Re-issued material)	
1946-1952	THE BIG THREE TRIO	
	If The Sea Was Whisky	Columbia 46216
	Money Tree Blues	—
	Lonely Roamin'	—
	It Can't Be Done	—
	Baby I Can't Go On	
	Without You	—
	Since My Baby Been Gone	—
	88 Boogie	—
	Get Her Off My Mind	—
	I Ain't Gonna Be Your	
	Monkey Man	—
	Big Three Stomp	—
	Hard Notch Boogie Beat	—

No One To Love Me	—
Don't Let That Music Die	—
Blip Blip	—
It's All Over Now	—
Tell That Woman	—
Got You On My Mind	—
Etiquette	—
Come Here Baby	—
Cool Kind Mama	—
Juice Head Bartender	—

(Note—Track listing and release date are tentative as of publication date)

Willie Dixon Labels

Willie Dixon was releasing material on his Spoonful and Yambo labels from approximately 1967–1974.

YAMBO 45s

108	KOKO TAYLOR: Instant Everything/A Mighty Love
109	MARGIE EVANS (W/CHICAGO BLUES ALL STARS): When I Make Love/29 Ways
1011	J.J. TAYLOR: I'm Not Tired/Tell Me The Truth
8915	HONEY DUO TWINS (W/CHICAGO BLUES ALL STARS): Come On Baby/Kiss Me
777-3	LUCKY PETERSON: 1,2,3,4/Good Old Candy
777-05	JAMES PETERSON: All On Account Of You/Sing The Blues Till I Die
777-13	MODERN TIMES: Why Must I Live Such A Lonely Life/Baby Just Maybe
777-15	WILLIE DIXON (W/CHICAGO BLUES ALL STARS): Petting The Baby/You Got To Move
777-20	McKINLEY MITCHELL (W/CHICAGO BLUES ALL STARS): That Last Home Run/All Star Bougee
777-110	SATAGANS: Smokin'/Lovers To Friends

YAMBO LPs

77701	E. RODNEY JONES: Might Is Right (Side 1)/LAFAYETTE LEAKE TRIO: Soul Wrinkles (Side 2)
77715	WILLIE DIXON (W/CHICAGO BLUES ALL STARS): Peace

SUPREME 45 RECORDS

1004	BUSTER BENTON (W/CHICAGO BLUES ALL STARS): Spider In My Stew/Dangerous Woman

SPOONFUL 45 RECORDS

777-26	McKINLEY MITCHELL (W/CHICAGO BLUES ALL STARS): Good Time Baby/All Star Bougee

WHY? 45s

WILLIE DIXON: It Don't Make Sense (You Can't Make Peace)/It's In The News. Released 1982

MCF 45s

MOJO EXPRESS: Willie Dixon (v); Cash McCall (g); Louis Satterfield (b); Al Duncan (d). AIDS To The Grave. Released 1987 as the B-side of Vernell Jennings: The Boogie Man (AIDS)

APPENDIX 2

There are over 500 titles in the Willie Dixon songbook. The following lists, as comprehensively as possible, the Dixon songs that form the backbone of his catalogue, the material that has been most eagerly seized upon by other artists. "Help Me," usually credited to Sonny Boy Williamson alone, is included here because of unresolved questions surrounding its authorship. The artist who first recorded the song is capitalized.

"BACK DOOR MAN":	HOWLIN' WOLF, The Doors, Blues Project, Frank Marino & Mahogany Rush, Shadows of Knight
"BIG BOAT (SOMEBODY TELL THAT WOMAN)":	BIG THREE TRIO, Peter, Paul & Mary
"BLUES YOU CAN'T LOSE":	WILLIE DIXON, Jack Bruce
"BRING IT ON HOME":	SONNY BOY WILLIAMSON, Big Walter "Shakey" Horton, Canned Heat, Led Zeppelin
"BUILT FOR COMFORT":	WILLIE DIXON, Howlin' Wolf, Taj Mahal, Eric Clapton, UFO
"CRAZY FOR MY BABY":	WILLIE DIXON, Charlie Musselwhite
"CRAZY, MIXED-UP WORLD":	LITTLE WALTER, Bruce Willis
"DEAD PRESIDENTS":	LITTLE WALTER, J. Geils Band
"DIDDY WAH DIDDY":	BO DIDDLEY, Captain Beefheart, Fabulous Thunderbirds, Sonics, Remains
"DO ME RIGHT":	LOWELL FULSON
"DO THE DO":	HOWLIN' WOLF, Top Jimmy & the Rhythm Pigs
"DOWN IN THE BOTTOM":	HOWLIN' WOLF, John Hammond, Siegel Schwall Band, Hubert Sumlin
"EGG OR THE HEN":	KOKO TAYLOR, Dave Edmunds
"EVIL (GOING ON)":	HOWLIN' WOLF; Eric Clapton, Canned Heat, John Hammond, Cactus, Luther Allison, Koko Taylor
"FIRE":	KOKO TAYLOR, Etta James, Lee Morgan
"HELP ME":	SONNY BOY WILLIAMSON, Ten Years After, Johnny Winter, Bo Diddley, Van Morrison
"HIDDEN CHARMS":	CHARLES CLARK, Howlin' Wolf, Kingfish, Nappy Brown, Hubert Sumlin

"I AIN'T SUPERSTITIOUS": HOWLIN WOLF, Jeff Beck w/Rod Stewart, Eric Clapton, Lonnie Mack, Megadeth, Tesla

"I AM THE BLUES": MUDDY WATERS

"I CAN'T QUIT YOU, BABY": OTIS RUSH, Led Zeppelin, John Mayall, Savoy Brown, Little Milton

"I GOT TO FIND MY BABY": MUDDY WATERS, Little Walter, Sunnyland Slim, Chuck Berry, Animals

"I JUST WANT TO MAKE LOVE TO YOU": MUDDY WATERS, Etta James, Chuck Berry, Ramsey Lewis, Charlie McCoy, Norman Luboff Choir, The Righteous Brothers, Lou Rawls, Timbuk 3, Foghat, Isaac Hayes, Van Morrison, Rolling Stones, Otis Redding, Rod Stewart, B.B. King, Earl Hines

"I LOVE THE LIFE I LIVE": MUDDY WATERS, Mose Allison, John Hammond, Georgie Fame, Carmen McRae

"I'M READY": MUDDY WATERS, Humble Pie, George Thorogood, John Hammond, Junior Wells, Freddie King, Buddy Guy, Albert King, Frankie Miller, Blues Project, Carey Bell Harrington, Luther "Guitar Junior" Johnson, Otis Spann

"I'M WANTED": WILLIE DIXON, George Thorogood

"I'M YOUR HOOCHIE COOCHIE MAN": MUDDY WATERS, Chuck Berry, Jimi Hendrix, Allman Brothers Band, Marshall Crenshaw, John Hammond, Dave Van Ronk, Sam the Sham & the Pharoahs, Steppenwolf, Bill Black Combo, Lou Rawls, Freddie King, Jimmy Smith, Buddy Guy, Pinetop Perkins, London Quireboys, Magic Sam, Jeff Healey

"INSANE ASYLUM": KOKO TAYLOR, Kathi McDonald

"I WANT TO BE LOVED": MUDDY WATERS, Rolling Stones

"JUST LIKE I TREAT YOU": HOWLIN' WOLF, Rod Stewart

"LET ME LOVE YOU BABY": KOKO TAYLOR, Buddy Guy, Stevie Ray Vaughan

"LITTLE BABY": HOWLIN' WOLF, Blues Project, Siegel Schwall Band

"LITTLE RED ROOSTER": HOWLIN' WOLF, Rolling Stones, Sam Cooke, Doors, Grateful Dead, Big Mama Thornton, Ronnie Hawkins, Jose Feliciano, Luther Allison, Z.Z. Hill, Eddie C. Campbell, Hubert Sumlin

"MELLOW DOWN EASY": LITTLE WALTER, Paul Butterfield Blues Band, ZZ Top, John Hammond

"MIGHTY EARTHQUAKE AND HURRICANE": WILLIE DIXON, Tina Turner

"MY BABE": LITTLE WALTER, Everly Brothers, Mitty Collier, Elvis Presley, Ramsey Lewis, Spencer Davis, Ike & Tina Turner, Nancy Wilson, Fabian, Bo Diddley, The Contours, Bill Black, Conway Twitty, Ronnie Hawkins, Gene Ammons, Lonnie Mack, The Uniques, Albert King, John Lee Hooker, Ricky Nelson, Lee Dorsey, Righteous Brothers, Mickey Gilley, Norman Luboff Choir, Steve Miller, Lightnin' Hopkins, Chuck Berry

"MY BABY IS SWEETER": LITTLE WALTER, Charlie Musselwhite, John Hammond

"MY LOVE WILL NEVER DIE": BIG THREE TRIO, Otis Rush

"PRETTY THING": BO DIDDLEY, Pretty Things, John Hammond & Dr. John, Canned Heat

"SHAKE FOR ME": HOWLIN' WOLF, Duane Allman, Siegel Schwall Band, John Hammond

"SITTIN' AND CRYIN' THE
BLUES":   BUDDY GUY, Willie Dixon

"SPOONFUL":   HOWLIN' WOLF, Cream, Ten Years After, Allman Bros. Band, Dion, Paul Butterfield, Harvey Fuqua & Etta James, Blues Project, Jose Feliciano, Bill Black Combo, Eric Clapton, John Hammond, Gil Evans, Jimmy Witherspoon, Climax Blues Band, Canned Heat, Koko Taylor, Delbert McClinton, Long John Baldry, Salty Dog

"TAIL DRAGGER":   HOWLIN' WOLF

"THE SAME THING":   MUDDY WATERS, George Thorogood, Grateful Dead, French, Frith, Kaiser & Thompson

"THE SEVENTH SON":   WILLIE MABON, Mose Allison, Muddy Waters, Dion, Johnny Rivers, Nancy Wilson, Peggy Lee, Climax Blues Band, Long John Baldry, John Cougar Mellencamp

"THIRD DEGREE":   EDDIE BOYD, Champion Jack Dupree, Johnny Winter, Eric Clapton, Barry Melton, West, Bruce & Laing

"THREE HUNDRED POUNDS OF
JOY":   HOWLIN' WOLF, Ronnie Hawkins, Big Twist & the Mellow Fellows, Roomful of Blues, Koko Taylor, King Biscuit Boy

"TOLLIN' BELLS":   LOWELL FULSON, Savoy Brown, Paul Butterfield

"TOO MANY COOKS":   JESSIE FORTUNE, Robert Cray

"29 WAYS":   WILLIE DIXON, Koko Taylor, Margie Evans, Johnny Littlejohn

"VIOLENT LOVE":   BIG THREE TRIO, Otis Rush, Dr. Feelgood, Oingo Boingo

"WANG DANG DOODLE":   HOWLIN' WOLF, Koko Taylor, Savoy Brown, Dr. John, Pointer Sisters, Dave Edmunds/Love Sculpture, Z.Z. Hill

"WHATEVER I AM, YOU MADE
ME":   KOKO TAYLOR, Nina Simone, Tracy Nelson

"WHEN THE LIGHTS GO OUT":   JIMMY WITHERSPOON

"WHICH CAME FIRST":   RY COODER

"YOU CAN'T JUDGE A BOOK BY
ITS COVER":   BO DIDDLEY, John Anderson, Hank Williams, Jr. with Huey Lewis, Billy Lee Riley, John Hammond, Tom Rush, Patti Labelle, Billy "Crash" Craddock, Dion, Stevie Wonder, Shadows of Knight, Cactus, Long John Baldry, Yardbirds, Roy Buchanan

"YOU GOT TO MOVE":   REVEREND BALLINGER, Willie Dixon, Nighthawks

"YOU KNOW MY LOVE":   OTIS RUSH

"YOU'LL BE MINE":   HOWLIN' WOLF, Dr. Feelgood, Stevie Ray Vaughan, John Hammond

"YOU NEED LOVE":   MUDDY WATERS, Savoy Brown

"YOU NEED MEAT (DON'T GO
NO FURTHER)":   MUDDY WATERS, Doors, John Hammond, Nighthawks, King Biscuit Boy

"YOU SHOOK ME":   MUDDY WATERS, Led Zeppelin, Jeff Beck, Heart

"YOUNG FASHIONED WAYS":   MUDDY WATERS, Sleepy LaBeef

APPENDIX 3

Willie Dixon's studio contributions for Chess and other labels extended beyond just writing blues songs. He was a musician hustling to make ends meet and session work was one avenue that offered the prospect of steady income. Dixon wound up playing bass on a substantial portion of the early releases on Chess—not just on the label's blues sessions—and he was landing a fair amount of studio work from other labels and producers before then.

But it was a time when documenting backing musicians was a haphazard process at best and hence discrepancies creep in. For instance, Dixon claims to have played on the sessions which produced the first Sonny Boy (John Lee) Williamson's "Elevate Me, Mama," but according to the discographies, it was Ransom Knowling playing on the track. Similarly, Dixon said his first recording session with Muddy Waters came at the same time—probably November 10, 1948—that he cut four songs with Robert Nighthawk and Ethel Mae for Aristocrat. There was a Waters session that weekend—which yielded "Train Fare Home," "Down South Blues," "Kind-Hearted Woman" and "Sittin' Here and Drinkin'"—but the credited bassist is Big Crawford. And the second Nighthawk session Dixon played on followed a Waters session—but Big Crawford is again listed as the bass player.

The following represents a partial list of songs that Willie Dixon played on during his years on the Chicago session scene. It seems likely that Dixon was present on virtually every Chess and Checker blues session from 1953 until his departure to Cobra in 1956 (and he apparently continued playing on Chess sessions fairly frequently between 1956 and his return to Chess in 1959).

But another problem rises in considering his input on Chess's 1960s recordings. Dixon largely stopped playing on sessions once the electric bass came into vogue around 1960 and moved into a more supervisory role in the studio. But precisely determining the extent of his participation on those sessions when he wasn't playing is nearly impossible since Dixon very rarely received official credit for his arranging and production contributions.

Dixon's studio presence extended beyond the normal realm of production assistance on Walter "Shakey" Horton's THE SOUL OF BLUES HARMONICA (Argo LP 4037, re-issued as Chess CH-9268) and two Koko Taylor albums, KOKO TAYLOR (Checker LP 1532, re-issued as Chess CH-9263) and BASIC SOUL (GRT LP CH 50018). Away from Chess, he supervised three J.B. Lenoir albums: ALABAMA BLUES! (L&R Germany, LR 42.001), DOWN IN MISSISSIPPI (L&R Germany, LR 42.012) and ONE OF THESE MORNINGS (JSP England, JSP 1105).

Much of the Cobra material Dixon produced has been issued by the Flyright label in England on: Otis Rush, GROANING THE BLUES (FLY 560), Magic Sam & Shakey Jake, MAGIC ROCKER (FLY 561), Otis Rush & Magic Sam, OTHER TAKES (FLY 562), SUNNYLAND SLIM (FLY 566), KING COBRAS (FLY 567), IKE TURNER AND HIS KINGS OF RHYTHM — 1958 (FLY 578), Harold Burrage, SHE KNOCK ME OUT, 1956-58 (FLY 579), Lee Jackson, FISHING IN MY POND (FLY 582), BETTY EVERETT & LILLIAN OFFITT (FLY 589), Otis Rush & Buddy Guy, THE FINAL TAKES AND OTHERS (FLY 594).

Willie Dixon played bass on:

REVEREND BALLINGER:
"This Train", "You Got To Move".

CHUCK BERRY:
"Maybellene", "Thirty Days", "You Can't Catch Me", "Too Much Monkey Business", "Brown-Eyed Handsome Man", "Roll Over Beethoven", "Havana Moon", "School Days", "Rock And Roll Music", "Oh Baby Doll", "Reelin' And Rockin'", "Sweet Little Sixteen", "Johnny B. Goode", "Memphis", "Sweet Little Rock and Roller", "Little Queenie", "Almost Grown", "Back In The USA", "Let It Rock", "Run Rudolph Run".

BO DIDDLEY:
"Diddy Wah Diddy", "Hey Bo Diddley", "Mona", "Before You Accuse Me", "You Can't Judge A Book By Its Cover".

EDDIE BOYD:
"24 Hours", "Third Degree".

BUDDY GUY:
"Sittin' And Cryin' And Singin' The Blues", "Try To Quit You Baby", "You Sure Can't Do", "This Is The End".

JOHN LEE HOOKER:
"Shake It Baby", "Let's Make It", "The Right Time", "I Need Your Love So Bad".

BIG WALTER (SHAKEY) HORTON:
"Hard Hearted Woman", "Back Home To Mama", "Have A Good Time", "Need My Baby".

HOWLIN' WOLF:
"No Place To Go", "Rockin' Daddy", "Baby How Long", "Evil Is Goin' On", "Forty Four", "I'm Leaving You", "Change My Way", "Wang Dang Doodle", "Back Door Man", "Spoonful", "Down In The Bottom", "Shake For Me", "The Red Rooster", "You'll Be Mine", "Just Like I Treat You", "I Ain't Superstitious", "Do The Do", "Shake It", "Love Me Darlin'", "My Country Sugar Mama".

LEE JACKSON:
"Fishin' In My Pond", "I'll Just Keep Walking".

J.B. LENOIR:
"Let Me Die With The One I Love", "If I Give My Love To You", "Don't Touch My Head", "I've Been Down So Long", "What About Your Daughter", "Daddy, Talk To Your Son", "Mama, Talk To Your Daughter".

LITTLE WALTER:
"Rocker", "Oh, Baby", "Got To Find My Baby", "Thunderbird", "My Babe", "Roller Coaster", "I Got To Go", "Crazy For My Baby", "Hate To See You Go", "One More Chance With You", "Who", "Boom! Boom! Out Goes The Lights", "It Ain't Right", "Flying Saucer", "It's Too Late Brother", "Teenage Beat", "Take Me Back", "Just A Feeling", "Nobody But You", "Shake Dancer", "Everybody Needs Somebody", "Temperature", "Ah'w Baby", "I've Had My Fun", "The Toddle", "Confessin' The Blues", "Key To The Highway", "Rock Bottom", "Everything's Gonna Be Alright", "Mean Old 'Frisco", "Back Track", "Blue And Lonesome", "Me And Piney Brown", "Break It Up", "Blue Midnight", "I Don't Play", "As Long As I Have You", "Just You Fool".

WILLIE MABON:
"Would You Again, Baby", "The Seventh Son".

MAGIC SAM:
"All Night Long", "Love Me With A Feeling", "Easy Baby", "Twenty-One Days In Jail".

MEMPHIS SLIM:
"Kilroy's Been Here", "Rockin' The House", "Lend Me Your Love", "Darling, I Miss You".

THE MOONGLOWS:
"Sincerely".

MUDDY WATERS:
"I'm Ready", "I Don't Know Why", "Young Fashioned Ways", "I Want To Be Loved", "My Eyes (Keep Me In Trouble)", "I Got To Find My Baby", "Sugar Sweet", "Trouble No More", "Clouds In My Heart", "40 Days And 40 Nights", "All Aboard", "Just To Be With You", "Don't Go No Farther", "Diamonds At Your Feet", "I Live The Life I Love", "Rock Me", "Look What You've Done", "Got My Mojo Working", "I Won't Go", "She's Got It", "She's 19 Years Old", "Close To You", "Going Home", "Muddy Waters Twist", "Tough Times", "You Shook Me", "You Need Love", "Little Brown Bird", "Five Long Years", "Country Boy", "My Home Is In The Delta", "Long Distance Call", "Good Morning Little Schoolgirl", "You Gonna Need My Help", "The Same Thing", "Can't Lose What You Ain't Never Had", "I'm Your Hoochie Coochie Man".

ROBERT NIGHTHAWK:
"My Sweet Lovin' Woman", "Black Angel Blues", "Annie Lee Blues", "Return Mail Blues", "Six Three O", "Jackson Town Gal", "Lula Mae", "Merry Christmas".

PILGRIM JUBILEES:
"Stretch Out", "The Old Ship Of Zion".

JIMMY REED
"Big Boss Man", "Come Love", "Meet Me".

JIMMY ROGERS:
"You're The One", "Sloppy Drunk", "If It Ain't Me", "Walkin' By Myself", "One Kiss", "I Can't Believe", "Rock This House", "My Last Meal".

OTIS RUSH:
"I Can't Quit You, Baby", "Sit Down Baby", "Violent Love", "My Love Will Never Die", "Groaning The Blues", "If You Were Mine", "Love That Woman", "Jump Sister Bessie", "Three Times A Fool", "She's A Good 'Un", "It Takes Time", "Checking On My Baby", "Double Trouble", "Keep On Lovin' Me, Baby", "All Your Love", "My Baby Is A Good-Un", "So Many Roads, So Many Trains", "I'm Satisfied", "You Know My Love", "I Can't Stop Baby".

SONNY BOY WILLIAMSON (RICE MILLER):
"Let Me Explain", "I Know What Love Is All About", "I Wonder Why", "Your Imagination", "Don't Look Your Eye", "Keep It To Yourself", "The Key To Your Door", "Fattening Frogs For Snakes", "I Don't Know", "Cross My Heart", "Born Blind", "Ninety Nine", "Dissatisfied", "Your Funeral And My Trial", "Wake Up Baby", "Let Your Conscience Be Your Guide", "Unseeing Eye", "The Goat", "It's Sad To Be Alone", "Stop Right Now", "The Hunt", "One Way Out", "Nine Below Zero".

OTIS SPANN:
"It Must Have Been The Devil", "Five Spot", "Had My Fun".

SUNNYLAND SLIM:
"It's You Baby", "Highway 51", "Everytime I Get To Drinking", "It's You, My Baby", "We Gonna Jump", "Too Late For Me To Pray", "Levee Camp Moan".

ROOSEVELT SYKES:
"Slave For Your Love", "Gone With The Wind", "Wild Side", "Out On A Limb", "Honey Child", "Never Loved Like This Before", "Last Chance", "Casual Friend", "Your Will Is Mine", "Hupe Dupe Do".

KOKO TAYLOR:
"I Got What It Takes", "What Kind Of Man Is This", "Blues Heaven", "Tell Me The Truth", "Good Advice", "Don't Mess With The Messer", "Whatever I Am You Made Me", "29 Ways".

SONNY TERRY:
"I Got My Eyes On You", "Sonny's Woopin' The Doop", "Burnt Child", "Whooee, Whooee", "Crow Jane", "So Tough With Me", "Whooweee", "Baby I Think I Got The Blues", "Ya, Ya", "Roll Me Baby."

WASHBOARD SAM:
"You Can't Make The Grade", "You Can't Have None of That", "I Just Couldn't Help It", "Soap And Water Blues".

JUNIOR WELLS:
"Two-Headed Woman", "Lovey Dovey Lovely One", "I Could Cry", "Cha Cha Cha In Blues (Cut My Toenail)", "Little By Little I'm Losing You", "Come On In This House", "You Don't Care", "Prison Bars All Around Me", "Galloping Horses A Lazy Mule".

BIG JOE WILLIAMS:
"38 Pistol Blues", "I'm A Fool About My Baby", "Pearly Mae", "Walking Blues", "Highway 45", "Meet Me In The Bottom", "Skinny Mama", "Jockey Ride Blues", "Coal And Iceman Blues", "Army Man Blues", "Black Gal", "Pallet On the Floor", "Levee Camp Blues", "Low Down Dirty Shame", "Gambling Man", "Ain't Gonna Rain No More", "Feel So Good", "Prowling Ground Hog", "Sugar Babe", "Tell Me Mama", "Studio Blues".

HOMESICK JAMES (James Williamson):
"Crutch and Cane", "Got To Move", "Dust My Broom", "Somebody's Been Talking", "Set A Date", "So Mean To Me".

SONNY BOY WILLIAMSON (John Lee Williamson):
"Mellow Chic Swing", "Polly Put Your Kettle On", "Lacey Belle", "Apple Tree Swing", "Elevator Woman".

JOHNNY WINTER:
"Mean Mistreater".

APPENDIX 4

Since this is "The Willie Dixon Story," the primary source of information was 60-plus hours of interviews conducted with Dixon and others who played important roles in his career and life. Written materials were only a minor part in constructing the narrative and were used principally for factual verification of the material contained in the chapter introductions.

Rather than uncovering new written sources, the research focused on recognized works in the field. The workhorse was Mike Rowe's *Chicago Breakdown* (Drake Publishing, 1975), still the most in-depth look at the Chicago blues scene available while Robert Palmer's *Deep Blues* (Viking Press, 1981) illuminated the Mississippi connection to that world. For contextual perspective on the milieu in which Dixon's career and blues unfolded, Nelson George's *The Death Of Rhythm & Blues* (Pantheon, 1988), Charles Keil's *Urban Blues* (University of Chicago, 1966), Arnold Shaw's *Honkers And Shouters* (Collier, 1978) and Charlie Gillett's *The Sound Of The City* (Pantheon, 1970, 1983) were valuable references.

On the Chess front, the chapter on Chess records in Peter Guralnick's *Feel Like Going Home* (Dutton, 1971) offered a time-capsule glimpse of the label's last days. More insight into the early years of Leonard Chess's life and the end of the Chess operation was provided by Peter Golkin's "Chess Records, Chicago: Blacks, Whites & Blues" (Northwestern University, Program in American Culture, published in *Living Blues* #88, 9-10/89, and #89, 12/89).

Gloria Coleman's "The Black Gold Coast—The Rise and Fall of the DuSable Hotel: An Oral History" (*Chicago Reader*, 11/9/84) furnished additional contextual background on the Chess brothers' pre-record label endeavors. Other periodical articles of use were Clarence Petersen, "The Chess Sound" (*Chicago Tribune Magazine*, 5/11/69), obituaries of Leonard Chess in the *Chicago Daily News* and *Chicago Tribune* (both 10/17/69) and Ray Brack and Earl Paige, "Interview with Leonard Chess and Willie Dixon" (*Billboard* magazine, Section 2, 6/24/67).

More general sources were *Living Blues* and *Blues Unlimited* magazines (the latter in particular for extensively researched interviews with Chicago performers published during the middle and late 1970s) for interviews with artists who provided snippets of germane information. Individual discographies of particular assistance were Bez Turner, "Eli Toscano's Labels" in *Blues Unlimited* (issue 134, March–June 1979) and Paul Vernon, "The Peacock Label: A Guide to the Gospel Recordings" in *Blues & Rhythm* magazine (issues 15, 16 and 18, 1985–86).

Liner notes of value were found on various Chess albums recently re-issued by MCA, along with Bruce Bastin's annotation for the collections of Cobra material on the Flyright label and those of Jonas Bernholm on the *Big Three Trio* LP for Sweden's Dr. Horse label. Also Sheldon Harris, *The Blues Who's Who* (Arlington House, 1979) provided factual background on Dixon's career and Jeff Titon, ed., *From Blues To Pop: The Autobiography of Leonard "Baby Doo" Caston* (Tufts University, 1974) provided supplemental information on Caston's career. Other discographical sources were previously detailed in Appendix 1.

APPENDIX 5

The following list covers major film and television segments featuring Willie Dixon. Historical footage—of Dixon and Memphis Slim's appearance on the "Today Show" with Dave Garroway in the late 1950s or other European segments which document the appearances of the American Folk Blues Festivals from 1962 through 1964—may also be available.

"I Hear The Blues," Granada TV, UK, segment on 1963 American Folk Blues Festival. Willie Dixon performing "I'm Nervous" and playing bass in backing band with Memphis Slim, Matt Murphy and Billy Stepney. Concert footage featuring Big Joe Williams, Lonnie Johnson, Victoria Spivey, Muddy Waters and Sonny Boy Williamson. 2 parts, approx. 35 minutes, 1963.

"The Blues," a Canadian Broadcasting Company Festival Production. Performance and interview footage featuring Willie Dixon, Muddy Waters, Sunnyland Slim, Otis Spann, Clifton James, Sonny Terry & Brownie McGhee. 60 minutes, 1965, unreleased.

"Out of the Black Into The Blues," French documentary on blues history. Willie Dixon interviewed at the Blues Factory studio in Chicago and filmed recording "Jelly Jam." Also featuring interview and/or live footage of Furry Lewis, Robert Pete Williams, Bukka White, Mance-Lipscomb, Roosevelt Sykes, Sonny Terry & Brownie McGhee, Junior Wells, Buddy Guy, Big Boy Crudup, B.B. King. Produced by Claude Fleouter and Robert Manthoulis for Neyrac Films, directed by Manthoulis, 120 minutes, 1971.

"Chicago Blues," UK documentary. Featuring a brief interview with Willie Dixon plus live and interview footage of Muddy Waters, Buddy

Guy & Junior Wells, J.B. Hutto, Floyd Jones, and Dick Gregory. Director Harley Cokliss, 50 minutes, 1972.

"Soundstage" segment with Muddy Waters and Johnny Winter filmed by PBS station WTTW in Chicago. Producer Ken Erlich, 60 minutes, 1974.

"Jump Street" segment on the urban blues filmed by PBS station WETA in Washington, D.C. Host Oscar Brown, Jr., approx. 30 minutes, shot in 1979.

"The Facts Of Life" docudrama, part of the "Were You There?" series for NET (National Educational Television), Nguzo Saba Films, Carol Mundy Lawrence director, 30 minutes, 1980.

"Live At The Maintenance Shop" concert for Iowa Public Radio Broadcast Network at Iowa State University, Ames Iowa. Featuring Willie Dixon and the Chicago Blues All-Stars, 60 minutes, 1981.

"Soundstage" segment recorded by PBS station WTTW in Chicago. Featuring the Blasters with special guests Carl Perkins and Willie Dixon, 60 minutes, 1982.

"The Living & The Legends," an RKO-Nederlander production of a Chicago concert. Featuring Willie Dixon, Jimmy Witherspoon, Koko Taylor and Otis Blackwell. Producer Niles Siegel, 60 minutes, 1982.

"Blues Explosion," concert footage filmed at the Montreux Jazz Festival, Montreux, Switzerland. Featuring Willie Dixon and the Chicago Blues All-Stars. Unreleased, 1983.

"I Am The Blues," interviews and concert footage at the Denver Center for the Performing Arts. Featuring Willie Dixon and the Chicago Blues All-Stars with special guest Baby Doo Caston. Heart Productions, 60 minutes, 1984.

"Ginger Ale Afternoon," Willie Dixon soundtrack for feature film. Producer Susan Shapiro, director Rafal Zielinski for NeoPictures. Released by Skouras Films, August, 1989.

INDEX

Index

Index

Index